The Other Side of the Fence

BRINGING HOPE TO
THE LOST...

Senior Chaplain Bill Potter

WESTBOW
PRESS®
A DIVISION OF THOMAS NELSON
& ZONDERVAN

This book is a work of non-fiction. Unless otherwise noted, the author and the publisher make no explicit guarantees as to the accuracy of the information contained in this book and in some cases, names of people and places have been altered to protect their privacy.

WestBow Press books may be ordered through booksellers or by contacting:

WestBow Press
A Division of Thomas Nelson & Zondervan
1663 Liberty Drive
Bloomington, IN 47403
www.westbowpress.com
844-714-3454

Because of the dynamic nature of the Internet, any web addresses or links contained in this book may have changed since publication and may no longer be valid. The views expressed in this work are solely those of the author and do not necessarily reflect the views of the publisher, and the publisher hereby disclaims any responsibility for them.

Any people depicted in stock imagery provided by Getty Images are models, and such images are being used for illustrative purposes only.
Certain stock imagery © Getty Images.

Scripture taken from the New King James Version® Copyright © 1982 by Thomas Nelson. Used by permission. All rights reserved.

ISBN: 978-1-6642-5210-3 (sc)
ISBN: 978-1-6642-5211-0 (hc)
ISBN: 978-1-6642-5212-7 (e)

Library of Congress Control Number: 2021924861

Print information available on the last page.

WestBow Press rev. date: 12/21/2021

Contents

Foreword

I was a volunteer under Chaplain William Potter at Delta Correctional Center (men's prison) in Delta, Colorado, for 11 years. I conducted and choreographed the men's choir and was a member of the local Good News Jail and Prison Ministry Presidents Council that supported him.

As a Christian, the longer I spent volunteering and planning fundraising events, the more I discovered that, in the Christian community, prison ministry is the poor kid on the block. The kid you love, but you don't brag about. Prisoners are not sympathetic figures like starving orphans in Africa. Prisoners are people who have committed crimes from DUI to drugs to theft to gang violence to murder. As Christians, we love and pray for these folks, but very few of GOD's people want to be in the same room with them! THAT is what makes people with a heart for inmates a unique group!

Prison ministry is not glamorous. It's not exciting (Unless, GOD forbid, there's a riot!). It's not going to make a prison chaplain famous or get him or her a show on Christian TV. Generally, prison ministries do not have crusades and concerts in huge stadiums that draw thousands of people, raise millions of dollars, and are shown on television all over the world. Usually, fundraising consists of mailers, media ads, small events, online and one-one donation requests, since most prisons are in areas far from cities.

Prison ministry is not for everyone. A jail or prison is a state or federal facility with very strict rules. Security and protocol are extremely important. Chaplains are not free to conduct their ministry any way they wish. They are not autonomous. They must preach GOSPEL while adhering to the rules of the facility that they are in, whether it is maximum or minimum security. That includes their interaction with the inmates. Any chaplain or volunteer who breaks the rules is told to leave and not return.

Prison ministry is humble. It is invisible. It is practiced behind walls and behind bars. It ministers to and saves the souls of "the least of these".

Prison ministry is REDEMPTION.

GOD could not have chosen a better man to put in prison that Chaplain William Potter.

Victoria Hearst, volunteer,
director Chapel of Hope Choir

Foreword

As iron sharpens iron,
so a friend sharpens a friend.
– Proverbs 27:17 *New Living Translation*

M y voice was one of many begging for this book. I wanted everyone to know what I witnessed: the many God interventions in the life of Bill Potter, so many things that could not happen in the world as we know it. But God . . .

Bill moved to Colorado from New Jersey to escape God's calling to prison ministry, he thought. I moved to Colorado from Ohio, via Texas, to pastor, I thought. But God brought our lives together in a town in western Colorado so that we could sharpen one another.

We have shared the tears and joys of life. There have been times of struggles and times of great victory. Together we have faced adversity and together we have enjoyed triumph. We have gone back and forth about who is in charge until we agreed that we are both servants and He is in charge.

We have walked with one another through times of grief and were still walking when the sunshine parted our clouds of sorrow. Bill has shown me what it means to hear God's voice and to walk in faith until God brings His promise to fruition. Our bond of friendship is strengthened by the friendship our wives share as well as that of our daughters.

Bill and Joan have taught Vicki and I a lot about serving God. There have been lessons in hearing God's voice, as well as depending on God to bring about His promise. Loyalty and diligence are traits that Bill and Joan have demonstrated in abundance. There are many stories about Bill "telling it like it is". I have seen and heard it in action.

When Bill first came to Delta as a "Religious Programs Coordinator" it was because he did not meet the educational requirements to be a chaplain. He began to take steps to change that. For several years Bill maintained a grueling schedule. He would begin long-distance education at 6 a.m. At noon he would eat lunch and head to the prison, Delta Correctional

Center, where he would counsel, teach, preach, and raise funds to perform ministry until he would go home at 9 p.m., and start all over again the next day. He was diligent and a finisher. By the way, he earned his Master of Theology and Doctor of Ministry degrees the hard way.

I was honored to serve Bill, Joan, and Jennifer as pastor. If there was ever a project that needed someone hands on, Joan was there. They purchased a home and Joan set about making it "their" home. She purchased a new refrigerator and had it delivered. When it came it was larger than the spot where the old refrigerator had been. While the delivery men stood there waiting for directions, Joan picked up a circular saw and cut away the decorative trim so she could get her new refrigerator in place. You do not argue with Joan.

I accepted a call to pastor in the suburbs of Denver and Bill continued there at the prison. When Bill accepted a new position with the Department of Corrections, he asked me to join him, which I eventually did. Even though both of our pay checks came from the state, we both knew that God was in charge. Bill flourished as a visionary, trusting me to put the pieces together. Many times, I saw Bill be obedient to God and God take control.

This book is not about Bill Potter. It is about a life that desires to be used by God. Let the same desire to be used of God be kindled in your heart. You may think it is impossible. But God …

Darryl Proffit Pastor, Volunteer Coordinator, Chaplain

Foreword

"The Bible calls us to love one another, and to open our eyes to the plight of brothers and sisters who are desperately in need of God' love. Bill Potter answered Gods call –even when he wasn't sure he was the right man for the job. As the saying goes, "God doesn't call the qualified, He qualifies the called' Bill Potter's calling was clear, and he followed it, first in a volunteer capacity, then as an ordained minister. For decades, he served the incarcerated with grace and humility. His devotion shows in the fruit his work produces. Today his story can inspire a new generation. The Other Side of the fence traces his path from reluctant servant to passionate advocate, showing what's possible when we surrender our own and follow God's leading."

Founder AlvedaKing.comPastoral Associate,
Priests for Life Creative Evangelist
Leader of Civil Rights for the Unborn

Foreword

My wife and I worked with Chaplain Bill for several as volunteers in the Chaplaincy Programs at Delta Correctional Center. Congratulations Bill, on the publication of your first book. Bill was and is a spiritual man and, also very practical. The main reason he was an effective chaplain (I believe), was his unconditional love for those to whom he ministered. He loved God and loved others, and he was loved in return, and he was trusted and as a result God used him to transform many lives. On behalf of those lives, thanks, Bill, for both your book and your ministry.

Bradford Kolman, Attorney, County Attorney
(retired).

This book is dedicated to my wife Joan.
Without her in my life I do not know how I would have ended up. She
is my best friend, the love of my life and my biggest encourager.

A wife of noble character who can find? She is worth far more than
rubies. Her husband has full confidence in her … Proverbs 31: 10-11a

Preface

Throughout our lives there are the good times and well, not so good times. There are times, I am sure that all of us have felt that we are at the end of our rope, whether you believe it or not, but remember that is when we think we need to stop and re-evaluate. Stop being focused on our own pity party and lean more of the meaning of life and focus on God and recognize the blessings that are all around us on a daily basis. Seek a better understanding of you creator (GOD). Find that someone who will help you work through the situation at hand. That individual must be a student of the Bible in order to properly guide you in a manner that will help you become familiar with how God the Father, Son and Holy Spirit want you to know them completely. If you do this "search" you will be blessed more than we will ever know. God is not to be feared He loves us all and is patient in waiting for us to return to Him. THIS MUST BE A LIFE-LONG FRIENDSHIP. SOMEONE WHO YOU TRUST INPLICTELY.

From a personal perspective, a blessing comes when you lose someone or something that is most dear to you. This book is about some of those instances that I have first-hand experienced and wondered where in the world am I going to find the strength to go on? I cried and cried some more. I screamed out of frustration. The world did not provide any answers. No matter how hard I would search. Out of complete exasperation did I turn to God and He reached out to me and in my sorrows and did I feel the embrace of God? You bet I did; and so, can you. Secure your heart (as I did mine), to the reputation of Christ.

> Your moods will come and go.
> Your world will change.
> But you will not be left alone.

You have discovered a contentment the world does not understand. Christ in our life brings peace and strengthens us.

Since no one can take Christ from us, no one can steal our joy.

Enclosed in the ensuing chapters of this book (I pray) you will understand that as we go through life with its lows and highs, that through it all God is there with us. It took a period of time for me to realize that God was to be praised through "it all" - the good as well as the bad. This is not what the world today will teach you. The questions like: "where is your God when you need Him most." Or: "How come 'your God' allowed that to happen." It is in times like this when I must stop listening to what the world around me is saying and look around at how God has "blessed" me and count those blessings, I mean really count them. That was when I became the proud owner of the things that can't be bought.

This book is all about getting to know God and being able to recognize that God will (and is) walking with us each and every day. God is omni-present.

I needed an appetite for God. [We all need an appetite for God.] I mean for as much as I have looked forward Thanksgiving with all the "fix'ns." I mean a mouth -watering - can't wait for the meal. Until that type of hunger grew within my soul for God, I never knew that God was always by my side. Let God know your hurts, He sees them anyway. I mean verbalize what hurts. Those down deep hurts, those down within the darkest part of your soul. Once I did this exercise several times over, crying out to God for help to show me the "real world" around me. The devil is wanting to destroy and conquer your world. Be strong in the Word. Let go of your selfish ways and reach out to the only One who truly has you best interests – God.

The hurts of life will begin to be healed. They will never go away, but I assure you that they will be healed. As I rolled up my sleeves and focused on God totally, was I ready for the Lord to use me to His Glory. It cost God the life of His Son on the cross to die for our transgressions. I also must remember the resurrection and the promise of the empty tomb. Christ's death and resurrection are no afterthought, as the enemy wants you and I to believe. Jesus holds the future to life for all of us.

The only way that I could spread God's love was by first to clean-up my life. Get my house in order and do the most difficult of actions – W A I T! what do you mean Lord, wait? As I prayed, I went to the Word to Isaiah: 40:31-

"But those who wait upon the Lord Shall renew their strength. They shall mount up with wings like eagles. They shall run and not be weary they shall walk and not be faint." (NKJ)

The Word brought a new life in me. I had to prepare myself, body, mind, soul and strength. As I went through all this, the heart-wrenching hurts of life so can you. Sometime the easiest of actions on our part become so difficult to accomplish. This is what myself, my wife and family went through. May you not only be blessed as you read through the book, but also challenged to move forward to do all that God has prepared for you. Yes! God has a plan for all of us. Believe it or not – it is true.

Before I begin in must recount the first (almost) half of my life as that presents a basis for my actions in what was in-store for my future, should I "choose to accept" the call of God.

My family I grew up in for the most part consisted of my mother and me. Union City New Jersey – in the shadows of New York City on the west banks of the Hudson River. Most people were of Italian, German or English ancestry. Gangs were call "clubs." Youth groups were part of certain adult organizations such as: Knights of Columbus; Masons and local churches.

When I was nine years old my father (for whatever reason), decided to leave us. My last memory of his was his fist knocking me out cold to the kitchen floor as he went out the door. I never have seen nor heard from him since. My mother had a rough, hard life after that. Initialing Applying for welfare to help get us back on our feet. If there was one thing, she instilled in me was we will survive. We will be better for this too!

Most mothers have a unique way of helping their children remember what is important and what we need to let go of as well. Sadly, to many of us refuse to let go. My mother died on Leap-Year Day 1960 at the age of fifty-three I was 22 years old. This would have and could have been devastating if I had not remembered my mother's words. "These things will pass." Yes, I cried a lot for a time, but things will pass, and healing will take place. While my mother made me attend church every Sunday, it did not have any major impact on my life until I was in my mid-forties.

One of life's great blessings is our children. Although for the "record" I was an only child, my mother berthed 8 children. I was lucky number 7 in line weighing in at 13 pounds even. Before I came on the scene for sure here was tragedy after tragedy in her life. First of all, for an astonishing 3 sets of twins before me, two sets of twins died of some birthing issues and the last set of twins in a streetcar accident at the tender age of 3 months. Then after me was a sweet girl named Margret Ann who was sadly dropped by a nurse the night before she was coming home, and the baby girl landed on her head and died of a massive brain hemorrhage. Was she "mad" at God? I do not know for sure, but she could have and with good reason. That did not deter her commitment to see me attend church regularly. I made my First Communion and Confirmation. For the most part all of this process was meaningless. My encounter with God was yet to come. Should I be blessed with children through marriage, I would find the joy and special loving bond with them and then the agony of separation by divorce that almost consumed me had it not been for God.

Shortly after my mother passed (six months), I married Patricia of Lodi, N.J. We had four children: Gerald, William T. Jr., Patrick, and Maria. What joy it was to have these gifts from God. Patricia and I were married for 17 years. These years with my children were unexplainably joyous. Only 25 years later my children from this marriage were reunited with me and have been close ever since.

At the age of 40, I married my wife Joan and was blessed with her six children to enter my life. They have ever since been an integral part of my life. They are Lynn, Billy, Scott, Keith (now in the presence of God), Jean and Jennifer.

We in 2021 celebrated our 44th wedding anniversary.

We also celebrated my 85th and Joan's 80th birthday!

THE HEARBEAT OF THE LORD GOES ON!
May you be blessed of God by this book.
Be challenged of God.
Respond to God.

Acknowledgements

When I thought of who to give thanks to for inspiring me to write this book (all throughout my life), I must admit that God is the first (2 Timothy 3:16,17). To him be all glory and honor. My mother taught me all about respect, respect for self, others and the love of God. I never would fully understand what she meant until so much later in my adult life. There were many others that have come into my life that I admired. Respect was far from my mind.

Then enter Rev. Sam Koons, an episcopal priest to first point me in the right direction, toward God. Most of all I give everlasting credit to my wife, Joan. Without her in my life I do not know how I would have ended up. She is my best friend, the love of my life and my biggest encourager. There have been others in my life that God would use as helper/encourager, but for the long haul it is my wife. The endless joy she has brought to me far exceeds explanation. Through it all, she was right there by my side, I love her, then there was Keith, one of our combined family of ten children (the Brady Bunch Plus four). He (at the age of 12), literally convinced us that we needed to go to church, period no discussion. So, "the next Sunday we went to church.

I have a list of many more people I could mention, but at the risk of leaving someone out, I will only mention two or three or more now.

These folks listed are all near and dear friends to me some of which I am still in contact with, others not so frequent as we all would like. First is Andrew Kaminski, one of many "encouragers," that God gave me. Darryl Proffit whom I consider not only a near and dear friend, but my brother. Buddy Bishop a colleague but a dear friend, pastor and confidant. Warden Bob Hickox (retired) also a close friend who always kept me "on track" (and still keeps trying today). Go Yankees! Helping with the editing were: Michael Reagor, Diane and Ruth Rogers, all of whom have put in endless hours of editing this for this "first-time author. Plus, Wendy for her editing prowess I am forever grateful.

Lastly, I like to mention a (more than) friend, whom Joan and I consider part of our family, Victoria Hearst. She has help guide me and my family many, many times. May God continue to richly bless you one and all!

"You are worthy, O Lord,
To receive glory and honor and power;
For You created all things,
And by Your will they exist and were created."
Revelation 4: 11

CHAPTER 1

"In the Beginning"
... New Jersey?

(Isaiah 6:8)

A s I sat in the kitchen of our home waiting for Pastor to pick me up, I was starting to re-think my decision to go on this weekend's retreat. How did I allow myself to get into this situation in the first place? I guess it all started two years ago. But you must first understand the circumstances surrounding the willingness to answer God even if we didn't know we were doing that.

First compelling issue: My wife and the children were going out of state on the same weekend as the retreat. We lived in West Keansburg, New Jersey, and they were headed for Bridgewater, Connecticut, for a soccer tournament and would be gone for the weekend, to supposedly return before I did on Sunday evening. Now please understand what I was about to say concerning my wife's driving and navigational skill and nothing more. She doesn't have any! Just the year before, while I was hospitalized for 10 days for back surgery, my wife (and I love her dearly), every other day or so, she would get lost coming to visit me in the hospital. The children were with her and would let her know that she was going in the wrong direction. She would insist that she wasn't and told the children to be quiet, and, eventually, she begrudgingly would turn around and go the right way to the hospital.

This spiritual weekend (a name I never heard of before), was called "*Cursillo de Christiandad*," whatever that means. I would find out by the time the weekend was over.

1

It is now almost 4 p.m. and no Father Sam. I was running out of patience and about to say "no" to the whole thing. Joan tells me to calm down, and with that the phone rings and its Father Sam. He said he will be there no later than 4:30 because he had an unavoidable emergency and extended his apology to me.

So, there I sat quietly pondering the situation. I start thinking about how I got myself into this whole mess and how it all started. Two years earlier, Joan and I were working with the boys — Billy, Scott, and Keith — who were all in the Boy Scouts. Keith, being the youngest and a Cub Scout, was about to transition from the Cub Scouts into the Boy Scouts. As a part of the process, he had to memorize the Boy Scout Oath and the 12 points of the Scout Law. As being a former boy scout myself, I, as the Cub Master of the pack that he belonged to, was helping him understand the meaning of the commitment he was about to make. He wanted to talk to me especially about the twelfth point of the Scout Law: "A Scout is to be reverent." He asked me the question, "How can I or we be reverent if we don't go to church?"

I feebly tried to explain that it isn't necessary for someone to go to church in-order to be reverent. That a person only must be good and respectful. It is not necessary to go to church. Well, Keith would not take that for an answer. For a week or so, he kept on saying that we as a family must help him fulfill the last point of the Scout law and *go to church*! Joan and I discussed this and decided that it wouldn't hurt for us to do that. She, being an Episcopalian all her life, and we were married in the church that she grew up in, so it would make sense to go there. So, the next Sunday morning we dressed and went to church. That made Keith happy and, as for me, I was pondering the matter at hand. I was raised in another denomination (Roman Catholic), other than Episcopalian. In this church the priest spoke in English. I grew up in the days of the Baltimore Catechism and the language (at that time) spoken in the church was Latin. Here in this denomination, the service seemed the same, only the priest spoke in English, and that I liked. So, we decided that the family would comply with Keith's request and start attending church the next Sunday.

When we walked into the church that day, little did I know how much of a life-changing move this was going to be. In a few months, we started attending church every Sunday. It must have been two months later the priest, Father Frederick, said he was leaving the church and that the diocese would send a replacement.

This is where Father Sam came into our lives and changed our entire attitude about what faith is and how we are to live it all the time. He would impact our whole family for the rest of our lives. Unknown to Joan and me at the time, the bishop of the Diocese of New Jersey called upon Father Sam to head up the Cursillo program and do whatever it takes to get it started in the diocese — and make it happen as soon as possible.

This renewal program originated in the Roman Catholic Church many years ago (1945 in Spain) and it became a great tool by the church to especially bring men back to the church body. The approach was to recruit married women to participate in the program, and what woman would not like a weekend off just to have a little R&R? But for that to happen, there came a big but: The woman's husband must first attend a men's retreat before they could go. So, the web was spinning. Joan was very convincing and persuasive, and I stubbornly agreed.

Suddenly Father Sam was at the door exclaiming how we must hurry to get to Bethlehem, Pennsylvania, where this Cursillo is going to take place. With a "little something" to eat we would be on our way. As I looked at my watch, I thought that if we need to hurry, the Amish dinner promised is by the wayside. No time must hurry!

I was thinking about not only this dinner, but I do not like to skip a meal. So, I said I needed to stop for dinner. He said, "don't worry, Bill. I brought something for the both of us for dinner." Now, Father Sam knew (I thought), how to pack a lunch or, even better, dinner. Was I in for a surprise! Soon after we got underway, Father Sam said for me (if I was hungry) to reach into the back seat where I would find a bag with some sandwiches. So, I pulled the bag up front, I took out a sandwich and asked if he wanted one now; he sheepishly said, "no thanks." So, I proceeded to rip into the wrapping, and was surprised to find a peanut and jelly sandwich! Not that I don't like one occasionally, but what a let down from an Amish feast to a peanut butter and jelly sandwich. I was not very pleased. The game changer was to make that sandwich the way I liked it. Now Father Sam knew how to make a PB&J sandwich the "right" way. First, he put real butter on both sides of the bread before getting to the main ingredients. Well, I have no other choice but to enjoy the sandwich or go hungry. I did enjoy them. They were good, all four of them. Father Sam didn't eat while he was driving, so I ate for the both of us.

During this time, I was being told of this great weekend and what an experience it would be. Going to Mt. Pocono to the Kirby estate with its tennis courts and swimming pool, after all, it really didn't sound too bad. I was also told that it would be about an hour or so bus ride from the church, but do not worry, the bus is a big "new" Greyhound-type bus with all the comforts. Now I was interested because I, from time to time, drove a bus and knew that these types of buses are very comfortable.

Again, I was in for a surprise. Since we were already very late from the onset, when we did arrive at St. John's Episcopal Church in Bethlehem, PA, I was shuffled about from registration on out the back door onto an old rickety school bus and was told to "sit down and be quiet." The weekend had already begun, and this is the silent retreat part of the Cursillo. No one is to talk until the silence is broken after breakfast.

I was ready to jump off that bus. Before I could even start to move out of my seat the door slammed shut. Then, to the surprise of us all, the back-door alarm went off and everyone turned to look. Lo and behold, an eight-and-a-half foot wooden cross was thrown into the back of the bus. A quick thought crossed my mind: *Who is going to be crucified this weekend?* The hour-and-15-minute ride up to that Kirby estate was the longest hour's ride I had ever took. I was experiencing all kinds of anxiety Why am I here? I should be with my family. My wife can't drive that way by herself. I made her promise to make sure she travels close to the other cars that are on their way to the game as well. She assured me that she would do that.

When we arrived at the Kirby estate, it was pitch dark and we couldn't see the outside grounds. We were given papers with room assignments and a map of the place so that we could find restrooms, showers, etc., without speaking. There were some bunk beds with a second deck, and by the time I got my instructions, all of the lower beds were taken. Being a big man that I was, although I tried, I could not manage to get up to the bed. The much younger gentleman that already was in bed seen my struggles and with some hand gestures agreed to take the upper bed. I was ever so grateful for I was resigning myself to sleep on the floor.

The next day after breakfast when silence was broken, the first thing I wanted to do was "escape." But much to my dismay, there was no escape from this mountain top, unless I was willing to walk about three miles to the nearest town. So, there I was, stuck on the mountain top for a weekend I did not want to be on. I must say this, the food was great, the classes were not, at least at that time, to me. I was preoccupied with concerns for my wife.

I did forget to mention that when the leader of the weekend got on the bus and told us not to speak, he also told us to take off our watches. We won't be needing them; we will be on God's time until the weekend is over. Well, nobody was going to steal my ability to know the time. Although I did respectfully take off my watch, I had a secret weapon. I had a pen that had a clock in the top of it, and for some unknown reason I brought it with me.

That evening, there was a service where the cross was used. It was what I would call a modern version of the "Stations of the Cross." We were directed by a pamphlet called "Every Man's Way of the Cross." It was very meaningful to most except me. It was not until days later that I fully understood the true meaning of that presentation, the purpose of the silent part of the weekend and how it fit in, like a well-crafted, intimate walk with God.

Well, Friday was a big bore, at least for me. My mind was elsewhere. Thinking about my wife traveling. I would say this: the food was great — wait, did I already say that? After the marvelous dinner, we gathered in the foyer and we were told we were going to pray for one another as the Spirit leads. I certainly wanted to pray, but, suddenly, I saw the others starting to hold hands for prayer. I was thinking, just wait a minute! I was not about to hold hands with some strange man I do not know. I felt pressured — panic, fear — all of which I was feeling most of the day. I felt the need to comply, but how would I do that? Well, I took the hand of the men on either side of me between my thumb and index finger and quickly closed my eyes.

As some began to pray, I tried to see what time it is by looking at the clock pen that I had in my pocket when, suddenly, I feel a hand on my head. I quickly look up and saw no one behind me. I then looked all around and saw no one even close to me. So, I closed my eyes once again and immediately felt that hand on my head. Once again it is a surprise to me to have that feeling of someone touching my head. I began to think about possibly there were psychotropic drugs put into the food! I was getting scared. I closed my eyes and thought, *whatever it is that is happening, God Help me!* I started to pray and ask God, "If you are as real as the people say you are, please be with my wife and family as they travel. Protect them from any danger on the road."

Then I heard a voice saying to me: *"My son, I am with your family right now. Trust me. I want you to be with me on this weekend. I want you to be closer to me, for I know the plans that I have for you. Come and follow me."*

Well, let me tell you something: I shouted, "MY LORD AND MY GOD! Forgive me!" I cried. That night, for the first time, I gave my life over to the Lord Jesus Christ. I was as free as I have ever been in my life. I was grinning from ear to ear. Hugging people. I found out what Cursillo meant. The full name of the program is called *Cursillo de Christiandad*, or "A Short Course in Christianity."

The rest of the weekend just flew by. I still don't fully know what was said, but I was free in my spirit, confident in God and all that He has planned for me, even though I did not know anything about it — yet. Well, the rest of the story is about to unfold.

When the men's group was driving back on the same rickety old school bus, it seemed like that Greyhound Scenic Cruiser. There was much comradery, singing, praising God, and celebrating — a party atmosphere, bar none. As I sat there taking this all in, I thought this must be like the bus ride to Heaven, if there is a bus ride to Heaven.

As we arrived back at the church, I noticed people scurrying around the grounds. Maybe there was a Sunday night service of some sort that we did not know about? Anyway, as we pulled up around the back of the church and parked, we were told to start singing our favorite song of the weekend: "DeColores"! This is of Spanish origin and has become part of the Cursillo.

We were entering the church singing this song, we were surely going to disturb the service. Well, much to our surprise, all the service was for us!

The final piece of the program was a closing service with the rest of those who had gone on a weekend prior to us. The leader of the weekend got up to speak to the attendees telling them of the weekend and the impact it had on the candidates. Then he turned to us and told us to "remember when we were told to write in our notebooks our feelings about the weekend? Now is the time to share those feelings."

They called each table. Tables consisted of nine people, six candidates and three team members, and there were seven tables. Each table had the name of a saint. I hoped that my table would be called first. I was sitting on the edge of my seat, wanting to shout to all that God is real! I felt like a little boy.

When all the formalities were over and the crowd was dispersing, I then started looking for Father Sam. At first, I did not see him in the crowd, but he was there smiling, hugging others, and then we made eye contact. I rushed toward him, and we hugged. As we hugged, I whispered in his ear, "do I have a miracle to tell you about." On the ride home, I just kept rambling on and on about the Lord and His mighty works. I wasn't worried a bit about the family. I knew that God was watching over them. I was confident that they would be home when I got there. It seemed like the ride back home was very short. We were there before I knew it. I saw the family car in the driveway and that was a great sight to see.

As I thanked Father Sam for taking me on this weekend retreat, I went inside the house to be greeted by Joan. It was late, and the kids were already in bed asleep. I recalled that as the meeting was being drawn to a close at the Kirby mansion, we were instructed not to reveal anything about the weekend process to our wives. We were told not to ruin the surprise of it to our spouse. Unpack your own suitcase when you get home. Just be low-key about the weekend. Now this in and of itself would provoke many questions, which we were told we could not answer.

Now back to my arrival home. As I hugged my wife, she asked me, "How did it go?" I told her it was one of the greatest weekends I have ever had and was blessed to be a part of! She stopped in amazement, and for a moment she was at a loss for words. Then she stated that she was not going on her weekend as scheduled. They changed you. You even look different! What did they do to you? Tell me! I was bursting at the seams to tell her all about the weekend but couldn't. I tried to make some feeble excuses up to her, but she wasn't listening to them at all.

The next morning at breakfast, Joan inquired about the weekend. I told her not to worry, it will be great for her, too. Boy, I was so close to telling it all. I learned not to reveal any of the message of the weekend. When you get into a situation where you feel you are so pressured by your spouse, pray. When I first heard this solution, I thought, *what good is that going to do?* But, with the Holy Spirit now alive inside of me, I can hold out. What I first thought was so trite of an answer truly was the answer! With the assurance of the Holy Spirit, I was learning, even this first day at home, taking small steps in the Holy Spirit. I was confident in my position that Joan would go on her trip.

All my wife did for the next few days was to keep on saying she was not going. Period. As that week passed by and no change in her opinion of not going, I suggested that she call her girlfriend and talk to her about the situation. They were planning to go together on the ladies weekend, even before I went. When she did, she felt a little bit consoled but not convinced enough yet to go. Oh, I so much wanted to tell Joan, to reassure her that all would be more than wonderful for her on the weekend. During the week, I was doing all sort of things around the house just to show her — yes, I was a changed man. Perhaps a better, more appreciative husband about the things she does, day in and day out, without any thanks. I started hugging her more.

She was seeing things in a "creepier" way, so, after a few days of doing these things and noticing how she was feeling about it all, I stopped — at least until she went on her weekend. I knew eventually she would, but it sure was a struggle getting her there. Thanks to her friend Sandy, who finally convinced her to go with her, she acquiesced and went on the weekend.

The day for Joan to leave had arrived. We got in the car and met up with Sandy and we drove to Bethlehem, PA, and got them off safely. It was a long weekend for me. I remembered how the flow of the weekend went and how the spirit gradually changed my focus. When my wife came home, she told me of the silent retreat part on Thursday night. The candidates were all informed not to speak to one another as they prepared for bed. They were told where the bathrooms and sleeping quarters were upstairs. But Joan in her understanding of things didn't quite get it right. As she stood in front of a locked door waiting to get into it, which she thought was the bathroom and someone else was in there. She stood for a half hour in front of what she found out from a team member was a linen closet. Even though (technically), the team member did break the silence, she spoke very quietly about that to her.

Later, they had a big laugh over it when the silence was broken at breakfast the next morning. I guess that was all I needed to hear. When I went to the closing of her weekend experience, she was beaming and overwhelmed with enthusiasm. However. Joan hasn't really said much about her weekend experience, except to say, "it was great! It changed my life!"

After 44 years of being together, I can say emphatically and with a shout of AMEN, I agree with her. The joy of the Lord has truly become our strength. To understand without a doubt, that God has your back, under any circumstance you can encounter, is truly a joy, not only for us, but most of all, unto the Lord! Our relationship jumped far beyond anything material into the true understanding of what it means to be two people joined by God and that no one can separate. There were times when we were challenged, just like most other relationships, but the love of God in our lives has pulled us together through it all.

When we got home from Bethlehem, PA, within days Father Sam was contacting us about becoming part of the formation process to get Cursillo started in the diocese of New Jersey. He wanted us to be on the ad hoc committee and get to work establishing a team for Cursillo #1 in our state. Now you must know that I have a habit of saying yes to things without really knowing what all is involved. This was the case here. Nevertheless, I agreed, and we were off to the first formation meeting.

Here we learned about the protocols to get the program underway. First, we needed to go back to Bethlehem, PA — this time to be part of the team for the next weekend. Being part of the team formation demands commitment. This meant going back and forth to Pennsylvania 10 different weekends for team formation and bonding, giving a talk to the candidates, and praying for all the team members every day; and they meant EVERY DAY, in deep prayer, and not only the team members but also all the candidates by name. This was extremely hard to do. Taking a block of time out of each day to do this is a serious time commitment. If we could not commit to it, we were told that maybe we need to consider not participating on the weekend. That is saying something. That was telling me, through the Holy Spirit, that if we as team were going to commit to this Cursillo, we are in 100%, nothing less.

The talk given to me to lead was about prayer. God got me on this one. I sure was of a "worker bee" mentality, but take time and pray? I don't know about that one. I really wasn't much of a pray-er. But give me a task to do, and I will see to it that it was done in half the time, that's the way I work. I usually find out that is the way God chose to get my attention and realize that He is the one who chose me, and He chose me to see that He is the one in control of the matter at hand, and I was His vessel.

I would say this: Praying is a humbling experience. It is a conversation with God. To approach the Throne of Heaven and even to speak, I found this very hard to do. I would spend what I thought was an inordinate amount of time listening, sometimes to nothingness, and, at other times in tears, but always feeling His presence. I would just mention a name and sit and listen. Many times, I would know that something was happening, but I didn't know what. It took me about five more years and going to Loveland, Colorado to find out what God was wanting of me. Now back to the Cursillo team training.

Not only did I have to give this talk to the team, but I had to go in front of a committee of men who had given this talk themselves, and they would analyze it see to it that I covered all the necessary points of the talk. If not, then I would have to do a re-write and present that to them again for approval. I didn't care for that so much, but God would see to it that all is well.

A peace came over me as I prepared for the talk. I prayed about it, and then wrote from my heart. When my turn came to present this talk to the committee, I was confident all would go well. Praise God, it did. You see, I was never much of a writer and less of a reader, but one thing I did know: "Through Christ I can do all things." I did not have to do a re-write. I finished what I thought the hardest part of this team formation process, the critique. Much to my surprise, these men were ever so loving and just suggested a few changes to my talk, but they indicated that if I choose not to make any changes, they would be okay with that. When the weekend came, it was beautiful weather in PA. The trees were in full autumn splendor. The team was fully prepared, and we were off to Kirby mansion in that same old worn-down school bus.

The Cursillo process is such a beautiful tool of the church to bring men of faith back to a renewed life in Christ. It not only renews the spirit within a man, it restores men back into the body of Christ. Its design is so magnificent. It is spiritually practical for everyone, regardless of the faith group affiliation, to experience. Nothing that I had experienced up to that point in my life has ever come close.

The following weekend, Joan, who was on the women's team, was told during the team formation process that she would be doing a talk on that weekend. I must say this: She did try to wiggle out of it, but there was no way that God (nor the team) was going to let her out of it. When I went to the closing service on Sunday, it was cold and damp outside. I wasn't really feeling well and had a sore throat, laryngitis, and couldn't speak. Considering all of this, I really did not want to make that two-hour trip to Bethlehem. But I did, because I couldn't find a ride for my wife to get home and God was pushing the matter, simply saying one word to me – GO! Besides, everyone that was going from our area had a full car.

The closing service was beautiful. The women were just beaming with the joy of the Lord shining on each of their faces. When the service ended, I quickly went looking for Joan so that we could leave. My sore throat was not sore anymore (my voice was starting to come back) when I spotted my wife just a few feet away from me. As I tried to get to her, I could see her smiling and talking to some friends of ours in a very loud voice. I grabbed her from behind and hugged her. She for a moment was startled. When she realized that it was her husband, she turned around and gave me a bigger hug. Before I could say a word, she immediately began to tell me that the night before she was to give her talk, she came down with a case of laryngitis and was afraid she would not be able to talk. The team members had the idea if they prayed, the Lord would remove the laryngitis and send it to someone else so that in the morning her voice would be restored and be more than able to do the talk. I then told her that I woke up that morning with her case of laryngitis. She just burst out in laughter. God does have a sense of humor.

Within a couple of days, Father Sam was calling the members of the ad hoc committee to a meeting in Farmington, New Jersey. It was time to bring the group together to see if there was enough interest to proceed with the program and permit Father Sam to report back to the bishop that Cursillo was ready to go. We also elected a leadership team required by the program. I was elected the vice chairman and Joan was elected treasurer. My responsibility was to meet with the pastors of the various churches within our diocese and persuade them of the benefits of starting a Cursillo community within his/her church. I was equipped with a letter of introduction from the bishop as a means of opening the pastor's door.

This wasn't too hard for me as I was working as a sales rep for a small business in Orange, New Jersey. My normal work activities required me to travel about in much of the same area as the diocese boundaries were. I was enjoying this work for the Cursillo almost better than my work. I was meeting with the various church leaders and explaining a program that would benefit a congregation in different ways: Small group participation, Sunday church attendance, more volunteers for church activities. It sparked their interest. Now for the essential point – the "Catch-22," if you will. The program specifically called for the pastor to go through a weekend before anyone from his congregation could attend a weekend. This raised several red flags. I heard many excuses such as, "I do not have the time right now. Maybe in a year of two; then I maybe can plan to take a weekend off," or "I just cannot devote the time for this program," or "its commitment is too demanding." As I tried (with some success), to explain the blessing this Cursillo program would have, not only within the church but in the greater community, some started to pay more attention to the program. It wasn't too long before requests came from pastors for an introduction to Cursillo.

By now, our first team formation meetings were taking place. The critique committees were organized and trained in the review process for the 12 talks of the weekend. The priests even had to have their talks reviewed. Humbling (for them), to say the least, but powerful for community building and team unity. A layperson telling a priest he may need to change his message to conform with the lesson plan? Intimidating, maybe, but strengthening the body of Christ.

When Cursillo #1 commenced in October of 1979, the team was pumped. God was ready, and God blessed everyone! With a heartfelt thanks to our brothers and sisters of PA, we were determined by His grace to get the job done. What God had brought together, no one would be allowed to tear apart.

As this group of people worked together, the Cursillo community was growing by leaps and bounds. But then came a game changer for this Cursillo community. One day about two years into the Cursillo program, I received a call from a Roman Catholic lady by the name of Pat. By now, I was the leader of the New Jersey Cursillo, after Tom had finished his time as the leader of the program. Pat started to tell me of a new program that she was heading up and needed to ask me to allow her to speak to the members of the Cursillo community of the Episcopal diocese of New Jersey. She introduced the KAIROS, a faith ministry like Cursillo but incorporating several faith groups and making it more appealing to the prison population.

A million thoughts were going through my mind: *Is she going to ask me to join them? Is she wanting money?* What could it be? Could I help her? I wasn't interested in joining them, I don't have any money to give to her that would be significant. I just wanted to hang up on her. But something prevented me from doing so. When she got around to the question, she wanted to ask my permission, and to give her a list of all the people that had gone through Cursillo so that she could call them and attempt to recruit some of our people to assist with the KAIROS program getting started in New Jersey.

I told her that I would provide her the list of people but could not be part of this for now. Then she asked me to consider being part of the ad hoc committee that was being formed. I felt relieved. *I can be part of a committee!* Sure, I would help you out there. So, she gave me a date for their first meeting, and I agreed to be there, and I asked her if I would be able to bring my wife. She said yes. How little did I know this would a life-changing time in my life, a time when I would attempt to run away from God. I found out you can't run from Him. He is Omnipresent — He is everywhere!

At that first KAIROS meeting, it appeared to be a "getting to know you" meeting. There were several people from other Cursillo groups as well as those from the Roman Catholic Cursillo. Now I must say, Pat and I started to not like each other. I mean, a personal dislike for each other. I came to find out that it was as real for her as it was for me. Why? To this day I still do not know. Although I have a thought or two about it. Just maybe the devil was trying to get in the way of this ministry and not even to go beyond this point. It didn't work, glory to God. He lifted many others to help Pat. I had told her to call those of whom she feels would be helpful in bringing KAIROS to New Jersey.

As this meeting adjourned, Pat called for prayer. In fact, she went as far as putting names in a hat and have each one of us draw one out and commit for a month to pray for that person every day. As I pulled a name out, I prayed, "God, please do not have me praying for Pat." Of course, I drew her name out. Thanks be to God, although no one disclosed whose name they had drawn, I knew she had drawn my name, just by the look on her face. I did not commit to anything after that meeting with the KAIROS committee — except to pray.

God can and does convict us when we make a promise to pray for each other. I didn't have much energy to pray for Pat. When God calls you to account for your prayers, or lack thereof, He already knows the excuses we are going to concoct. Accountability for each of us is important. He keeps us accountable, each to the other, but I was convinced that prayer works when it comes from a faithful heart. We, as representatives of the Lord, must live up to our actions and deeds. If there is any lack of piousness within us, we must repent and, as we repent, God then acts on our behalf to repair any damage we may have done so that we can move forward from within ourselves. He restores our strength, gives us courage to move on, knowing His forgiveness coupled with our faith can move mountains.

CHAPTER 2

How Beautiful Are the Mountains …

In time, Joan became involved in KAIROS and went into a New Jersey prison for KAIROS #1. The event was held at the New Jersey State Prison for Women in Clinton. I now had an obligation to attend that closing service. As the leader of the Cursillo in New Jersey, I was obligated to be there for the closing service of the KAIROS. Joan could have gotten a ride home, but I had to go anyway, so I dutifully attended.

What an outpouring of the Holy Spirit on that weekend! Those ladies were on fire for God. Testimonies of how God showed them they needed to forgive themselves before God could or would forgive them. The stories of abusive relationships with the men that were in their lives were horrific. These women were, on the outside, hard, callous, and some looked outright mean. Only through Jesus Christ are they made whole again. When they took off their masks (and several had more than one), they felt the healing presence of the Lord. I was touched!

As the KAIROS men's team was preparing for their first New Jersey weekend, which was to be in the Bordentown Prison for Youthful Offenders, I was called and asked to reconsider and join the team. I respectfully declined because God was not calling me into prison work. I really did not want to ask Him. I was avoiding what the Spirit was telling me to do. Although I did hear a portion of what God was telling me, I perceived that He was calling me into a ministry, a formal ordained role, within the church. I spoke to Joan about that and she seemed to be okay with it. We then prayed for God's will to help me accomplish this call I was feeling in my life. She said she would support my call to ministry.

I set up an appointment with Father Sam. I then asked him about his thoughts of me becoming a clergyman and what route should I take in pursuit of the call from God. He advised me to contact the bishop and seek his advice about the matter.

Bishop Van Duzer was a hard man to get ahold of. I tried several times to set up an appointment but never was I able to do so. However, I did get to the right person (through Father Sam), and I was on my way via a special path for "older" persons to follow, what is fondly called the "old man's canon." This is a special path for seniors who feel called later in life to be in a formal ministry role in the church. I was excited to be enrolled in the Bishop's School of Theology. I knew God had things under control. The Cursillo ministry was going strong, and as far as I knew, the KAIROS was growing as well.

The world around me was heading for a recession in the late 1970s and early '80s. My expenses were rising and income was not. I was becoming stressed out. My boss, Nick, asked me to prepare a presentation based upon current sales and projected sales for the upcoming sales year. I would specifically ask for a 1¼% increase in my commission only on the fall selling season. Nick was impressed with my presentation and agreed with my projections. But, I knew there would be a "but" that would be a fly in the ointment. He told me that was non-negotiable — period. I then told him that I was going to consider what options I had. He replied, "go for it." He would not stand in my way if I could improve myself. Years later, Nick would say that was one of the worst business decisions he had made.

I went looking. When I was exhibiting our product line in August of 1981 at the New Jersey Bandmasters Association, the exhibitor next to me was a man I knew from Red Bank, New Jersey. He worked for a company that he was so proud of, to the point of being on the brink of obnoxious. Not that this was the first time we exhibited next to one another. This was planned on by both of us. We had become acquainted with one another a few years earlier at a similar convention in Atlantic City.

He was very outgoing and always bragging about the company he worked for – the Gordon Bernard Company (GBC) of Cincinnati, Ohio.

This day would be no different. Today, however, would be somewhat different on my part. Marty, in his big exuberance over his work, asked me if I knew of a good salesman in Kansas, Colorado, or Oklahoma that was looking for work. (I thought to myself, *I got you now…*) All the bragging you do about this great company that he worked for … we shall see about that! So, I responded to him, "If the person was good, he would be working already. But I just might be interested in the position if things were right." Besides, he always was mouthing off about this great company he worked for. What I really meant was, I want to know more. I would now find out for myself just how great a business the Gordon Bernard Company was or whether Marty was just being a big bag of wind.

He started to look very excited. "Really!" Marty, with some measure of composure grabbed my arm in his excitement and said he would call the company on Monday and pass along my name to them. I said, "great."

Monday came and went. So did Tuesday through Thursday. Then on Friday I received a phone call from Bob Sherman, national sales manager for the Gordon Bernard Company. After exchanging cordial greetings, Sherman asked me if I would be interested in working for the company. I responded that if they needed someone immediately, I was not the man. I had made a commitment to the company where I was currently employed. Bob said he could respect that kind of loyalty. He then responded by saying, "If you are the kind of man we think you are, we are willing to wait until January of 1982."

I was blown away! I told Bob I was interested. "Where do we go from here?" I asked. Bob said he would be in touch with me in early December for an onsite interview. When I told Joan about this conversation, she stated she did not believe they were going to hire me. She wanted to know how far we'd have to move. I said it is only about 10 inches away from us on the map.

As the ensuing months passed, I was thinking: *God, is this your will for me to uproot the family, take the kids out of their comfort zone?* I must state now that an integral part of the Cursillo program is the formation of small prayer groups to uplift, support, and hold up various needs of the group. Joan and I called upon our prayer group to lift up the concerns we had about the possibility of relocating somewhere out west. Meanwhile the KAIROS was making great strides in the prison ministry. Inmates were seeking God's forgiveness, turning their lives around, and accepting Christ in their lives.

I went to a few more closings, this time in the men's prison. I was uncomfortable at these closings. I felt God calling me, but was He? I need to get out of here — as soon as possible, or maybe sooner. My prayer was for God to GET ME OUT OF HERE! How little did I realize my panic attack would change my life forever!

In retrospect, Joan and I were very "comfortable" in our church. She was the church treasurer, I was the junior warden in charge of building and grounds. We had a great relationship with the pastor. Plus, Joan and I were the youth pastors. I was studying to be a deacon in the church. Life was good. One day in particular comes to mind with regard to the youth ministry. It was mid-August. I was preparing a devotion to share with the kids, but I just couldn't find any subject matter. I prayed and prayed some more — nothing. "Lord," I said, "please give me something from your Word. You know they need to hear from You. It doesn't matter whether or not they like it! They needed to hear it." Still, nothing came. So I gave up. Besides, it was dinner time. After dinner, we left for the church.

We always arrived 30 minutes early to give the kids time to unwind from their summertime days and get a cold drink and prepare for the program. Besides, it was always interesting to eavesdrop in on the kids to know what they were talking about. At this time, I still had no idea of what I was going to say to them that night. Then I overheard one of them say they were going to the movies after youth group meeting that night down at the boardwalk theater. Wait a Christian minute here. That movie was R-rated. How are these 12- and 13-year-old kids getting in? They need to be accompanied by an adult in order to get in. "Wait a minute!" I interrupted. "Who is the adult that is going with you? You know that movie is R-rated, don't you?" They said, "yes, they knew, and all you have to do is pay your money and they let you in. No questions asked."

Wow! I thought. Then it came to me: "Thank you, God! Now I know why You didn't give me anything at home when I prayed. You wanted me to listen to the kids and to know about their plans to go to the movies, and to ask them to invite You to go with them!" That deserves another WOW!

I then was inspired by the Holy Spirit as to what to say, and I gave it to them, both barrels. I was so thankful and humbled as well. I asked them to consider taking Jesus with them to the movies. Leave a seat empty next to them for Him. Know that He will be there anyway, whether or not they actually ask Him.

I knew that it was all good. All good, or so I thought. After the youth group meeting ended, I overheard the boys saying they were still going to the movies anyway. I was devastated, mad, and angry all at once. Why did I waste my time talking to them, Lord? I gave it my all, but it seems that my words fell on deaf ears. Frustrations were weighing in. Now I somewhat know how Jesus felt when no one listened. Maybe that was my lesson here, to feel what Jesus felt. Feel rejected, no one paying attention. Seeking only their own agenda. The children were doing the same thing. "But God, they are only children. Shouldn't they listen? Your Word says, "bring unto Me the children.' Why, God, don't they listen?"

There was a youth group trip planned for that following Saturday, and I was driving the bus. I was considering cancelling the trip because of how mad I was at those kids. However, Joan was telling me to calm down. Things would be okay. That didn't help me with being mad. Saturday came. I picked up the bus and went to the church to pick up everyone who was going on the trip — including the "moviegoers." Now this trip would be about an hour's drive from the church. About 15 minutes into the drive, the moviegoers were singing as well, and whole-heartedly, I might add. "Hypocrites," I said to myself. *Just look at their smiles. How can they do that! God, what is going wrong here?* I was about to turn that bus around and take those sinners back home. They don't deserve to go to Great Adventure.

Just about then, one of the ring leaders of the moviegoers makes his way up to the front of the bus and shouts out to me, "Hey, Mr. Potter, we took your advice and did not go to the movies. Instead, we took Jesus to the boardwalk and He was with us." I almost cried with joy! "Thank you Lord," I said. "They did hear!" As I was thanking Him, I heard that voice, that inner voice of God, telling me to trust in Him to do the work in others. "Just continue to follow Me. I will be with you." Most of the time, I listen.

When we arrived at our destination, I dropped them all off at the front gate and parked the bus and prayed for all to have a safe, fun-filled time. What an experience in learning to be humble and contrite.

It was a few months later that I got a call from the Gordon Bernard Company. Bob, the sales manager, called and asked to meet with him on Monday of the following week. "How will you send me the tickets to fly to Cincinnati?" After a momentary pause, he replied: "We do not normally send tickets to any individual for an interview. After a successful interview, we would reimburse a new hire." I responded, "I'm sorry, if you want to interview by phone, that would be okay with me." He said he would get back with me and hung up rather quickly. I thought that was history and I would not hear from him again. Within an hour after, Bob called me back and said that the tickets would be waiting for me at the airport on Sunday and someone would pick me up from there to take me to the hotel. Wow! I was blown away.

It was intimidating and exhilarating at the same time. This is the first time that I took a step of faith in my life. Even to ask for such a consideration is a big "wow!" for me. I knew from past experiences that this was very significant. I ran to tell Joan about the call and to plan what I would ask for salary and moving expenses.

She kind of took the wind out of my sail by saying, "Go, enjoy yourself! Besides, they are not going to pay you the salary you are asking for, no way. Plus cover the costs of moving?"

Six days later I was boarding a plane from Newark to Cincinnati. When I arrived, there was a driver who welcomed me. As we proceeded to the car (a limo), he advised me that we were going to the Helmsley Hotel in downtown and that I would be picked up at the hotel at 9 o'clock sharp the next morning. Everything was top shelf. I did not have a good night's sleep. I had a lot to go over in my mind. I thought, *is my prayer group really praying for me to be guided by the Holy Spirit in deciding whether to take the position, even if offered?* My wife saying, "enjoy your weekend, they are not going to give you what you are asking." I determined that if I did not get these items fully, I would respectfully decline the position.

I was ready and in the lobby by 8:45 a.m. The driver who dropped me the night before picked me up. As I entered the building of the home office of the company, I noticed that this also is where they made the products that they sell to businesses, schools, high school bands, etc. Bob came down from upstairs where the corporate offices were located and greeted me with a big smile and invited me to go upstairs. As I followed, I noticed that the building was older, the old 1930s type of brick. Very well kept, I might add. The staff that I met were pleasant, friendly, and very welcoming. Bob took me to a conference room, told me to sit and that he would be right back. Within a few minutes, (it seemed like an eternity to me), two other men came in with Bob. He introduced the men as Mr. Gordon Bernard, President and Mr. Robert Sherman, Vice President, (Bob's dad and Mr. Bernard, his uncle).

After exchanging some pleasantries, we gathered round the table and I was asked why I was looking to come to work for this company. I explained my circumstances to them. Then, as if the Holy Spirit Himself stepped in, I spoke of my prayer support team back in NJ praying that I would be guided by God in making this decision. I explained my involvement in the Christian community. We would come to terms if that was God's call.

Mr. Bernard stepped in and asks me some basic questions, like my anticipated salary, then asks Bob what were they going to offer. Bob's response was written on a piece of paper, turned upside down and slid across the table to Mr. Bernard. He picks it up, looks at it, pauses for a moment, then said to me: "Bill, we're planning to pay our representative $500 a month more than you are asking for! That's our offer. Now as far as the moving expenses go, we have never paid for anyone's costs that is a new hire, but we are not opposed to doing that." Then he motioned to the two others and said, "let's go out and talk about this – Bill we'll be right back."

I figured this is the catch-22, this will be the deal breaker. It seemed that the door that they went out was just closed when Mr. Bernard came in with his arms wide open as said to me: "DeColores!" He gave me a hug. I was speechless. He reached into his vest pocket, took out his personal checkbook and proceeded to write me a check for the moving expenses including the plane tickets for my wife and two accompanying children. He then told me, if that isn't enough let him know, and conversely, if that is more than enough, to return to him any excess funds. He then stated that his prayer group was also praying that he made the right decision whether to hire me. He then called the two other people back into the room.

We talked about where I could live in the area I had to cover: Colorado, Kansas, and Oklahoma. The company officials thought it best that I live in a central location and suggested Liberal, Kansas. I was also firm in saying that I would live in Colorado Springs, Colorado. My theory was that if they had the confidence to hire me, they should also have the faith in me that, no matter where I lived in that tri-state area, I would do my job. I informed them there was a strong Cursillo community there and that my wife and I would make friends quickly. (That was intended to be the convincer for Mr. Bernard.) This location was critical to me, as was my family's adjustment to this new city. Reluctantly, they agreed. Now Bob Sherman, the Senior Vice President of Sales, took me on a tour of the facilities. He introduced me to the office staff, then took me downstairs to the production part of the building. I met the men and women who put the product together.

When the tour was completed, Mr. Bernard came in and took me to lunch. At lunch, he explained the company's history. I was very interested and somewhat overwhelmed. This company was all that Marty said it was and more. I firmly believed that I would have a long and successful relationship with the company and was looking forward to getting things underway. As we were heading back to the office, Mr. Bernard not only reiterated to me about the relocation expenses, but also said, "If your wife is not fully willing to relocate, just call me and tear up the check." I assured him as best I could that Joan would be on board.

As we arrived back at headquarters, my ride to the airport was waiting for me. I had a 6 p.m. flight back to Newark, and it was already 4:30 p.m. I said my goodbyes and off we went to the airport. As I sat on the plane thanking God for this opportunity for me and the family to start a new life in Colorado, for a moment I paused. I thought, *This conversation with God needs some extra thanks and praises. No need to sweat over incoming phone calls about pressuring me to get involved in this prison ministry called KAIROS. Hurrah!!! GLORY TO GOD!*

As I landed in New Jersey and was deplaning, I saw Joan and ran to her and gave her a big hug and said, "WE ARE MOVING TO COLORADO!" I saw an almost empty look on her face, as if to say, "where in the world is that? What are you talking about? Moving?" She was totally confused. She thought I went to Cincinnati for the weekend and that no way would this company agree to the things we agreed upon for us to take the position. On the ride home, I told her all about the job, about the meetings, and the "raise" we were getting even before we started.

Now for the details of the move. It was the middle of December; the holidays were upon us, and we had to pack a house and move by January 1? I assured her we did not have to move by the first. "I will be leaving on January 2nd with our car packed with as much as we could of breakable items, and a moving van will do the rest of the moving for us." Yes, we needed to have a moving/packing party with some friends, so that most of the small items would be boxed and ready to go, but a moving company would transport our furniture. Now this was major stuff for her, never having been outside of the community where we were living. But she was up for most anything, so she said, "let's go, if that's what you felt the Lord is saying to us."

This must have been answered prayer. Then it clicked in my head: *Be careful about what you ask for, Bill!* No, this is nonsense. God doesn't play tricks on people, or does He? Our holidays were spent with saying our goodbyes to family and friends. We met with the New Jersey Cursillo family and gave them our farewells and best wishes. We turned over the helm of that program to others, including the treasurer's position, which was held by Joan, and the leadership position, which I held. None of this was easy, but our friends knew God was sending us to Colorado. My wife's brother George kept saying, "What do you want to go there for? It is always cold, and they get a lot of snow, too." "That's in the mountains, not where we are going to live," I replied. I was thinking to myself, *Don't look up the annual snowfall in Colorado Springs, thank you very much.* Suddenly I was overtaken by *What have I done? You don't even know where you are going? You have never done anything like this before! Don't be stupid. You have a good job here, why are you going out into the wilderness?* I started to tremble. My knees were almost knocking. While everybody else was wishing me well, I was now asking, "what have I done?" *Wait a minute, don't panic. Look at Joan, who is so calm about this move. Or is she feeling like I am right now? Is she putting up a good front just like me? Do you think God has His hand on you as you run away from His work? Am I being a coward by leaving the Cursillo ministry? Leaving St. Mark's Church? Leaving all of our friends and family?*

There were some other issues that I wanted to get away from as well. That had to do with my children from my first marriage. It's always hard to discuss matters of the heart. I love kids. Joan and I have 10, her six and my four. Joan and I had never talked about her kids versus my kids. They were always "our" kids. What a great relationship to love one another and accept the children of both families as our own. No double standard. No arguing or disputing issues with the children. We would either agree or agree to disagree, and we would ponder that one together and, at some point, come to a proper solution. This process has worked for us for 44-plus years. Our children refer to us as "mom and dad." We were going to Colorado and the "fear factor" just came over me.

When time came for me to visit the Potter kids up in Lodi, New Jersey, there always was an issue that would delay or cancel my visits. I was never notified before I left Keansburg, which was an hour-and-a-half drive. It bothered me, and I was sure it upset the kids. Sometimes I would just catch a few minutes with my daughter Maria while she was on her recess time in the school yard, and that was through a fence. Moving away to Colorado would limit my visits, but would that stop the emptiness, hurt, and dismay? What would those kids think of their father leaving like that?

I recalled recently attending my son Billy's high school graduation in Lodi. He called me and asked me to please sit in the balcony, not in the orchestra area, as he did not want his mom to know that his dad was there. "Don't worry, Son, I will sit in the balcony." He asked me to meet with him on the east side of the auditorium after graduation because he wanted to see me. When we did meet, he introduced me to his girlfriend (now his wife), Karen. I inquired about going for something to eat, and Billy respectfully declined because of the other graduation activities that were happening that day.

As I drove back home, I stopped at one of my favorite places for a quick lunch, Callahan's. The best hot dogs in the world! If hot dogs are served in heaven, this is what they will be like. Every time Joan and I would go to New Jersey my first stop would be to head to Callahan's. Sorry to say that there is only one restaurant in New Jersey that is open. I still go there any chance I get.

> "For God has not given us a spirit of fear, but of power, and of love, and of a sound mind." -2 Timothy 1:7 (NKJ)

Fear is not a word that I should allow to overtake my thoughts. Thoughts that God had given me to start fresh in Colorado. Do not let these thoughts consume me. Onward, upward, to Colorado! Then I remember what the Lord said about worry.

> "Therefore, do not worry, saying, 'What shall we eat?' or 'what shall we drink?' or what shall we wear?' for all these things the gentiles seek. For your heavenly Father knows that you need all these things. But seek first the kingdom of God and His righteousness, and all these things shall be added unto you." -Matthew 6:31-33 (NKJ)

God, You always have the answer! Why then does it take so long for us humans to get into your Word? Pressure, that is the answer. There are so many outside issues to deal with these days. All of the internet has to say or tell us what we need. The answers are found in Your Word, Lord.

On December 30th, there was a gathering at our home with some of our closest friends to bid us farewell. It was a melancholy time. Sharing memories of times gone by. Yet praying for the future of the New Jersey Cursillo program, too. It was getting late, around 10 p.m., and although most were reluctant to say goodbye, and all saying, "if things don't work out …." I would be off to colorful Colorado on January 2nd!

Little did I know of the plans that the Lord had in store for me. He had more than a surprise or two in store for me upon arrival in Colorado!

CHAPTER 3

"For I know the thoughts that I think toward you …"

-Jeremiah 29:11-14 (NKJ)

As I left New Jersey that cold-but-bright sunshiny day in January of 1982, *I thought, I hope and pray that I was truly following your lead, God.* The weather was great all the way across this great country. I always thought that the state of Pennsylvania was a big state — then came Kansas. Although I must say that the first 200 miles or so was very nostalgic for me. Those amber waves of grain … however, no purple mountains majesty. That would come later. After six hours of waves of grain, they lost the amber shine. It seemed like I would never get out of Kansas. I was about to click my heels together and holler for Auntie Em! (But that would have still been in Kansas.)

Then, it seemed like out of the distance I could see what looked like mountains. Could it be that they were the Rockies? A half an hour went by and I didn't seem to be any closer. In fact, the image I was seeing looked even further away. Then all I was seeing were cumulous cloud formations. I still had another 200 or so miles to go to get to Colorado. It was then that I decided to stop for the night somewhere west of Salina, Kansas, get a refreshing night's sleep and a fresh start in the morning.

Well, so much for a good night's sleep. I tossed and turned repeatedly. Finally, at 4:30 a.m. I got up, took a shower, and made some coffee (it was terrible). The only thing I could say about the coffee was that it was hot! At 5:45 a.m. I started out for "The Springs." Little did I know what was about to happen. I saw a sign that said: "The Shortest Way to Colorado Springs - U.S. Hwy 40." I still had not seen any mountains, so I decided to take the "shortest" route.

About 75 miles down the road, the right front brake rotor seized up and I almost lost control of the car. Praise the Lord that I did not lose control and crash. Here I was, out in the middle of "nowhere" Kansas. I sat in the ditch on the side of the road. No cell phones back in 1982. Off the major interstate highway, I waited and finally a farmer came by and asked if I needed help. "YES!" He said he would take me into town.

The town consisted of one new car dealership (Ford), one motel (mom & pop) consisting of 12 rooms, a café and not much else. The Ford dealership also did whatever towing necessary for the area. I had no other choice, so the tow truck driver and I went out to my car and towed it to the dealership. Now, my car was a 1979 Dodge Aspen Wagon. When we got back to the dealership, I was told they would not be able to look at my car until Monday morning. As I was explaining my situation, I was told to hold on. "We folks out here do things in an orderly and right manner. I have other jobs to finish before I can get to yours. Now calm down, get yourself a cup of coffee and we will do you right soon on Monday."

I had to cool my heels in Sharon Springs, Kansas for two days. There were some nice folks at that motel, which was just down the street. They even provided me with breakfast the two days I was there, at no charge, or so I was told. On Monday morning, I was at the Ford dealership by 7 a.m. to check on the status of my car. Tom, the mechanic, told me I was correct, my right front caliper needed to be replaced. Tom also checked out the left caliper as well and he said that they both should be replaced at the same time.

I said, "Okay, when can this be done?" He responded and said, "We don't stock Chrysler replacement parts here, we are Ford people here in these parts." They would have to be ordered from Topeka, and they should be here tomorrow morning, coming in on the Greyhound bus. "Al- right," I said, "go ahead."

Tom said I needed to talk to Fritz in the parts department about pre-payment for the parts. Fritz told me that it could take up to three or four days before my car would be ready. Now, I was about to be in panic mode.

I was just starting a new job in Colorado, my car broke down some 220 or so miles away. Where do I go from here? I decided to call Bob Sherman at HQ and advise him of the matter. As I spoke with Bob, he asked me if I could rent a car for a week or so until my car is ready. I thought, *Why didn't I think of that?* "I would get back to you on that, Bob."

I was still at the dealership and I asked Fritz if there was a place I could rent a car for a week. He said, "Nope, afraid not. But tell you what I would do for you: You can use my car. I would rent that out to you for $200 for the week. How's that going to work for you?"

I responded with a big Y-E-S. By noon, I was on my way to Colorado Springs. I did call Bob back and apprised him of the situation. He replied to make sure I got all or most of my personal matters covered during that week, such as finding a place to live, setting up my at home office, arranging for my office supplies, and obtaining a mailing address so that the company could send me supplies necessary to begin work. I asked him to send all my necessary materials care of the main Colorado Springs Post Office and said I would pick them up there.

About an hour from Sharon Springs, lo and behold, I started to see mountains. I mean, the *real* thing, the Rocky Mountains, specifically Pikes Peak. I was getting excited about this great adventure that I was about to begin. A fresh start — no pressure about prison ministry, or so I thought.

Upon arrival in Colorado Springs, I went to a modest-priced motel, Travelodge Motel on North Nevada Avenue, and registered for a week-long stay. In the lobby, I spotted two newspapers, *The Gazette-Telegraph* and *The Colorado Springs Sun*. I asked the clerk at the desk which paper was the better one? Did I get an earful about *The Gazette*! A very opinionated clerk proceeded to give me his bent on that paper. He wouldn't read that paper "even if it was the last paper on earth." I bought *The Colorado Springs Sun*.

I went back to my room and opened the paper to the classified ads, the rental apartments. I had a specific list of home requirements that Joan had given me: three bedrooms, fireplace, patio/balcony, and all kitchen appliances included. So, as I scanned through the ads, almost immediately I came across a promising ad that included all that she asked for. I called right then, and someone answered the phone. The gentleman on the other end told me that he just placed that ad and that it wasn't to appear in the paper until the next day, and I was the first caller.

"How soon may I see the place?" He said the earliest he could do that would be Saturday morning. We met Saturday at 10 a.m. at the apartment. It was a second-floor apartment that was perfect. It had all of what Joan had requested. She said "make sure" over and over. When I saw the place, I said to myself, "perfect!"

Now for the particulars, like rent, security deposit, etc. This was the easy part, I was shocked to find out. We signed the lease agreement and nothing else. There was a balcony off the living room. As I stepped out, I saw a church about 50 yards away — up the hill a bit. I asked John, the owner of the apartment, if he knew what flavor of Christianity it was. He replied that he did not know. After I gave him a deposit to secure the place for us to move in on February 1, we shook hands and departed.

I decided to go and find out what kind of church it was, just a few yards from where we were planning to live. When I researched what Episcopal churches there were in Colorado Springs, I learned there were three. I intended to visit all of them before we settled on a church home. Can you believe that the church just a few yards from where we are going to live was St. Francis of Assisi Episcopal Church? I went there on Sunday. All I can say is, *Wow!*

That's the way God is, just look around you and not only see the wows, but experience them! They are all around us. Take time to stop, look, and listen to what God's people are doing (James 1:22). This church was having a "folk" mass. Or, as I would later comment, a contemporary service. I was excited; in fact, I was overwhelmed.

Oh God, you are more than all powerful, wonderful, and all consuming. I have followed Your call to relocate to Colorado, you have provided a place for my family to live, and a nearby church to worship. If that's not a wow, I do not know what is! The *coup de grace* was that the largest Cursillo community in Colorado Springs was right there at St. Francis! I wept.

After I got myself together, I called Joan on Sunday, January 10th, and said, "There is no need to look around for a church, I found it. All we need is within walking distance from our townhome. I have rented a furnished

29

two-bedroom apartment. Make plans for friends to handle the movers when they come and you're out of there."

She responded, "I love you and miss you, too." Then I told her I had already changed their flight to Thursday, January 14th. She said, "What?" I gave her four days (really, only three) to get our house packed and clothes for her and the kids until the movers arrived sometime early February. I must add that Joan is and always has been a "can do" person. She loves challenges, and this was a challenge which she passed with flying colors. I must repeat here that she said, "I miss you, too!"

On the day before Joan was going to board a plane, it snowed along the East Coast, causing air travel difficulties. There was a plane crash in Washington, D.C. the day before she was leaving, and friends were calling Joan to make sure she knew all about that. She was appreciative, but really did not want to hear all that info. Too much info — thanks, but no thanks!

Joan's oldest daughter, Lynn, was to drive Joan, Jean, and Jennifer to the airport. Joan learned as they started out that Lynn did not have heat in her car and the temperature was below freezing. I guess that was Lynn's way of helping her mother and sisters get used to the "Colorado" cold. When she arrived at the airport, thankful for the warmth of the terminal, flights were not leaving the airport yet because of the snowfall and cleanup operations. After a short wait, boarding operations started, the runways were cleared, and de-icing operations began. The plane with my family on board was the first in line for takeoff. Between the cold, snow, and the terrible crash the prior day, there was also the tension, stress, and emotion of this move. But all went well, and they landed safely at Stapleton Airport. It was a delightful day, sunshine, temperature in the 70s, and it was January 14th!

CHAPTER 4

"I would give you a new heart ..."

– Ezekiel 36:26 & 27 (NKJ)

I arrived at Stapleton airport, after getting lost — I first went to a small private airport, Cherry Creek in an area of south Denver, and quickly found out that the airport I was looking for was somewhat north of where I was at. I was 45 minutes from Joan's scheduled arrival time, so I was in a rush to get to Stapleton. I was just going a "little" over the speed limit on the highway when, of course, a state patrol car sped up behind me. *Oh no, that can't be for me.* And it wasn't, thanks be to God!

As I arrived at the airport, I was immediately in a panic. Traffic all around, unfamiliar with the parking there, I was driving somewhat slower than I would have, so the cars behind me were flying by me, beeping their horns and one driver was giving me the "fickle finger of fate award." Finally, I found a place to park and headed into the airport. Now, in the pre-911 era, I could go out to the gate where they were to arrive. I was right on time. Joan's flight was not. As I was waiting, I couldn't help but wonder what was going through their minds. Don't have any friends. Don't know where to buy food. Have no idea of the housing arrangements I made, and, last, they were coming to a place where snow was a regular part of life. And, Joan doesn't like snow! What a drastic change and culture shock they were in for.

When the plane arrived (about 45 minutes late), I was excited to greet them. As they de-planed, I first spotted Jean, then Joan and Jennifer, smiling (at least Joan and Jennifer were). As they approached me, I noticed how they were dressed. Heavy coats, shoes, gloves, and boots. They looked like they just came from Alaska! Here I was in a light wind breaker because it was 70 degrees and sunny outside. We hugged and kissed and went to the baggage claim area and they began to un-layer their clothes. They were dressed to the hilt with one layer after another. They removed enough clothes to get comfortable for the drive to our temporary living quarters in south Colorado Springs. We lived in a furnished apartment on Airport Road till the end of January and then moved into our permanent residence at Snapfinger Woods.

Within a few days, as I was getting my home office organized, Joan was registering the children for school and all was starting to settle into normal family life. Our plans for this new stage in our lives was coming together —BUT THEN GOD.

Joan packed all winter clothing because everyone was telling her she was going to "snow country." Jean and Jennifer were going to a school where no one knew them, and they were dressed like Eskimos. They were the "new kids on the block." The kids were immediately in for the moderate Colorado Springs climate. This was an unusually warm January, there in 1982, and temperatures were in the 70s! So out to the store we went to get new clothes for the girls.

One morning, while I was reading the newspaper — the Colorado Springs Sun, of course — on the front page was an article about a suicide at the county jail. First thing I thought was to pray for this person who had no other hope but to take his own life. How sad this was to me. A few days later, another suicide! Oh, how terrible a situation for the jailers to have to deal with this once again. I went to pray again. As I prayed, I heard a voice (in my head) saying, "Stop praying and do something. Go!"

No, no, I must be hallucinating. I left New Jersey because I didn't want to go into places like that. I was in shock. Then there was a third death in the same jail that month. As I prayed, I kept hearing the word "GO." I tried to make a deal with God, I would pray and financially support anyone that God would send to that jail, but please, I was begging, not me. All I heard was GO! I went to my prayer group at our new church and asked them to join me in prayer for God to send someone into the jail, but not me! Show me some support, my prayer group! Their support came in a way I never would have dreamed of, and I was sure they didn't either. They responded in the exact way God wanted them to. What other way would it have been? I continued to pray for God to send someone other than me. God wants someone there, and it must be someone other than me.

I must sell calendars. That's what brought us to Colorado in the first place. I had to work. I had a big territory to cover. So, I started to do what I was hired to do. I headed to Oklahoma in early February. I was gone for a week but had little success. I sold two previous accounts and established one new account. While I was on the road that night I had time to pray and think and pray some more. I kept hearing in response, GO! Then on that last night before I returned home, for one more time I pleaded with God, *please not me, Lord!* As many people know, God's Word never changes — but I thought with some pleading, it just might. But alas, He still was saying GO!

I have been told that at times I can be thick-headed, stubborn, and obstinate, which is true, but God does not give up. When He calls you, He calls you! I put all my objections before Him, but the Lord said to me, "I have prepared a way for you, GO!" I went down on my knees and wept. I mean, truly wept. I did not have a good night's sleep. I tossed, I turned, I wrestled with the blankets most of the night. When morning came, I packed my bags and started to head home. I found a Christian radio station and I was singing so happily along the way that I didn't even watch where I was going and missed my turnoff from the interstate. I went 31 miles out of my way, but it was all good. Just singing and praising God, I truly felt God's presence and His love all around.

Upon arriving home, I told Joan about my encounter with the Lord and that I felt a calling to go. But I argued it couldn't mean God wanted me going into a jail (or so I thought). I didn't want to do that. In fact, that's why God helped me find a good job and leave New Jersey, to get away from all that jail and prison stuff, right?

For the next four months, I secretly struggled with that call of God that was in my heart. Our prayer-and-share group was praying for and with me about the matter. In reality, I was not wanting to give in to God. In the past, I had asked Him for a lot of things, and He was generous to me. But now, He was asking me to do something I didn't want to do. After all, this is big time stuff, life-changing stuff, and this was not for me. *No thanks God, I will take a pass on this one.*

I might as well have been in jail or prison myself. There were a few things that I had done over my 40 or so years that I was not very proud of. This type of ministry was not for me. But God does not give up. He just quietly keeps on pulling and pulling. He keeps putting you in special circumstances where special people help you listen and listen some more to hear and discern the Word of God. At first, I thought I was being pushed, manipulated, and outright pressured to do something that my prayer team would not do themselves. I even called out one of them and challenged them to go there and leave me alone.

By April, we were just about settled at our Snapfinger Woods townhome and looking forward to planning our first vacation later that summer. As Joan and I were planning the trip, we thought we would plan our vacation around the annual company conference that was held in Cincinnati at the end of May. The conference would be for three long days, or so I was told by a colleague, Marty Scanlon, and no one brings their children to this meeting. Now we were in a pickle.

As we were planning vacation time to correspond with the conference, Joan came up with an idea. We all were feeling a little homesick and somehow wanted to get back to New Jersey to see our friends, and besides, the kids were asking about that as well. So, we decided to drive from Colorado to New Jersey and drop the kids off for a few days. Joan and I could then fly out of Newark Airport to Cincinnati for the conference and, upon our return, visit with our friends for a few days, and then go to Virginia Beach to see Joan's brother Fred and other family members. Then we could drive to Lynchburg and see one of our grandchildren. It was a round-about-way to head home, but it would allow us to see our family.

So, at the end of May we started the trip. We left on a Monday morning and had a great drive to New Jersey; no incidents, just a boring drive (so the kids thought). But Joan and I enjoyed seeing America. What a beautiful country we live in. When we arrived in New Jersey, we dropped the kids off at their friend's home and spent a few days with Joan's brother George and his family. On Saturday night, we decided that it would be a great idea to go to St. Mark's Church, our old home church. Besides, we could visit some friends at the same time.

So, on Sunday morning we went to St. Marks. Lo and behold, as God would have it, the bishop of the diocese of South Jersey was there, confirming some of the children. I thought, *Wow, what a special day!* Joan and I had a hand in teaching these kids early on. Now they were making their commitment to serve the Lord. What a great day. Then God slapped me on the side of my head.

As part of the bishop's sermon, he preached from Matthew 25:36b: "I was in prison, did you visit me?" Now that in and of itself was (to me) not so significant at the time. This message was not specifically meant for me, was it? Just coincidental, right? Man was I soon to find out how wrong I was!

The next morning as we left for the airport it was raining and the outlook for the rest of the day was not good. When we arrived at the airport and got our boarding passes, we headed toward the gate and heard an announcement that our flight was delayed about an hour. At about 10 a.m. we were told that the flight was delayed again. The flight, which originated in Boston, was still on the ground there and, because of the bad weather there, the airline could not say when our flight would leave. It was about 1 p.m. and I started to panic. We needed to get to Cincinnati for our conference. So, I went up to the podium and asked if there was another flight so that we could get to our destination today. The agent at the podium was polite but not very helpful, telling us that there was not any availability on another airline at that time. I did some of my own research and found nothing, so we were going to have to wait.

At about 3:30 p.m. the agent called me up to the podium and stated that if we were willing to take a short flight to Philadelphia, we could catch a plane to Cincinnati. I replied with a resounding YES! So off we go to the other side of the airport to board a twin prop Allegheny Airlines plane to Philly. It seemed like it was taking forever to takeoff. The plane was going from one runway to another. I thought we might see the pilot get a toll ticket to drive us there. Mind you, the weather was stormy. As the plane took off, the pilot came on the intercom and said that we needed to keep our seat belts securely tightened as it was going to be a bumpy ride all the way to Philadelphia. I know a good part of the terrain, even from the sky, and after about 20 minutes, I could see we were beginning to fly in circles around the area of Atlantic City. And it was getting to be bumpy. The turbulence, the tossing around, we felt like we were on a roller coaster ride. Besides, I suffered from motion sickness. This was a tough flight! Suffice to say I was sick. After about 30 minutes of circling around Atlantic City, the pilot reported that we have been diverted to Scranton-Wilkes-Berry Airport. We were told that there would be a Frontier Airlines plane waiting for us when we arrived. That was somewhat consoling. As we landed at Scranton Airport and we taxied up to the gate, out of the corner of my eye I saw a Frontier plane pulling out of an adjacent jet wing. Now what was up with that! Sure enough, that was the plane that was going to take us to Cincinnati. Now we were informed that there would be another Frontier Airlines plane in two hours. I was somewhat relieved that there would be a two-hour wait. That would give my stomach some time to quiet down. It most assuredly did calm down. It was getting late, almost 9 p.m. I was thinking we would not get into Cincinnati until after midnight. I was not a night person and did not enjoy this airplane madness. Finally, a plane arrived, we boarded it and were told that we are going to Pittsburgh to connect to another plane there to take us to Cincinnati. WHAAAT?!

After I calmed my wife down, we (once more) boarded another Frontier Airlines plane. We were about to give up getting to Pittsburgh and call it a night and go the rest of the way in the morning. Joan reminded me that there was a welcome breakfast by the company and we were expected to attend. So off we went to Pittsburgh, arriving there at approximately 10:30 p.m. Now, the last leg of our journey: getting to Cincinnati. We were told that there is only one flight leaving for Cincinnati that night and there were only a few seats left on this Pan Am flight.

Now I was truly in panic mode! Being just five months with the company and I was going to miss this welcome breakfast. No way. We were going to get those last seats and be on time for the meet-and-greet breakfast. Now this would be the third airline we would have been on that day. So, in a quizzical voice, I ask, "Do you think our luggage will be on the plane when we get there? Well, when the agent looked at our itinerary, he was holding back from an out-right laugh and said, "we can only hope!" I said to him I would pray for our luggage to be there when we de-planed. I wish I could have called that agent and told him that our luggage was the first to come off that plane. Praise God!

The meetings in Cincinnati were as expected, partly interesting and mostly boring, at least for the "old timers." But I was soaking it all in. I was excited about meeting the other sales reps. I had never been part of such a multi-national sales team and I was loving it. But, the honeymoon would soon be over. This was a well-oiled machine, precise in every facet: from sales, to printing, to delivery. I was extremely excited to be part of this team. But God had even more for me to get excited about after the conference was over!

CHAPTER 5

May 1982 — The Real Work Begins

"Ask and it will be given to you; seek and you will find ..."

- Matthew 7:7 (NKJ)

When Joan and I arrived back in New Jersey to pick up the kids and plan our trip back to Colorado, she asked me about how far it would be if we were to take a "detour" to Virginia so that she could see her brother Fred? "That's just about taking us in the wrong direction, literally south instead of west." But we could take an extra day or two if she really wanted to see her brother.

"Yes," she said. So, we went to Virginia Beach to see him. We decided to take the scenic route, driving directly south on the New Jersey Turnpike to the Cape May ferry. We got there just in time, as the ferry was about to leave. We were the last car to board. If we missed this one, we had to wait for the next one the next morning. We got off on the east shore of Maryland and continued our drive across the magnificent Chesapeake Bay bridge and tunnel into Norfolk, Virginia and then drove on down to Virginia Beach.

Our visit, although short, was a blessing to Fred and his family. We spoke of the work Joan and I were doing. On Sunday, Joan and I were going to church. Joan asked her brother Fred if there was an Episcopal church nearby. He didn't know for sure. We looked in the phone book and found several churches in the Virginia Beach area. As we were selecting one, Fred said, "that one is not the closest to us." But we chose that one anyway — another "God coincidence." When we arrived at the church, there seemed to be an exceptionally large crowd assembled. This was not any particular church holy day, or so we thought. It turned out that it was an extra special day for this church.

The bishop of the diocese of Virginia was coming and he was going to perform the sacrament of confirmation at this service. Joan and I thought it would great to attend this service. We decided to stay. After the opening portion of the mass, the bishop got up to speak. As he began his message, he informed the congregation that he was "taking bishop's privilege" and was going to use last week's gospel and preach on Matthew 25:36: "I was naked and you clothed Me; I was sick and you visited Me; I was in prison and you came to me." (NKJ)

I just burst into crying, sobbing and visibly overwrought. So much so that the bishop paused momentarily. After a few moments (which seemed like an eternity to me), I gathered my thoughts and composed myself enough for the bishop to continue. As for the rest of the service, it went along without any further interruptions on my part. I knew from that day on that God had a specific purpose for me and my family. It was not to sell calendars!

Immediately after returning from this business/vacation trip, I was in contact with the county sheriff's office to find out information about volunteering in the jail. I was referred to the chaplain, who was an Episcopal priest (how about that?) out of Manitou Springs. Wow! I was overcome with joy that the chaplain was from the same denomination as mine. Our meeting should be a slam dunk. He would want or need volunteers, and for sure another Episcopalian.

When I spoke with Father Scott, he was very supportive, but not receptive of needing another volunteer at the jail. He did, however, refer me to a chaplain in the state system. Father Scott indicated that the state system used a lot of volunteers and that I could be more effective in that environment. After sharing my story, and, feeling somewhat rejected, I went home.

I prayed that night and asked God to help me find the direction that He wanted me to go. *I need Your touch, to feel Your presence. Please, somehow, give me a sign as to what to do.*

During this time, I am employed with the Gordon Bernard Company and my job was to sell, sell, sell. So, I planned a trip to eastern Kansas to call on some accounts already established and to cold call on some other potential clients. The trip was scheduled for a week. While I was there, I renewed a few old accounts and established some new ones. On my way home, I was enjoying the scenery and I decided to take the "shortcut" road into Sharon Springs once again, thinking that I might stop there again just to say thanks for the help that I had received the first time heading to Colorado. That's where I had those car issues, and just maybe, I might get an introduction to someone within the local school district to show my wares and help the school district raise funds for one of their projects.

Then about five miles outside of Sharon Springs, my car broke down AGAIN. No, no that can't be, but here I was again! It was Friday AGAIN, and of course, I had the same vehicle, and of course the local garage did not stock the part I needed. The part I needed would be in on the Monday morning Greyhound bus. Three days in this one-garage town! I needed to be doing something, but what?

I prayed a lot. I slept a little. On Monday, I awaited the bus arrival with the part (a fuel filter). But when the bus arrived, the part did not. I went to the garage to see what was happening. I was told that the part did not get to the bus stop in time and therefore missed getting on the bus. They told me it would not be there until Tuesday. Here I was without a car and an appointment with someone that might be interested in our community calendar.

In spite of this, I sold the program to the local Rotary Club and was back on the road that late afternoon. Unknown to me at that time, the garage owner himself went to Wichita to pick up the part needed to fix my car. That's hospitality at its best. I was overwhelmed. The next day I phoned the chaplain at the state facility in Cañon City. I found out that the chaplain, a Catholic priest, was on vacation. I was told to call back next week. Bummer. But, if anything, I was persistent. God was teaching patience.

As I was driving home that day from a few appointments for the calendar business, I was listening to Christian music. A flash came to me from God. "Remember that KAIROS prison ministry you thought you left behind forever in New Jersey? Guess what, Bill Potter, you are here and right where I wanted you in the first place. Now get to work for Me. Time is running out!"

What does that mean, "Time is running out?" I instinctively responded with a resounding "Yes, Lord!" but received no answer.

The next week (it was now the beginning of June), when I called back to Cañon City, I spoke with the chaplain and set up an appointment for the following week. In the meantime, the chaplain suggested that I see a man up in Denver who was currently a volunteer. He would give me the rundown of the ins and outs of volunteering in the Colorado Department of Corrections. The man's name was Bill Fay. The next morning, I called Mr. Fay and went up that very afternoon to meet with him. I did have to cancel some other appointments in order to meet with him. God told me that was Priority One. Stop the presses and do it!

As I was sharing my testimony with him, he just sat there with this big smile on his face, nodding his head in approval. When I finished talking (after almost an hour), Bill told me that he had been praying for God to send him someone who had the organizational skills to do Cursillo in prison as he had started a Curisllo the prior year and felt the call to develop that program behind prison walls.

BINGO! The lights came on, the bells were ringing! KAIROS! LOUD AND CLEAR. THIS WAS TO BE THE MISSON – KAIROS. Get it established in Colorado. I asked Bill if he had ever heard of the KAIROS Prison Ministry. He responded in the affirmative, but he stated it was too expensive. There was no money for startup and there were costs involved to get an instructor from Florida and to teach the course to the volunteers (a requirement of the KAIROS ministry). "Let's pray," I said. "We will see how God moves."

In Matthew 7:7 it states: "Ask and it will be given you; seek and you will find, knock and it will be opened to you." (NKJ). Bill and I prayed for a while, then I left with a renewed spirit to drop what I was doing and seek God in His fullness. Little did I know at that time, what I was doing and its cost, not only to me, but also to my family. Could I quit my job and trust and rely on God fully? The trials were yet to come. Was I being foolish? Was this all wrong? Or was I intended to work for the Gordon Bernard

SENIOR CHAPLAIN BILL POTTER

Company? I would find out shortly that was not going to be good enough for them. A year later they would terminate me.

Bill Fay contacted me a week later and asked me to meet again on Friday. I agreed. On that day we began to put together what we thought God wanted us to design.

We strategized our next moves:

- Recruit people to participate in the ministry (BP)
- Raise funds (both)
- Introduce/explain the program to the prison staff (BF)
- Set dates, time and prisons we would be invited to go into (BF)
- Contact KAIROS national office to get the particulars on setting up the ministry in Colorado (BP)

Bill Fay would be "Mr. Inside" and I would be "Mr. Outside."

At our respective churches we began to speak out about the ministry. Some were interested, most were not. All this was to be expected. After much prayer, the Lord directed me to contact KAIROS national about the training needed so that we could start the ministry under their umbrella. Initially, I was informed of the up-front costs to have the training and that at least 45 to 60 people were needed to attend the training. Costs would include airfare for the trainer plus housing and food and a car rental. This was estimated to be approximately $3,000-4,500.

"WOW! That's a lot of money," Bill Fay said, when I called him about my conversation with KAIROS. We determined, after much prayer, that God, if He wills, will provide. Both of us will enlist our prayer warriors to lift this matter in prayer. In the meantime, we would continue to recruit potential team members.

What seemed to be coming out of nowhere was call after call to give presentations to various church groups, Curisllo meetings (Ultreyas), about KAIROS. When you are in God's will, things just "happen." Needless to say, the meetings were an outpouring of the Holy Spirit. Team member interest was overwhelming. I was so excited. In a matter of a few weeks, there were over 100 people signed up to attend a training session. All we needed now was the funds to get the trainer here.

I called Bill Fay and he told me that some funding had come in, but there was still a long way to go. "Don't worry, "God will do it," I responded. "Let's plan a training date for some-time in July."

"Great!" Bill said, and I agreed to call KAIROS to let them know that we wanted to set up a training date for some time in July.

The next morning, I called the KAIROS office and, with excitement, I told them how the Lord was moving in Colorado. However, there was one stipulation that we did not know about: The chaplain or warden of the intended facility must attend a Cursillo first. The intention was to ensure that the ministry would have someone on the inside who knows the ins and outs of the program and be its most ardent supporter.

This could potentially be a major stumbling block for the program, but to God, who can do all things, nothing is impossible! Therefore, no training was scheduled at that time. I was deeply distressed. I felt like I was letting people down. In my prayers, God told me not to sweat the small stuff. What did that mean? I would soon find out.

Bill and I met for coffee at a Denny's in Castle Rock a few days later to discuss how we were going to proceed from here. I was pleasantly surprised when Bill told me that the next Monday we had a meeting with the warden at the Colorado Women's Correctional Facility (CWCF), in Cañon City, a prison where Bill volunteered. A glimmer of hope from God. Bill told me that he knew of the requirement of KAIROS and that is why we were having the meeting. He suggested that we pray about the outcome of that meeting.

That Monday, Bill and I met at 10 a.m. at the prison for our scheduled meeting. After the usual introductions, we got down to business. Attending that meeting were captains from the security, housing, and food service departments. As we explained the total program, they had many questions about the process. How many volunteers and inmates would be involved? Would the food service department feed the volunteers? How many guests would attend the closing service on Sunday? All of these we answered to the best of our knowledge, mostly to the satisfaction of all, especially the warden. That was a plus, for sure.

After the meeting concluded, the warden invited Bill and I to stay for lunch. While I was not too excited about eating prison food, Bill agreed for both of us. The warden took us in the dining hall and left. He told us he had to make an important phone call. He returned a short time later and asked if we would be able to go to the Fremont Correctional Facility (FCF), at 2 p.m. Bill had also volunteered there. He gave a quizzical positive look, so I agreed. Up to this point, the warden had not agreed to go on a Cursillo weekend. A lot of issues still needed to be resolved.

After lunch, the warden had his head of security give me a tour of the prison. It was a small prison in comparison to most. An old facility, built in the early 1900s, it housed a maximum of 96 women. Thus, the tour did not last very long. We chatted for a while in the warden's office before we left for FCF. During that meeting the warden told us that his counterpart at FCF was having a staff meeting that day and that a time was set up for us to speak on KAIROS at that meeting as well. That was a surprise to me. Bill had forgotten to tell me about that one.

That meeting was a blessing in disguise. The warden there had heard about the ministry while attending a conference. Another warden from South Carolina was sharing with him the tremendous blessing KAIROS has been to his facility and encouraged the Colorado warden, saying if he ever had the chance to have that ministry at his prison, he would see the positive effect on the entire population. So, God was in action before we thought of it.

This meeting was a shoe-in. In fact, it was almost funny. The warden knew about the stipulation that either he or the chaplain needed to attend a Cursillo. He asked if it would be okay for his assistant warden to go in his place. We gave that a conditional approval and would check with the national office, and the wardens knew the dates.

The next day, I called and received permission for the associate warden to go instead of the warden. Calls were made to the prisons to inform them of the go ahead. Now we had to find out when and where the next Cursillo was happening. This is when the associate warden called me to tell me that he did not go anywhere without his wife. This was certainly a fly in the ointment. Cursillo weekends, I later learned, for the most part were men only or women only, though there were a few co-ed weekends. So, right away I made a few phone calls and found out that there was a co-ed weekend coming up in about three weeks in San Antonio, Texas. I then called the warden at CWCF and asked him to clear those dates. I learned the associate warden at FCF could go and they could attend together, and he would bring his wife, too. Then it was cleared for the two couples to go together to the Cursillo in San Antonio.

All we needed was to buy the plane tickets and cover the additional $400 costs for the weekend. I also needed to find out if there was room for two more couples and whether someone could pick them up at the airport and bring them back on Sunday night to fly home. An awful lot to ask of people you don't know. Only God could work it out! And He did. Everything went without a hitch. In fact, both were amazed at how it all came about. People in San Antonio who did not know these people from Colorado picked them up (we sent pictures) as they de-planed, without even name cards, and walked right up and introduced themselves and took them to the weekend seminar. The questions they had when they returned were, "how are we going to do this?" Not we can't do this. We were all amazed. Only God.

To those who do not understand the workings of KAIROS, it literally is an invasion of the normal operations of any prison. The number of volunteers can be over 200, home-cooked meals must be prepared for each offender, 400 dozen homemade cookies must be baked, and personal letters written to each offender. All this certainly can impose a security nightmare.

CHAPTER 6

"Trust in the Lord with all your heart"

- Proverbs 3:5&6 (NKJ)

"There is no currency in this world that passes at such a premium anywhere as good Christian character. The time has gone by when the young man or the young woman in the United States has to apologize for being a follower of Christ ... No cause but one could have brought together so many people, and that is the cause of our Master." - William McKinley, 25th President of the United States (1897-1901) APB

By mid-August, Bill and I (by God's grace) had our meeting with the wardens. After that, Bill and I put our heads together and developed a plan to bring the first ever KAIROS weekend to Colorado that October. We knew that only with God by our side directing our steps would we succeed.

Bill Fay was going to coordinate the needs of the program from the security side and get preliminary approval for a location to hold the 3 ½-day event and the equipment we were planning to bring into the prison. I was to continue to recruit volunteers from the Colorado Cursillo community. I was also going to work with KAIROS national office to arrange training.

Before I called KAIROS, I had called upon my prayer group to join in praying that God would help us find a solution to what appeared to be an insurmountable task. That following day, about mid-morning, I called KAIROS and the person I needed to speak to was not in that day. There was, however, a member of the board who was in the office, and he agreed to talk to me. In my conversation with Dick Day, I learned he was one of the "original nine old men" that founded KAIROS. After the obvious questions I had about the training costs, and the disclosure that we had yet to raise the money, he said if we could get enough people together in two weeks, he himself will do the training at "little to no cost!" I was (almost) speechless. Dick said, "Hello? Are you still there?"

After a few seconds, I regained my composure and said, "Yes." He went on to explain that he had a pre-planned business trip to Denver at that time, which would end on Thursday. If the two training sessions could be scheduled for that Friday night and all-day Saturday, he would change his plane ticket and return on Sunday instead. I immediately responded with a resounding "yes!" Little did I know how difficult it would be, but with God, nothing is impossible. I was almost in panic mode, until I went to the Lord in prayer. I was on a learning curve and little did I know that prayer would become a key part of my life forevermore.

I told Bill of the great news about scheduling the training for the following weekend and that it was going to cost us ZERO! He responded, "Wow!" He was as surprised about this as I was, but could we pull it off? It was going to take a lot, but with God all things are possible.

The task of calling everyone (about 40-100 people) would have seemed impossible in the short time frame before the scheduled meeting. To get 45 or more people together in that short period of time, with potential conflicts and all, would have to be a miracle of God. Of the 45 or so we called, only two declined due to other commitments. I was amazed! Some even asked if they could bring an extra guest or two? Without hesitation, I responded with a resounding "yes!"

Bill made the arrangements for the site to hold the classes. I made the arrangements for lunch on Saturday and for other refreshments as well. When I looked at my Day-Timer for the calendar company, I was scheduled to be out of town on a business trip. I really needed to keep those scheduled appointments. In my anxiety, excitement, or whatever else you want to call it, I cancelled all those appointments and, much to my dismay, I was not immediately able to reschedule any of them. *Oh well,*

I thought, *something else will come up. God will provide. My company will understand — they are Christians.*

The Friday of the meeting, 45 people showed up for the training. As I entered the room, I could immediately sense the presence of the Holy Spirit. There was an obvious air of excitement. Almost as if we were waiting to see God come through the door. It was only Mr. Day, but the Spirit of God was certainly with him.

The essence of the first meeting was how important it was to build the team. This unity that Dick was speaking about was to become the cornerstone of the ministry. First and foremost, each and every team member must be fully open to the Spirit of God to effectively minister to offenders, but also to the prison staff, through a humility that could only be attained through God's Spirit living and breathing within each team member. This team, and all the teams that would follow, needed to know that God had to be first in their lives. They must be able to display that love of God not only while working in this ministry, but develop a new openness, a new way to openly show how much God loves them by the words through which they lovingly share their testimony with others. As time would prove, KAIROS would become the premier example of that love to all who met its members, volunteers, team members, prison staff and, obviously, the offenders.

On Saturday morning, this session was to go through the nitty-gritty of the outline of the weekend, the nuts and bolts of what each talk was about. Although KAIROS was a similar type of presentation as Cursillo, there are significant nuances that Dick noted. One bullet point of the class was to show the utmost respect to the staff. We were invading their territory, as guests in their "house," with a program that most did not want there in the first place. This could lead to great conflict if we let it. This reminded me of my military days when we were instructed to "always obey our last order first." That meant that no matter what, if an officer told us to do something, our response was to be, "Yes, Sir." No questions asked, period! This approach was (almost) a showstopper for some. You see, many of the attendees were self-made businesspeople and military types, from career enlisted to officers. Some owned their own businesses or were managers of some sort and were used to giving the orders, not taking them. A hard nut to swallow.

At this time, KAIROS national was also in its infancy. They were still trying to get organized insofar as getting a formalized manual of operations and talk outlines for the start-up ministries that wanted affiliation with the national office. Mr. Day did have with him a sample manual of how to conduct a weekend. He did explain to all present that this was a "living document," anticipating changes. The last two hours of training were devoted to helping to set up a "ministry infrastructure," explaining how the nuts and bolts of the ministry "ideally" should be run.

I want readers to understand that I was never and still am not a person who always does things in an ideal manner. Not that I fly by the seat of my pants. But some would say that I have a "full speed ahead" mentality. I was not a "nuts and bolts" type of a person. My wife Joan would develop into that person for me and the ministry. After the training session ended, a few of us wanted to take Dick out to dinner to pick his brain a little more. He explained that he would be taking a red-eye flight back to Florida that night, as he could not get a flight out on Sunday. Most assuredly we knew that we had a lot of work ahead of us and not a lot of time to get it done before our first weekend, which was scheduled for October 1982 at the Colorado Women's Correctional Facility.

Right before the attendees were dismissed, I asked them to remain for a few moments. Bill Fay and I put our heads together and presented a proposal of what we felt necessary for a weekend #1 in October. We planned a meeting for the following Saturday at the same place, at the same start time, 9 a.m. There was a pressing need to form a council to oversee the start-up operations and pursue funding, which was estimated to be around $2,000. Most said they would be there, but a few were non-committed. Dick Day, who remained and was listening, interrupted and suggested charging team fees, as was commonly done throughout Cursillo. Also, we could have the various churches represented in the team/community prepare the meals and bake the cookies. All agreed. We needed approximately 1,200 dozen cookies for the weekend! (I would explain why in the next chapter.) Meeting was adjourned.

So much material was covered, but I was not good at taking copious notes. Thank God, Joan was. Plus, I had the only copy of the authorized manual. I hoped to prepare about 10 or 12 copies before our meeting on

Saturday. I was to be out of town that week on a business trip to Oklahoma, leaving Sunday night and not returning until late Thursday. As I prayed about that trip and was looking at the preparation needed for the pre-KAIROS team meeting Saturday, there would not be enough time to get it all done, so I revisited my schedule to see what changes could be made. If I left early on Sunday, I might be able to make some calls to possibly move up some dates and times of some meetings to complete all my appointments on or before Wednesday evening. Much to my dismay, that was not going to happen. So, I did the next best thing. I tried to reschedule for the following week. That didn't work either. I had to cancel four meetings until September or October. My company did not like that very much.

I initially did not give the company a detailed explanation of the need to make those changes. They would confront me about all the changes to my scheduling at the annual sales meeting in June. The company ultimately terminated me the following January. At the time, I thought (and prayed) it was all good. I was reminded to "Trust in the Lord with all your heart and lean not on your own understanding" (Proverbs 3:5, NKJ). In addition, I felt that my talents were very marketable, being the salesman that I was.

I would soon find out that I needed to get the I's out of the way and let God work in and through me —a tough and hard lesson to learn. I have always been in control in my BC days (Before Christ came into my life). Hard, hard lessons to learn and it would take a lot of time to learn these lessons. I was ever so thankful that during this time God had given me the most wonderful, understanding helpmate in all the world. Joan stuck with me through it all. Glory to God for His love and mercy, for His mercy endures forever!

Before the people gathered for the first-ever KAIROS team meeting in Colorado, they were asked to pray over who they felt God was calling to lead this ministry through its infancy. There would be needed approximately 12 people to be on that ad hoc committee, which would eventually become its governing board and prayer support. The group came with lots of enthusiasm, prayed up and ready to go, or so I thought. There happened to be a few clergy in attendance this time who were not there previously. They would become a nucleus for the recruitment of additional clergy in the future. There were others in attendance that were not at the training sessions but wanted to participate in the program. This would create a minor problem that our prospective trainer, who would be selected at a future meeting, would resolve.

Bill Fay had received volunteer applications from the CDOC for all to fill out. Some volunteers objected. Some had minor offenses, misdemeanors, some had family in prison, some had friends that are incarcerated and were on their visiting list. These were all disqualifiers. That eliminated about six or seven volunteers. Now came the issue of clergy. They would visit from time to time at the various prisons in Cañon City and conduct services as well as counsel some offenders, and even hear confessions. The question was, "Will this preclude them from participating in KAIROS?" No one (at this time) knew the answer. Fortunately, I found out later, it did not. While no one fully understood the responsibilities of any of the leadership roles, all positions were filled that day. Bill Fay became "Mr. Inside" coordinator with the prisons; Bill Potter became "Mr. Outside" coordinator of recruitment, funds, cookies, and meetings. Boy, I would soon find out that I had bitten off more than I could chew.

I knew we needed some $2,000 or more for the weekend expenses. In addition, we needed lodging for the team, which would be around 40 people. That would mean at least 20 rooms in a hotel for three nights. This would be an added expense, over and above the $2,000. I was thinking, not praying, about this, and the challenge was consuming me. I was getting irritated, though Joan would call it something else.

As I was trying to figure it all out, I thought, prayer might help, or would it? What if this is not part of God's plan and only mine? Maybe a few others as well. But I decided to talk to Abba Father. I even took the time to pause and listen. Then, it came to me, thanks be to God, an inspired revelation. Go talk to the three Roman Catholic bishops in the area and the one Episcopal bishop, too. Four bishops in total. For the start-up team included Roman Catholics and Episcopalians. If each bishop would provide $500 from their funds, we would be in good shape. So, I set about arranging appointments through the clergy that were in attendance.

On Wednesday of that week, Steve, one of the prospective team members, called me about possibly attending a Catholic Cursillo closing service in Colorado Springs that Sunday afternoon. One of the bishops of the diocese would be on that team and he would try to get him to talk to me about this "KAIROS" ministry. I gladly accepted the invitation and asked him what time the closing would be held and where. He informed me that it would be from 3-4 p.m. at the Catholic Church in Widefield and that he would be looking out for me.

As I arrived at the church parking lot a few minutes early (2:45 p.m.), Steve came out to greet me. The expression on his face was that of overflowing joy. I knew he must have been on the team for that weekend, the overwhelming joy of the Lord was that obvious. I asked, "How is the weekend going?" with a grin from ear to ear he stated, "What a powerful weekend!" And he even had a chance to mention KAIROS, and it seems as if there was some interest aroused amongst everyone, including the bishop. In fact, the bishop wanted to see me after the closing and was making it a point to do that.

As the service started, I took note of the people that were there for the weekend. I could almost pick out the team members from the candidates, or so I thought. I found out later that I was almost totally wrong. The clergy types were obvious to pick out with their proper attire. But which one was the bishop? There were eight priests in total on the team, from a rather young redhead priest to one that was much older. I once again was trying to "pigeonhole" people, and I picked the wrong one. I thought that most bishops would normally wear proper clerical attire suitable for the office of bishop. Wrong again, Bill.

The last person I thought to be the bishop was the young redhead in the group. But that was him, Auxiliary Bishop Hannifin of Denver. I later found out that the Denver diocese was to be split and there would be a new diocese of Colorado Springs, with Bishop Hannifin to be appointed Archbishop. As I spoke with him, I immediately felt the overwhelming presence of God with him. He was radiant, beaming if you will, and almost glowing. Glory to God. I knew that he would be open to receive what the KAIROS ministry would mean to the offenders who were incarcerated in Colorado. As we spoke, his interest was stirred, and he immediately told us that we would be able to talk better at his office the next day. He said he would clear his appointment schedule in order to meet with me at 3 p.m. Monday afternoon. I thanked him and went and shook Steve's hand and asked if he wanted to join me at that meeting. He declined because he had to work the next day. I told him that I would call him that night after the meeting.

Driving home late that Sunday afternoon, I was so overwhelmed by the Holy Spirit that I started to cry. So much so that I had to pull over for a few minutes as I prayed and contemplated what had just happened. Simply stated, God was at work to bring salvation to the lost, the prison. "When I was in prison and you came to me?" (Matthew 25:36 NKJ). Every time from this day forward those words would keep echoing in my mind whenever I went into a facility to visit.

While I was living in New Jersey, I was preparing for the ordained ministry. Since I was over 40 years of age, I could qualify for the process through what was known as the "old man's canon." Although at the time I took personal offense at the phrase "old man's canon" (I was not thinking of me as an "old man"), I did appreciate that I did not have to go through a formal seminary process, which allowed me to take courses of study through the Bishop's School of Theology in New Jersey, a home study plus weekend seminars with the bishop or his designee.

When I arrived in Colorado, I inquired if the diocese had such a program and was informed that they did, so I enrolled. *Wow,* I figured, *He, God, wanted me in Colorado, to be a prison chaplain.* The exact place I did not want to be in New Jersey, but why Colorado? I was asking God. Never did get an answer to that question. As I did look at the Rocky Mountains, I believe there was my answer. There is a song that I was not so sure of its title, but in part it goes: "If God doesn't live in Colorado, I bet He spends a lot of time there." I understand that! These mountains are spectacular.

CHAPTER 7

"The steps of a good man are ordered by the Lord, and He delights in his way."

- Psalm 37:23 (NKJ)

"Should not the Bible regain the place it once held as a schoolbook? Its morals are pure examples, captivating and noble ... In no book is good English so pure and so elegant, and by teaching all the same book they will speak alike, and the Bible will justly remain the standard of language as well as faith." -Fisher Ames, author of the First Amendment (taken from the American Patriot Bible)

My plate was quickly overflowing and about to burst. Something had to give! Between traveling for work, study for ordination and the KAIROS prison ministry getting started, I was at the brink of physical exhaustion. I had a dilemma. I couldn't stop working, as I needed to pay the bills. But I needed to complete the ordination process, to be recognized in a formal way by the Department of Corrections to add credibility to the ministry. I could not stop serving KAIROS for the ministry to grow.

Wait a minute, I needed to stop ... and pray. As I did so, God said to me, "It's about time you stopped to listen to Me instead of all the I's you have placed before Me." Wow! Here I was again, putting me before the Lord. Losing sight of Who it is that Bill Potter should be following. Get out of the way and start to follow His Way. I would from time to time thereafter get in His Way and keep trying to do things as Ol' Blue Eyes would always say "my way." (By the way, for some of the younger folk, that person I referred to as "Ol' Blue Eyes" was Frank Sinatra.)

As I was praying and listening, God spoke to me, not so much in an audible way, but through that inner peace that you sense in your heart and mind from God as the right thing to do. I started to set-up appointments to see the various Catholic bishops in Denver, Colorado Springs and Pueblo. In addition, I was also going to see the Episcopal bishop who was also in Denver, Bishop William Frey.

First, I went to see Bishop Hannifin in Colorado Springs, since I lived there too. The bishop was very receptive and was willing to offer support in any way he could. First, we needed prayers, people, and money. He said that he would for sure pray and open the door for help with recruitment, by endorsing the ministry in his next weekly/monthly letter to his churches. About the money, he was not so sure. Funds were tight, and it depended on the amount we were looking at. I explained that if all the bishops would be able to give an equal amount of $500 dollars, the first weekend's basic finances would be covered and that the team fees from this team would be the foundational support for the next and ensuing weekends that would follow. So, this was, in essence, seed money. It seemed that the bishop (who also was involved in prison visitation), took all of a blink of an eye, and he was on the phone talking to someone about a check for $500. Then, he said, "I'm in," that he would be honored to the first bishop in the state to offer his whole-hearted support for KAIROS.

After he hung up from that call, he called the bishop in Denver and, hitting the mute button, asked me when this week I could get up to the Denver archdiocese to meet with the Bishop Dolan. I told him as soon as possible. He then proceeded to ask, "when would the bishop possibly have an opening" to meet with me. I got an answer right away. The Bishop had a last-minute cancelation that following day at 3 p.m. I responded, "I'll take it." Bishop Hannifin added that the Denver diocese prison chaplain would also be in attendance, if that would be okay with me. "Sure," I replied.

It is an amazing God we serve. How He orchestrates our path is awesome, we just need to allow ourselves to take His advice and follow. A great lesson that needs to be learned over and over and over, I would find out many more times in my life. As I left Bishop Hannifin, I stopped and called Bill Fay to see if he would be able to join me at that meeting. He respectfully declined due to a prior business commitment. I just said I would keep him informed of my progress. When I told him about the $500 check from Bishop Hannifin, he just shouted, "Hallelujah, God is good!"

It was a dark, gloomy morning that Tuesday as I drove up to Denver. Rainy in Colorado Springs but snowing as I approached Monument Hill. I mean, an almost blinding snowstorm. As I slowed down due to the conditions, others were beeping at me and speeding by, including semis and other trucks and cars. But I was not going to speed up for anyone, as I was not too sure of the road conditions, having never driven them up until now. As I came down from Monument Hill, there was a monster eight-car/truck pile-up that stopped all traffic in either direction for almost two hours. I was glad that I left with plenty of time to spare just in case of such an event. Fortunately, the accident was on the opposite side of the road and the delay only impacted the northbound side for the short time that it took the emergency crews to arrive.

As I was coming through Castle Rock, the snow, much to my amazement, just stopped. I mean, like I had come through a curtain and there I was on dry roads the rest of the way to Denver. So, I decided to get off the highway and relieve the stress of the drive and get lunch before I continued to the meeting.

As I came into Denver, I was pulled over by a very polite and friendly state trooper. As he approached my car, I noticed that he had his ticket pad out. I wasn't speeding or driving erratically. He asked for license and registration. As I was getting the documents he asked for, he said, "Do you know that you have a taillight out?"

"No sir," I responded.

"I am issuing a warning. Please get it fixed soon."

"Yes officer."

He said have a great day and left. *Thank you, Lord,* I said to myself and drove off.

When I arrived at the Roman Catholic Cathedral parking lot, there were no parking spaces available. I had to park on the street, by a parking meter. Not having any change in my pocket, I quickly looked around to find some place where I might be able to get some. I saw a meter maid on the next block. Now what to do? There was a restaurant there and a few retail stores. People walking around shopping. Out of the blue a young man approached me and said, "do you need help? You look confused."

I responded that I didn't have any change. "Can you change a dollar?"

He reached into his pocket and gave me a quarter and said, "It's on me."

Wow! It's rare these days that people do such things. Again, a "thank You, Lord" was appropriate. God watches over and supplies our every need. "And my God shall supply all your needs according to His riches in glory by Christ Jesus" (Philippians 4:19 NKJ).

When I entered the Catholic diocese office (arriving 15 minutes before my scheduled appointment) and introduced myself, the receptionist said, "Go right in. The archbishop is waiting for you."

I later learned that Archbishop Stafford wasn't waiting for me. He was expecting Father John, his diocesan prison chaplain, so that he could get the lowdown on what KAIROS was all about. Upon exchanging some pleasantries, I noticed that he kept clanking at this watch. Finally, he asked me to explain some things concerning this prison ministry. In conclusion of somewhat of a dissertation about how KAIROS works, Stafford said, "How can I help?"

That's why I came here in the first place, I was thinking to myself. I further explained that Bishop Hannifin and Episcopal Bishop Frey had already donated $500 each for seed money, and, would he be able to match the same amount? After some thought, he agreed. He called to the finance person and had them issue a check immediately to KAIROS of Colorado. I told him that a report would be forwarded to him with details of the impact this first weekend had on the inmates, staff, and the prison. He shook my hand and directed me to the door and had his assistant bring me to the finance officer, who handed me the check.

Just as I was headed out the door, the archbishop's assistant came running up to me and asked me to come back in because the archbishop wanted to speak to me again. *Uh oh,* I thought. He had changed his mind and wanted the check back.

When I entered his office, there was a priest in there with him. I learned that it was Father John, the priest in charge of Catholic prison ministry for the archdiocese. This meeting was just a "get acquainted" one. Father John asked me if I would like to have dinner with him that evening. I respectfully declined and told him, because of the snow coming down on Monument Hill, I needed to get home before that portion of the highway might be closed. I did ask for a raincheck, which he gladly gave to me.

On the way home, I rejoiced at God's marvelous blessing this day and how humbling a feeling that He had selected me to do this work. Didn't He know that I left New Jersey because I did not want to go into this crazy prison ministry called KAIROS? A little rhetorical, maybe, of course I knew that God knows all things. But maybe, just maybe occasionally, something or someone slips through the cracks?

Newsflash, Bill: There are no cracks in God's plan! Glory to God. The key to the churches coming together is the common understanding that the one and only thing that could cross the denominational borders is the Bible (some translations excluded). What joy filled my heart that this understanding could be reached. The fact that KAIROS is an interfaith ministry that strongly holds to those precepts was the moving force for the seed monies coming forth from the bishops throughout the state. Glory to God!

One last mountain to climb (I thought would be the easiest): the Bishop of Pueblo, Bishop Arthur Tofoya. I understood that he was the strongest supporter of prison ministry, having been rescued from drowning several years before by an outside inmate work crew as he was in a river fishing when his boat capsized. Much to my surprise, I would soon find out it was quite the opposite.

I initially had a tough time scheduling a meeting with Bishop Tofoya because he was traveling out to the western slope of Colorado. It was not until mid-September that I would be able to see him. Bill Fay and I talked things over and we agreed to go ahead with the assumption that the remaining $500 would be forthcoming from the bishop upon our meeting. Bill would contact the Denver folks, and I the Colorado Springs people. The team formation process would begin in a week or so with the first one taking place in Colorado Springs at Holy Spirit Episcopal church. The ad hoc committee was meeting that Saturday to set up the teams, with this first weekend to be held in the Colorado Women's Correctional Facility in Cañon City. The leader would be Sandy Browning, a person from our initial prayer group. By the way, the rest of the women from our prayer group were on the team as well. The ones who at one point in time said, "Oh no, not me." God is great and greatly to be praised.

Bill and I had already planned to be "servants" on this first team, to be the all-around gofers to take care of any last-minute errors or omissions. We saw to it that all was taken care of. Besides, Bill and I had to make sure if there were any major staff concerns security issues, we would handle them.

The first meeting was designed primarily as a team "get acquainted" time. Assignments were to be handed out. The talks, of which there were 14, were handed out as well with the understanding that each would be critiqued by the team before the weekend. This would be done before all weekend seminars, in order to keep the method of the ministry protected in its original intent by the authors.

It was approaching lunch. All were instructed to bring a sack lunch and beverages would be provided (coffee, iced tea, etc.). I was going for some coffee and a lady was standing by the pot and I just couldn't get around her, so I said, "Excuse me, but I would like to get some coffee and you seem to be blocking the pot. By the way, I am notorious for not remembering names, so what is yours?"

She smiled and said, "My name is Louise."

Then I asked her, "Are you 'Roman?'" (meaning are you Roman Catholic?) She replied, "Oh no, I am Mexican!" Well, did we have a laugh about that one for many years, in fact, I still have a chuckle every now and again.

Back to meeting with Bishop Tofoya. At the appointed date and time, I did arrive in Pueblo at the Bishop's office. I was excited that finally the last part of the funds would be in hand. This was going to be a matter of explaining — asking for the funds. But (and there always seems to be a "but" clause) the bishop was much opposed to the idea of contributing to this ministry. After all, this did not start within his diocese, nor was it exclusively Catholic.

I proceeded to explain that this ministry was an off-shoot of the

Roman Catholic Cursillo program that started in Spain back in 1945 and that it was brought to the U.S. by the Spanish Air Force trainees while they were training at an air force base in Texas. He really was not impressed with my background knowledge of the ministry. Bishop Tofoya stated that he was late for a dental appointment and was excusing himself, when I interrupted him to remind him this "first weekend" was taking place in his diocese with the support of the other Roman Catholic bishops of the state, plus the Episcopal bishop. It would be a shame if his name was omitted when sponsors were around. He then took a very pregnant pause and contemplated my words. He then said I made a very persuasive point.

After another minute or two, he picked up the phone, hesitated a moment, looked at me and said, "This is a one-time request, right? Yes? You have a very convincing way about you, Mr. Potter."

Then he dialed a number and spoke with the diocese treasurer and requested a check in the amount of $500 made out to KAIROS of Colorado. I then let him know when the closing service at the prison would be and that an invitation was extended to him, if he wished to attend. I shook his hand and went out by the reception area to wait for the check. As I was waiting, I did notice that the bishop never left his office. Strange, I thought, but nevertheless, after about a half-hour wait, I received the check. I went on my merry way, thanking God for His love and mercy.

As a matter of fact, I missed some appointments for the calendar company. I did not realize the foremost reason I was in Colorado was GOD! Thanking Him for all He was providing, but inwardly I was thinking about what I was doing for God. Later that night, as I was reading from His Word, I was deeply humbled, and I asked God for His forgiveness for acting in a prideful way.

Here is that Scripture: "Trust in the Lord with all your heart and lean not on your own understanding. In all your ways acknowledge Him, and He shall direct your paths." -Proverbs 3:5-6 (NKJ)

CHAPTER 8

"I will never leave you nor forsake you."

- Hebrews 13:5

D riving home from Denver late that afternoon, I thought of the work I was doing to establish KAIROS in Colorado and the work I was putting aside that was my livelihood.

Lord, I prayed, what do I do or where do I go from here? There is so much to do for the ministry, yet I need my job to support my family. Or do You have something else in mind?

I really need an answer. I never asked such a direct question of God before, but I needed answers, and I needed them soon. Work selling calendars was being neglected, yet I knew I was doing what God wanted me to do. Right? Still, I was doubtful. I wouldn't keep this job for very long unless I start producing. *Help me Lord, please.*

Nothing. Not a word.

I arrived home about 6:30 p.m. and Joan was cooking. I said to her, "Let's go out to eat."

She immediately turned all of the burners off and said, "Let's go, I'm ready." She called the kids up from downstairs and we all went out for pizza. I had a sleepless night, tossing and turning all night. I had a few appointments locally the next day, and I was not in the mood for them, but I got up early, dressed, and left for my first of three appointments that day in and around Pueblo.

I really wasn't feeling up to par, with not much sleep that night before, but God helped me through this first one, and I even impressed myself, and sold a program. Wow! My next appointment was in about an hour. It was only about 20 minutes away from where I was. I spotted a nice enough looking local diner and decided to stop there for a light lunch. Well, my lunch had nothing light about it. A big chorizo and beef stuffed burrito. Hot and spicy! Yummy. I would regret eating that in the not-too-distant future.

I really worked fast through the second meeting, and — surprise, surprise — sold that account, too. Maybe that was the answer God was giving me. Surely, I would not make it three in a row, if I can make it through that last appointment. Praise God, all went well, I was able to get to that last appointment without any further problems. I sold that account as well. Glory to God. In addition to that sale, I made my quota for the month for the first time since I started with Gordon Bernard Company. I was elated. Not only did I meet my quota, but I felt that I got my answer from God as well (or so I thought).

This talking to God is cool! He really does supply our needs. Psalm 55:22 says, "Cast your burdens on the Lord, and He shall sustain you; He shall never permit the righteousness to be moved." Words I would never forget.

After I processed those orders, I went to my KAIROS folder to see what I needed to do for supplies for the weekend. Tables and chairs needed to be rented along with a truck to bring them to the prison. Team applications needed to be filled out and turned in rather quickly. Security background checks on them all must be completed before anyone can get into the prison for the seminar.

The one thing that Bill Fay and I sort of neglected was the need to have the chaplain at the prison attend a Cursillo weekend. But not really. You see there was not a CDOC staff chaplain currently assigned to the prison. A dilemma? Maybe not. What if the warden were to attend such a weekend? Would that even be possible?

The KAIROS national office was emphatic that someone in a position of authority from that facility needed to attend an "outside weekend" before KAIROS could be held, period. Now what do we do? A meeting was set up with the warden at CWCF for the following week. In the meantime,

Bill and I had a meeting with the warden at FCF the next day to see if arrangements could be made for the first KAIROS weekend at that facility next spring.

Upon entering FCF, we were escorted to the facility conference room. We were alone in the room for a while when the doors were flung open and this angry looking man in uniform entered and just said, "follow me." Okay. To the wardens' office we went. Once in there, a group of six people entered, some in uniform, some not. No Warden McGoff, though. The air seemed somehow very thick. No one was talking. We did exchange a few pleasantries, but then silence, a silence that seemed to last an inordinate amount of time, but actually about five minutes.

When Warden McGoff entered the room, the ice was broken. He was a warm, friendly man, and it was obvious he was sympathetic from his opening remarks about KAIROS. When we first met him about a month earlier, he was all questions about the ministry. Questions like, "How long has the ministry been doing the seminars and where?" "What kind of space would be required for the weekend?" "How many people?" etc. As we were explaining how the program worked, I happened to mention a prison in North Carolina where KAIROS had been for a long time. McGoff stopped me and said, "That's all the information I need. I will make a phone call later." He said, "Thanks for coming and have a great day." He would get in touch with us.

That seemed strange to Bill and me as we were talking on the way home. We never did get that phone call. But the meeting that was to take place the following month went as scheduled. After the warden entered the room, things were okay. We were asked to explain the nuts and bolts of the ministry. We addressed the concerns that the security staff brought up. When there seemed to be an impasse, the warden said to the staff, we can work it out, not to worry. Wow! Then came the biggest question of all: There was no chaplain at that facility at that time. Someone had to attend, but who? There was a momentary (pregnant) pause. Then Warden McGoff looked over to this assistant and said, "That would be a great thing for you to do, Ben."

Ben Johnson was the associate warden at FCF. What else could he say but "okay, boss"? I informed Mr. Johnson that the trip would be a "no out-of-pocket expense" for him. Mr. Johnson then said, "We have to talk." As I walked down the dull, drab, almost colorless corridor, Ben had a quick pace that I almost had to make a trot of sorts to keep up with him. We entered his office and, much to my surprise, the atmosphere changed in an instant. This office did not look like anything I would have expected. It was well taken care of; almost meticulous. Clean would most certainly be an understatement. Everything has a place, and everything in its place.

Benny (that's what he preferred to be called) invited me to sit down. We needed to clarify a few matters. "First, I do not go anywhere without my wife," he said. "I really do not want to go on this "Cursillo" weekend. I will do all within my power not to go. Do you understand me?"

"But …"

And before I could say another word, Mr. Johnson pointed his finger at me and said, "What don't you understand about I DO NOT WANT TO GO ON THIS WEEKEND?"

Needless to say, he was very intimidating, cold, firm, and calculating. I gulped and said, "Let me put your concerns to rest. This is a wonderful opportunity to share Christ's love for everyone."

I soon found out that Benny was a believer. What joy filled my heart. In addition, I picked up some measure of dislike for "jailhouse religion." I explained to him the "KAIROS" method is so designed to weed out those types very quickly. For him to understand the method, he would need to partake in a similar weekend himself. Then, and only then, would he completely know the process and outcome of the weekend.

He reiterated, "I do not want to go on any weekend program. Period." I could see we were at an impasse. Then, as I looked at my watch, I remembered that if I didn't leave FCF at once, I was going to be late for my appointment with Warden Dick Mills at the women's facility. I expressed to Benny that I had to leave because of the meeting. Then, much to my surprise, Benny put on a big smile and said to me in a much more friendly way: "If you convince Warden Mills and his wife to go on this 'Curisillo' weekend, my wife and I would go with them!"

Well, that got me excited and I almost shouted "hallelujah." I was excited as I left Mr. Johnson's office and headed to CWCF. "Thank you, Lord, for this opportunity to bring your Word into these two prisons. May, by your grace and mercy, KAIROS be able to explain how important it is for the Word of God to be delivered to these offenders who feel that they have been abandoned by family and friends because of their actions."

As I approached CWCF, I felt an overwhelming presence of the Lord come over me, a strange (but awesome) peace. I was greeted by a uniformed officer at the front door who knew my name and said that warden Mills was expecting me. He escorted me into a conference room, offered me coffee, and I accepted. He then informed me that the warden would be in shortly.

Well, shortly became almost an hour. When Warden Mills came into the room, he brought with him a group of about eight others, some in uniform, others in plain clothes and one woman in prison garb. Warden Mills introduced the group to me and indicated that each of these "team" members would have some strategic input as to whether this KAIROS program would be welcomed to his facility.

Warden Mills stated his concerns: 1. The facility population was 96 offenders; 2. KAIROS asked for 42 offenders to participate on a given weekend; 3. The facility would allow only 24 offenders on a weekend program; 4. Would this adjustment of attendees be permitted by KAIROS?; 5. How soon would a weekend be held/scheduled?; 6. What kind of space will KAIROS need for the program?; 7. What about feeding the team members and offenders?

As I was prepared to respond to these questions, I felt the Holy Spirit overwhelm me. I thought of Proverbs 8:35: *"For the one who finds me finds life and finds favor with the Lord. (NKJ)"* I soon not only answered all of these questions to everyone's satisfaction, but (by God's Grace) they seemed to be "fired up," anxious, even eager to help in any way. I was overwhelmed. But there was one there who seemed to play devil's advocate. The security manager, Major Marriott, was throwing all kinds of stumbling blocks in the way. God kept on giving me the correct answers for all the concerns she had.

When the grilling process was over, I asked to meet the facility chaplain. Much to my chagrin, I was informed that the facility currently did not have a chaplain. I knew ahead of time that there was not a deputy warden, and that the second in command was the security manager, Major

Marriott. Here came the game breaker, or so I thought. But God had His plan in place long before I stuck my nose in.

When I approached the subject that one of the facility officials "must" attend a weekend before KAIROS would consider holding a weekend, the warden interrupted and said, "we will talk at the conclusion of the meeting."

"Okay," I said, and then without any further matters to discuss, I said, "wait a minute." We needed to schedule a date for the first weekend in the state prison system, which was to be tentatively held at the women's prison. I guess since the prison's executive director had already sanctioned the concept of KAIROS for the system, he felt that if there were to be any kinks, glitches, or any other types of problems in the program, CWCF would be the place where the least amount of damage would incur. But a date needed to be set. The warden said we need to talk about that. He wasn't exactly ready to do that. These things will be discussed at our one-on-one meeting after this meeting concluded.

After a few more pleasantries were exchanged, the warden adjourned the meeting. The warden said he had some urgent business to tend to and Major Marriott gave me a tour of the facility. As she showed me the facility, I was looking out for possible places we could hold the weekend. In reality there was only one: the gym. In talking with the Major, she indicated that it would be virtually impossible to use the gym on a weekend. That was the place for most recreational activities on the weekend. There would be a lot of upset inmates if their weekend recreational facility was taken away for even just one day, let alone an entire weekend. As she ended the tour, she was not interested at all in the KAIROS program.

By now, we reached the administration building and the warden's office area. His administrative assistant advised me that the warden was on the phone and would be with me shortly. She offered me a bottle of water, which I gladly took, as my throat was parched. Within 10 minutes, the warden's door opened, and he invited me in. Warden Mills seemed very openly warm toward me as he expressed his interest in the KAIROS program. He said he has heard a lot of positive things about the program at a warden's conference that he had recently attended. Then he asked, "What are we going to do about the requirement of the facility chaplain attending a weekend? As you know, we do not have a chaplain currently. We have a few applicants we will be interviewing soon. I was not sure if we can meet any time frame this year?"

(Oh, Lord! What or how do we deal with this situation?) I shot a quick arrow of a prayer and I heard Him: "Ask the warden if he would want to go." Then I remembered what Benny Johnson said to me:" If the warden at CWCF would go, so would he. That's it, that's the answer … Mr. Mills and Mr. Johnson go together on the next Cursillo weekend.

Hold everything. There is one more stipulation: Mr. Johnson also amended his conditions for going on this weekend, and that was that he does not travel overnight without his wife. Where could we find a co-ed Cursillo weekend? Bill Fay indicated that there were a few of those types of weekend encounters in the U.S. and that he would check and get back to me.

Sure enough, Bill found a co-ed weekend near San Antonio, Texas that was happening in about a month. I immediately contacted Mr. Johnson and Warden Mills and informed them of the dates of that weekend in Texas and that all expenses would be covered for both, plus their wives. They indicated that they would get back to me after checking their calendars. I put a firm contact date and time for two days hence. While Mr. Johnson grumbled a bit, he finally agreed to my conditions. "Thank you, Lord!" I cried out — after I hung up, of course.

CHAPTER 9

"Be kind and compassionate to one another, forgiving each other, just as in Christ God forgave you."

- Ephesians 4:32 (NIV)

The days seemed long until I knelt in prayer and Bible reading. Time was no longer of importance. What was important was contemplating God's Word. Being filled with the joy of His presence in my life, and moreover, God with me here and now. A total emergence, a blending of my will with His Spirit. What a tremendous, overwhelming experience. Learning how to wait upon the Lord and its true meaning.

In the meantime, Bill Fay was working on the preliminary arrangements for the trip for the Mills' and the Johnson's. Finding flights, Mr. Johnson stated that they had to have nonstop flights for he has not, nor will not in the future, make any type of flights that involve connections. Talk about trying one's best to get out of something! Meanwhile, not a word from Warden Mills. Curiosity was getting the best of Bill Fay. Seeing as he had planned to visit CWCF in the next few days, Bill decided to plan a visit with the warden.

Bill invited me to join him on that day and he would see if they would give me a tour of the facility. I jumped at this opportunity to possibly check out the "joint" logistically prior to the proposed weekend in October. On that long drive to Cañon City, I was amazed at the natural beauty of the surroundings. The bright colors of what seemed to be almost desert-like surroundings were awesome. Too many times I had driven this same road and not noticed all the colors, rock formations, and of course, the occasional varmint running across the road. What could I have previously been thinking? Perhaps my mind was so preoccupied that I missed all this amazing creative splendor of God's hand? Daydreaming, maybe? But in any case, God blessed me with this time of focusing on His world, His mission, and His work that was presenting itself then.

I was contemplating all this and praising God at the same time. Suddenly, a profound and abrupt shout blasted through the quiet saying, "Hey, are you sleeping? Want to stop for coffee in Florence?" Bill quizzically asked.

I never refuse an opportunity to have coffee, but I said, "as long as we are not late for our appointment."

"Plenty of time," Bill exclaimed. Great!

Florence is a sleepy, quiet town off the highway where many businesses had already closed their doors. There were signs of a once-thriving western town. Most places were boarded up, and many houses were abandoned … almost a modern ghost town. But nestled in what once was a thriving town square was a little coffee shop. You knew that this was one of the few businesses open because of the trucks parked in and around this coffee shop. As we pulled in, some people were leaving the shop and they waved to us. Friendly, or so it seemed, I did not know them, but Bill lowered his car window and waved back.

Upon entering the shop, a woman behind the counter shouted out a bright "hello," and Bill responded, "I'll have the usual." He then turned to me and asked. "What will you have?"

"Coffee and a doughnut."

"No doughnuts here, fella," said the woman.

"Get a cinnamon roll," Bill quipped.

"Sounds good to me," I responded.

We then went to the nearest empty table and sat down. Our coffee was waiting. Bill chuckled and said, "don't be surprised. Once these folks get to know you, this is what they do."

When that cinnamon roll was placed on the table, my eyes almost popped out of my head. I had never seen such a huge roll in my life. It was the size of the plate. Warm, sugary topping. I said to Bill, "I couldn't eat all this."

"Don't worry," he replied. "That's why there are two forks; I'll help you eat it."

All this was great, but I was anxious to get to the meeting, tour the facility, and get things finalized for our October weekend at CWCF. (On several occasions thereafter as I traveled to Cañon City, I stopped at that same coffee shop and had a cinnamon roll, eating the whole thing!)

As we arrived at CWCF, I was somewhat surprised to see women working outside the fences. *Wow, maybe there is some measure of leniency with incarcerated women,* I thought. I then spotted an officer there with them. That made me feel a little more at ease.

We approached the main entrance to the prison. I saw locked doors, bars on the windows and a "call-in box" to the control center. Bill proceeded to ring the access bell and a voice comes through asking the question, "who goes there?" Bill identifies us and indicates that we are there to attend a meeting with the warden. With no other communication, the door buzzed open and we proceeded to enter. As I looked around, I noticed that the entrance appeared to be in a general reception area, with one exception. Straight in front of me, about 50 feet, were bars. I mean, bars straight across the whole wall, floor to ceiling. They were painted in a drab military style beige. Chipped, paint peeling from the ceiling, the entrance obviously in much need of repair.

Off to the left was a much nicer appearing entrance to what was the executive offices. Wood grain, solid oak door, glass enclosed office area. A stark difference. Almost looking out of place. So neat in appearance. Looking freshly painted. The warden's administrative assistant was on the phone. I could hear her telling the warden that his 10:30 appointment had arrived. When she got off the phone, she instructed us to be seated and said the warden would be with us shortly.

"Shortly" soon became almost an hour. What was happening here? Is there some possible glitch? My mind was thinking all kinds of wild thoughts. What possible obstacles were going to be put in our way? I stopped my wayward thoughts right there. I began doing what was right: Praying. Calling upon God to bring His peace "which passes all understanding" into my mind. I started to rebuke satan's distractions that were trying to fill my mind and seek God's presence during this time.

As quickly as those thoughts of panic came in, God's peace surrounded me. What a peace, what a joy, what an overwhelming calm came over me. The words: "Calm down, Bill. Don't let the moment steal your excitement and joy. It's all good." Patience is a virtue that I once prayed for, but not much anymore. I was ever so slowly learning because God would be throwing potential or perceived circumstances to help me truly understand the meaning of patience. It was working, but every now and then ... well, I think you understand what it is that I am trying to say. Right?

The door to the warden's office suddenly flung open and out came a woman dressed in uniform. She approached us in a cordial manner, shook hands with Bill and, as she turned to me, reintroduced herself as Major Marriott, security chief, and invited us into the warden's office. After exchanging some niceties, we quickly got down to the "nitty gritty" of why we were gathered there.

I was amazed at how quickly and so smoothly this meeting was going. The warden was agreeing with everything. Bill Fay had things well in hand. I just sat there, took notes, and said very little, until it came to the part of traveling to San Antonio. When Warden Mills asked about the travel arrangements, I thought here we go, now is when things could fall apart. Mr. Mills indicated that he had spoken with Mr. Johnson and all the arrangements appeared to be in order. I was taken aback by that comment. The Johnsons and the Mills had already agreed about the travel arrangements? That was great.

I chimed in, "All we have to do is to set up the travel to the airport, right?"

Mr. Mills said that they will get there on their own. Just two weeks from then, they would be on their way to attend a Cursillo weekend. Glory to God! Now Bill and I needed to get busy getting *palanca* letters* ready and sent to these folks for their weekend. The excitement for the first KAIROS to be held in Colorado was starting to build. The Colorado Department of Corrections would never be the same again. Glory to God.

We also started a prayer clock for the weekend. This is a clock listing the names of the Mills and the Johnsons and letting them know that there were people praying for them every hour they were attending this weekend, around the clock for 72 hours of continuous prayer. Prayer that God's love would reach down to touch them so personally and deeply to have them understand the importance of a close and meaningful relationship with Him, that inmates deserve the same privilege to experience this personal relationship with Him, and that KAIROS was the vehicle that God wanted to use, and that they were to back this endeavor 100 percent.

The accomplishment and impact they would experience was for them and them alone. Whether or not the weekend would be approved was not our intent in sending them on this weekend. Rather, we wanted them to understand the impact of God in an individual's life (an inmate). Of course, we were hopeful that the overall presence of the Holy Spirit would erase any negativity of this type of program being introduced into the prison system. None of us ever thought of the close personal bond that these two couples would develop out of this weekend. Praise God!

Bill and I had an almost sleepless weekend. Between praying and calling others to pray during this weekend, we were kept busy making sure that all that was planned, went off like clockwork. On Sunday evening (after the time that they were to get home), Bill unsuccessfully attempted to contact both.

On Monday morning, Bill and I were to meet with them, each at their respective facilities. About 5 a.m. I received a call from Bill saying that our meeting was postponed till Wednesday. We were to be at FCF by 9:30 a.m. and meet at CWCF at 2 p.m. Little did we know that all was good. Warden Mills and Deputy Warden Johnson needed to clear some perceived obstacles before they could meet with us. They too knew the system and, little did we know at the time, they were preparing the way for the weekends to take place.

They held a meeting with the executive staff in Colorado Springs headquarters for the CDOC, not leaving until they received their support and approval on Monday. Then they met with the staff at their respective facilities on Tuesday, going over potential issues and perceived problems and how they were going to get staff "buy in."

I wish I had the opportunity to sit in on those meetings, but I did not. Nor did I ever get any input as to the discussions. However, I did eventually get some understanding of where the battle lines were going to be drawn, what was expendable and what was not, from a KAIROS point of view. Although, ideally, the program was to be presented entirely as designed, our understanding of the methodology of KAIROS was only a matter of conversations with KAIROS officials. We (staff and volunteers) needed to be flexible in the Spirit so that the ministry would produce fruit.

Bill and I also met on Tuesday at his office to go over some strategies in anticipation of objections. Bill and I decided to call KAIROS headquarters in Winter Park, Florida. As we talked with them, they helped us better understand possible objections we might encounter and how to address them. What is normal in daily life is not typical in a correctional facility. We would not have all the answers needed in response to their questions, but we could anticipate what they would be. KAIROS headquarters also filled us in on some possible answers to questions that they have had to reply to. As we have learned repeatedly, pray, pray, and pray. God truly has all the answers. All we need to do is listen.

(*Palanca letters are love letters to a person attending a KAIROS or Cursillo weekend, letters of encouragement from other Christians who have attended a similar weekend, who may not know that individual personally but have a relationship with Christ.)

CHAPTER 10

"Fear not, for I am with you; Be not dismayed, for I am your God. I will strengthen you, yes, I will help you. I will uphold you with my righteous right hand."

- Isaiah 41:10 (NKJV)

When I awoke on Wednesday morning in the middle of the night, before my feet would hit the floor, I began to pray. Tears of joy flowed from my eyes. Later I referred to my "eyeballs beginning to sweat." The Lord was preparing me for battle. He was filling me with an air of excitement, enthusiasm, and overwhelming joy. I must have spent close to three hours with the Lord in prayer and meditation. His unending peace was assuring me of the outcome of this meeting. "Don't worry" God was telling me in my spirit, but it has always been my nature to worry about everything. About 7 a.m. I got out of bed and showered. Joan must have heard the shower going. By the time I got out of the shower, she had coffee for me. I got dressed and proceeded into the kitchen for breakfast, which Joan had already prepared — cereal, toast, and another cup of coffee. I was all wired for the day.

The morning traffic on Academy Blvd. was typically congested for this time of day, the morning rush hour. As I approached the checkpoint entrance to the east prison complex, a 5-prison complex, I was stopped by the entrance officer and asked to identify myself and the purpose of my visit. After the officer verified my request for entry, as I was proceeding forward, I noticed in my rearview mirror that Bill Fay was behind me. Interestingly, the front gate officer just waved at him and let him enter.

Bill and I met up in the parking lot in front of FCF. As I went over to Bill's car to chat with him for a minute or two, Bill said let's get inside the prison first, then we can go over any last-minute issues. Once inside, we were escorted by an officer to the warden's office. We were told by the warden's administrative assistant that there was a meeting in progress. As we were waiting, we were offered coffee or water. Well, I never refuse a cup of coffee. Bill asked for water. So, we waited, and waited, and waited some more.

Almost an hour later, the warden came out from his office very apologetic and invited us into his office. Warden McCoff introduced us again to his administrative and food service crew, and security staff — 14 people in all. I was taken aback by the number of people who were in attendance. I started to get a little nervous. As I took one deep breath after another, Bill leaned over to be, touched my arm, and ever so softly whispered to me, "it is okay." By then I was shooting arrow prayers to the Lord – *help!* As God has done so often to me, I heard Him say, "it's alright, I am with you, I will give you the words you need to say. Don't worry, Potter, I still am the molder of the clay."

Just then, a calm came over me like I never felt before. I had to hold back from laughing out loud. That's how I was so full of the Lord's peace, joy, and happiness. I just wanted to shout it out that no matter what you say, My God is in control. Of course, I did not say that. But with some boldness, exuberance, and joy was I able to address all the concerns of the warden and his staff, and all of this within 30 minutes. Bill Fay could not get a word in edgewise, at first!

That afternoon at CWCF the meeting went equally as smooth. The one issue was the size of the prison: only 96 female inmates. KAIROS asks for 42 inmates to attend any given weekend. Warden Mills explained, "if 42 inmates attended at one time, that would cause a major security issue." The time required for the program consisted of 40 hours over 3 ½ days. A team of 40 volunteers would arrive at the prison with lots of supplies that needed to be security checked-in before any of the materials would be allowed into the prison. This is a nightmare for all the prison staff, from the warden to the line staff.

My mind was now racing. Hold on everybody, stop the music! This is such a small facility, why such a clamor? Maybe because it is such a small facility, there could be a fear for the safety of volunteers. I was thinking that this is not going to be easy to convince every prison staffer here that we, KAIROS, have years of experience in these matters and that all would go well. While I could not guarantee any of this, I was trusting in the mighty hand of God that all would be alright.

Bill and I addressed all concerns, and we even volunteered to take over the food service department and feed the whole facility, staff included, for the entire weekend. The food service captain was elated that we would volunteer to do such a thing. All is well that ends well, Glory to God. Our date for KAIROS #1 was set for October 14th.

As we were about to leave, Bill mentioned the closing service that takes place on Sunday. There would be approximately 200 people that will request to attend this event. There was a deafening silence that came over the conference room. Each one was looking at another in dismay. They never had so many people come to the prison at any given time. The warden broke the silence with a chuckle. He then stated that "There is not a place in the prison to handle such a large group of people except in the gymnasium. If we use that area on a Sunday, that's not going to work. The inmates use that area heavily on weekends. There will be problems, I assure you. Using that area is virtually impossible."

There was a momentary silence. Then the warden, his right hand on his chin looking as someone who was deep in thought, said, "Bring me proof, in writing, that you will produce all those people wanting to attend that closing service. I want their full name as it appears on an official state ID. Their social security number and current address. No ex-felons, no one under the age of 21, or relatives of the prisoners. Background checks will be needed, and that information must be turned in by September 10th. No latecomers will be accepted."

I interjected, "Why so early a deadline to have such forms turned in to you?"

Warden Mills then stated that "we need time to process all those applications. That will take a lot of man hours." Looking rather convincingly at me, he said, "that ends that."

It's August, we had less than 30 days to get all those applications out to the team, they needed time to distribute them, get them back to us for review, then turn them in to the facility by September 10th. Wow. It seemed impossible to get it done in the allotted time frame. Then the warden reiterated: "That ends that, period!"

It was by all outward appearance that this was the game changer of the weekend. Do we postpone the weekend? Do we move it into November? Bill asked if we could have a minute to discuss this matter. "Sure, use my office." So, Bill and I went into the warden's office. "What are we going to do?" Bill asks me. "Let's pray," I replied, "see what God has to say."

As we began, a scripture almost immediately came into my mind: Deuteronomy 31:6 *"Be strong and of good courage, do not fear nor be afraid of them, for the Lord your God, He is the One who goes with you. He will not leave you nor forsake you. NKJ)"* As we shared this scripture, peace came over us and we knew we would be able to meet these requirements and be on time.

When we returned to the conference room, I noticed that about half of the staff had left the room. I thought they just left for a break, but much to my disappointment, the warden let us know that were not returning. Mr. Mills then asked, "what is your decision?" With smiles on our faces, Bill said we would make/meet all the requirements on time and in order. I thought Mr. Mills was going to slide right out of his chair in utter amazement. I then said, "We will keep in touch weekly as to our progress, and that as soon as we get the visitor applications, we will turn them in." We shook hands and left CWCF.

In the parking lot, Bill stopped me and asked, "How are you planning to get this done? I cannot devote the time necessary to do it."

"I will handle it."

Little did I know how much of a life-changing statement that would turn out to be. On the drive back to Colorado Springs, all kinds of thoughts were going through my mind. (*How am I going to handle it? God, help me. I need you. I want you more. HELP! Am I biting off more than I can chew?*

77

Lord, I have a job that takes me not only out of town, but out of the state. I need answers as to how I will handle the situation.)

Suddenly, I start singing "How Great Thou Art." I had to pull off the road, for tears of joy started filling my eyes to the point of distorting the view of the road. God's peace was overwhelming me. A sense of joy came over me. The words that Jesus uttered to the first disciples: "...*then He said to them, 'follow Me, and I will make you fishers of men.' They immediately dropped their nets and followed Him.*"

I arrived home about 6 p.m. that night and was so excited. My wife greeted me at the door, and I was just rambling on about what happened that day. She laughed and said, "Slow down. What is going on? What happened?" As I caught my breath, I explained to her what a blessed day it had been. Two of our daughters (Jean and Jennifer), were living with us at the time and were just a little perplexed at how I was acting. Joan, being the mother that she is, explained that Dad was just overly excited about the prison ministry. They both looked at each other quizzically and left the room.

There was a team meeting scheduled for that weekend at All Saints Episcopal Church in Colorado Springs. Joan and I spent most of the rest of the week preparing for the meeting, making sure that we had enough copies of the KAIROS manuals for all. There was a meeting with Sandy Browning, who was the designated leader of the first weekend. We went over the details of the meeting format and prayed over the names of the team members as to what assignments each would have for the weekend. In the ensuing weekends it would be much easier, as many people were to repeat the same talk that they could hear on this first weekend.

There were two tasks we were overlooking. First, we needed to critique each talk before they presented the "finished" talk to the team. The KAIROS formula strictly requires ensuring the overall message of the team is consistent each time a weekend seminar takes place. Yes, there is time to include personal testimony in a talk, but the overall message must be the same — each and every weekend — and that being God loves you, the people of God love you, and there is another (better) way to life than the lifestyle you have been living. Freedom means setting your eyes on God and His plan for your life (Jeremiah 29:11-13).

Second, we had to focus on SECURITY, SECURITY, SECURITY. Each volunteer had to turn in their completed CDOC volunteer application form. The way that a prison operates is by protecting the public from offenders until they serve their time and are released. This is what all corrections staff always say is their primary concern: safety. Safety for the "stakeholders" — you and I.

Further, they are unwilling to compromise in this environment. This is a para-military environment, for sure. You do as instructed by each uniformed staff member with a "yes, sir/yes, ma'am." You can ask questions later (much later). There is so much information to cover in the short period of time we have at this meeting. Put first things first. Send/call the team members and stress the importance of attending all the four scheduled meetings. To miss one may mean you will not be able to be part of the inside team. If that happens, there is need for extra support outside the facility for the inside team. The hardest part of the pre-weekend team meetings is teaching the team members that security must remain paramount for all of us or we could be escorted off the grounds and that will be that.

Saturday arrives, Joan and I headed to All Saints Episcopal Church, arriving there about 7:30 a.m. The church appeared to be closed. I called the person who was to meet us there and open the fellowship hall for us and, much to my surprise, we woke him up! He told me that he would be there as soon as possible. Well, we could have held the first 30 minutes of the meeting in the parking lot before he showed up.

Filled with much fear and trepidation, we quickly entered the fellowship hall. When can we start? Is there something that can be eliminated from the meeting schedule so that we can cover everything? Confusion was all around us. Then Father Scott Frantz, an Episcopal priest from Manitou Springs, stood up and shouted out: "Quiet! Let us pray right here and now for the Lord to intervene and settle us down. Bring His Spirit to guide us and direct us."

So, we prayed, and prayed, and then we prayed some more. I was getting nervous because time was slipping away. Then the Lord said to me in my spirit, *"Let it go, let it all go, this is My time and I am in control."* I started to weep. Forgive me, Lord, for getting in Your way. I know You are the all-powerful, holy and Almighty God. A peace fell over me the likes of which I had not experienced in a long time.

After the prayer time, Father Scott said, "let's have coffee and take some time to get acquainted with each other." Normally I would have objected to this coffee break, but I just smiled to myself and thought, *It's okay, God has this one.*

All the materials were distributed, applications filled out and handed in, and, praise God, we finished on time. However, we did lose two team members because of conflicts in scheduling causing them to miss two of our meetings. Sandy Browning, the team leader of the weekend, as well as the remaining meetings coordinator, with Joan Potter her assistant, and Bill Fay and I were to coordinate the menu and purchase or find donations for the necessary supplies.

The joy of all this was to come from the team members' churches for the funds necessary for the weekend. There was a financial matter that had to be considered. It would cost each team member $125 for the weekend, which included the motel room (double occupancy), to stay over three nights. In the ensuing weeks that were ahead of us, we would discover that there was a Roman Catholic abbey in Cañon City that did have a school with two dormitories which were not being used as the school had closed a few years earlier. On Monday, I went down to Cañon City and checked out the abbey. I met a monk named Brother Martin and he gave me a tour of the facility. As we talked, he mentioned that he was familiar with the Cursillo program and its methodology. Brother Martin was more than willing to allow us to use the facilities and the rate was a lot less than the hotel. I booked it for the team and canceled the hotel.

CHAPTER 11

"But those who wait upon the Lord shall renew their strength; they shall mount up with wings like eagles. They shall run and not be weary, they shall walk and not faint."

- Isaiah 40:31 (NJK)

Warden Mills and I met to decide how we were going to select the inmates for the weekend. Flyers had been posted weeks prior, notifying the inmates of the weekend seminar and that they needed to apply in order to attend. Warden Mills had previously agreed that 24 inmates would be allowed to attend. Today we were going to sort through the applications and select who would attend. With two weeks to the seminar, it was necessary for the inmates that were selected to be notified so that they had adequate time to notify their people on their visiting list, not to come that weekend. Also giving the inmates time to decide on attending the seminar or not.

When I arrived at the prison front door, I was greeted by Tammy, the programs supervisor, and taken to the conference room. In the prison conference room was the warden, four case managers, and the security manager. Spread out on the table, in front of each case manager, was a stack of papers and several piles of files. The warden opened the meeting by introducing the case managers to me. I asked if I may say a few words, to which the warden nodded yes. I began with a prayer and then asked how the sorting of the names was to be conducted. Warden Mills then interrupted me and stated that he had a prior commitment and had to leave. The team, as the warden called them, will assist with the selection process with the security manager chairing the meeting.

There were a total of 96 inmates at the facility, and we needed 24 of them attend the seminar. Almost a quarter of the census. Some could be out to court or hospital or possibly transferred, paroled, or released over the next two weeks, creating an operational nightmare. Impossible to accomplish according to the security manager, Major Marriott. I was thinking, *nothing is impossible*, and remembering Matthew 19:26 — "But Jesus said to them, 'with men this is impossible, but with God, all things are possible'" NKJ— I said to myself, *how do we, Lord, convince these people that it will work?* Then, I received a Word from God: "Tell them that with the food we will be bringing in, we will be able to feed the entire facility. Prepare, cook, serve all offenders and staff on board for that weekend. The warden, Bill Fay, and I had previously discussed and agreed upon that matter. It appears that the warden had not passed that along to the rest of the staff. I assured them that was the case.

With that in mind, we moved forward in the selection process. There were 63 applicants for that seminar. KAIROS had set a max of 42 for the weekend and up to six alternates, with the understanding that any candidate who did not show up on Friday morning would be replaced by an alternate. Once that happened and the original candidates showed up, the selected inmates had to return to their normal prison assignment for the remainder of the weekend with no visitors permitted to see that inmate. The purpose of this rule was to remind offenders that if a visitor showed up to visit them, they would be turned away. Some offenders will call a loved one on Thursday evening, after a seminar, to tell them what they have experienced and how blessed they are feeling. We would see this happen time and time again.

The selection process goes quickly from this point forward. One of the case managers informed me that an inmate in his case load informed him that she had previously attended a KAIROS weekend in a Florida prison.

I thought that was great and suggested she could be our first inside "team member," if that was okay with them. They agreed.

What a great addition to our team! However, as I gave it more thought, if she (JJ) already attended a weekend in Florida, what happened that she is now in a Colorado prison? I could not help my curiosity. I decided to call her case manager. I did go through the warden, of course, for approval to ask about her incarceration in Colorado after her Florida vacation. The warden said yes, and he had his assistant connect me with JJ's case manager.

The conversation was brief (after a chuckle), with the case manager informing me that there were corresponding charges on her and Florida had the first "dibs" and when she concluded her Florida obligation, she was extradited to Colorado. So, all this occurred before she accepted Christ into her life. I was happy to learn this.

As Saturday rapidly approached, Joan and I had a meeting with Sandy Browning concerning the "musts" to be accomplished at that meeting. These were absolutes as far as the team was concerned. The biggest was processing the applications to attend the closing. Bill and I were predicting that there would be in excess of 200 applications. When we initially informed the warden and his security manager, they almost choked. The security manager (Major Marriott) said that there was no room in the facility to hold such a crowd. Warden Mills interjected (tongue-in-cheek), saying, "You bring me those closing applications, and if you have those 200-plus, we will make room for them all." Major Marriott looked at the warden with a quizzical facial expression, more of a gasp for air as she almost choked again. The warden gave her a hand sign as if to say, "Don't worry, that's not going to happen."

I asked Major Marriott when she would need those closing applications and she told me to bring them in on Thursday of the weekend. If we are planning on 200-plus applications for the closing, how in the world would she get them all cleared before Sunday? I found out after the weekend that the only concern (at the time) was that the people were not on any offender's visiting list. That made sense. In the future, all closing applications would have to have complete background checks for an individual to attend a KAIROS closing.

Saturday's meeting went as planned, just like clockwork. As we prayed, there were 234 closing applications. Prayer is the key to the success of a KAIROS weekend. When people pray together, *really* pray, they develop a bond through the Holy Spirit that is so unique it is hardly comprehensible to non-believers (the ones who have never experienced such a closeness to God through another person, let alone a team of 30-plus members united in prayer). To humanly explain the uniqueness of such a team bonding process is almost impossible. When the Holy Spirit of God works in this way, unless you experience it firsthand, you wouldn't understand. Prayer is not just words asking for God's favor, it is worship in its purest form. When Christians come together expecting, I mean with excited anticipation, God meets with them — miracles happen.

Yes, God is still in the miracle business. The KAIROS team formation process is just that, expecting God to do what He said He will do: Unite His people as one with Him.

"My sheep hear my voice, and I know them, and they follow me. And I give them eternal life, and they shall never perish; neither shall anyone snatch them out of my hand. My Father, who has given them to me, is greater than all; and no one is able to snatch them out of my Father's hand. I and my Father are one." (John 10: 27-30 NKJ). Just as Jesus and the Father are united, so is the team united in their love for God, united as they prepare to go into the devil's playground — prison. The enemy would be defeated on this weekend, glory to God. A light will shine from the GREAT CITY.

On Monday before the weekend I was absolutely filled with much anxiety or excitement. I could not figure why, but I was about to burst at the seams if I did not turn in those closing applications before Thursday. I went to Cañon City early that afternoon to turn in those 234 applications. All the way down to the prison I was singing praises to the Lord. It is amazing how an hour-long drive can go by so quickly when you are in the presence of God.

Pulling into the prison parking lot, I saw the programs coordinator getting into her car. I pulled up behind her, blocking her from getting her car out. I jumped out of my car so excited that I caught her before she left for the day. However, I came to find out she wasn't as happy as I was.

She was taking the afternoon off because she would be working on the weekend.

When I told her that there were 234 applications for the closing, she looked at me with an expression that was inexplicable. I didn't know if she was glad or mad. She informed me that earlier that morning she was told that she would have the responsibility to check all those applications to see if any were on the visiting list of any attending inmates. She reluctantly came with me into the prison and into the security manager's office. After exchanging a few pleasantries, I handed her the enormous stack of closing applications and she immediately turned them over to Mary, the programs manager. Major Marriott directed her to complete them as soon as possible. Mary grunted and took them and turned around and left. I asked if there were any questions. Major said no, so I left.

The rest of the week, Joan and I stayed busy, mainly coordinating last-minute prep for the meals for the prison. Now, in addition to feeding 24 candidates (inmates) and 30 team members, there would be another 79 people (54 inmates and 25 staff). Thank God for Louise Abeyta, the team kitchen leader. Her team had organized the Roman Catholic churches in the Denver area to prepare the food and deliver it for the weekend. Keeping the food hot during the transporting from Denver to Cañon City was the challenge. Louise told me that she had that under control. I wasn't so sure. Then I remembered what Paul said in Philippians 4:4]: "Rejoice in the Lord always, and again I say rejoice."

To realize that God knows what is going to happen before it happens is not only refreshing, but rejoicing needs to take place before, during and after, that's what rejoicing in the Lord always means. Get with the program, Potter! It wasn't "what more can Bill and I do," but what the Holy Spirit does within a team that is united. Hard lessons to learn when you are accustomed to being/wanting to be in control. The phrase, "Let Go and Let God" has become a constant challenge for me since then.

It's Thursday and God's team is on its way to Cañon City on schedule and with all supplies in hand. Pulling into the prison parking lot, we noticed a state highway department road grader clearing a field off to the right of the prison parking lot. I guess the warden figured we were serious about the number of people coming to the closing service on Sunday. We all got a laugh out of that. All the equipment we were bringing in had to be inspected to make sure it was not "contraband." The staff was very polite, professional, and almost friendly. Little did they know how much they would be touched by God on this weekend. We as a team didn't know how much we would be blessed, too. That is what our God is about — blessing His people.

"Behold, how good and how pleasant it is for the brethren to dwell in unity! It is like precious oil upon the head, running down on the beard, the beard of Aaron, running down the edge of his garments. It is like the dew of Hermon, Descending on the mountains of Zion.

For there, the Lord commanded the blessing — Life forevermore." (Psalm 133, NKJV)

When all was said and done, only three items were not allowed: large kitchen/butcher knives. We should have known that … understandable. However, the logistical nightmare was just beginning. The devil was trying to interfere, but our prayer team was already at work. The part of the team that I have not mentioned until now had been at work for months preparing the way for us. Binding the spirit of darkness from attacking us successfully was one of its primary purposes. As well as praying for the rest of the weekend activities, candidates, and prison staff.

Some of the spaces we thought we were going to be able to use turns out were "off limits" to volunteers. We were shown two other areas (small rooms) close to the cafeteria/dining hall. As it turns out, these rooms were better logistically for us anyway.

The gymnasium was setup to be the primary location for most of the weekend activities. All things considered, the setup of the gym, the food supplies, cookies was exactly what we needed. Christians from all over the Eastern Slope (Front Range) of Colorado made cookies to be served all during the weekend throughout the prison – in the administration area, control center. After each daily session was over, the candidates who had their fill of cookies were given a big bag of cookies to take back to their living unit to share with the other inmates who did not attend the seminar. Needless to say (but I would anyway), everyone in the prison by Sunday night was on a sugar high.

Bill Fay and I were the only men on the team and were to serve in any capacity that was needed: gofers, grunts, and comforters. We learned many valuable lessons on what it meant to be a servant. The gym was set-up, the other rooms were as well. All this done by 3 p.m., although all team members were not scheduled to arrive at the prison until early evening. A set-up crew of eight arrived in the morning. Too many team members could cause problems in the set-up process, bumping into one another, or standing around, or talking to inmates (which we were told was not permitted until the actual seminar started). We did have the one inmate (J.J.) who was permitted to help in the setup. She was busy, smiling, and most pleasant. She was everywhere, doing whatever needed to be done. What a great example she was to the outside team members (volunteers). The team left the prison to head to the abbey to clean-up, have dinner, and return to the prison for the beginning of the KAIROS seminar.

Most of the team arrived as scheduled. We ate together, discussed what the schedule was going to be, and explained the check-in process at the prison. We reminded all that no jewelry, earrings, body piercings, necklaces, etc., apart from a wedding band/ring would be permitted. Before we left the abbey, we gathered in the living room to share in the team communion. What a blessed time it was, with each team member serving the others. What Jesus Christ did for us was more deeply understood by all. The servant heart of Christ was what we were taking into the prison with us. Maybe for the first time, many of us began to understand its meaning, but not fully until the closing on Sunday night.

The shake-down process was a first-time experience for many of us but not all. Some had family incarcerated in other facilities and knew the drill. Others were almost embarrassed with the pat-down. Nonetheless, by the end of the weekend, the team members were comfortable. The team moves together as a group, which is the process for the entry and egress from the prison for the entire weekend. We gathered for prayer before the candidates arrived. Each inside team member had a name or two to greet their candidate(s) upon arrival. Getting them coffee, tea, their name tag, and escorting them to their assigned seat for the evening session. After all team and candidates are seated, Sandy Browning, the rectora as she will be known for the duration of the seminar, shared opening remarks and explained the night's format.

After she completed her remarks, a short break followed. The next portion of the seminar was quiet time, designed as a time to reflect, but solemn for sure. Women always seem to be more emotionally responsive than men, and this night would be no different. I noticed some of the candidates faces, and they were looking around the room to see if others were similarly responding. When the tears started to flow, many of them just let go and let them flow. As the first session ended some three hours later, the schedule for the next day was discussed, questions asked and answered, and the session closed.

The clergy (all seven of them) were equally busy Friday and Saturday, dealing with forgiveness as well as many other iniquities. Healings were taking place, old wounds were closing and, to the glory of God, the joy of the Lord was abounding all around us.

Meanwhile in the *palanca* room (the supply/prayer room, for those who have not been through a Cursillo-type weekend), some of the more "mature" ladies on the team by late afternoon Friday were suffering from tired and aching feet. Bill and I became foot massage therapists for the remainder of the weekend. When my wife got wind of what we were doing, she made it known that I had never given her a foot massage. Was I in trouble or what?

There is a special moment on every KAIROS weekend for any holdouts who had not accepted the invitation of Christ and the Jericho walls around a person are broken down. Late afternoon, while the candidates were attending a chapel visit, a bag with their name on it was placed in front of their assigned seat. Each table leader then led the group in a prayer. At the conclusion of the prayer, the candidates were allowed to open the bags. Then, without any further instruction, the team members left the table.

Inside the bags were "love letters" from people on the outside who had never met the candidate, yet, with the love of Christ in them, had written letters of encouragement, testimony, and love. Some of the candidates had not received any letters from the outside since the beginning of their incarceration. In their cases, the letters were opened and read by prison staff to make sure there was nothing in the letter that was incriminating or any form of contraband enclosed.

This is where the uniqueness of this bag impacts the offender — the letters are in SEALED envelopes! Unheard of, even unthinkable in this environment. In the early planning stages of the weekend, the bags of letters became an issue with the security staff. They insisted that sealed envelopes could not be used. When Bill and I met with Wardens Mills and McCoff prior to the administrative staff involvement, we went over what were perceived as the "stumbling blocks" of the program. Sealed letters would be a big one. Initially that was a no-brainer for the wardens. We encouraged the wardens to contact other states' prison systems to check out the program's effectiveness and the overall importance of "sealed letters." We gave them several locations where the KAIROS ministry was active within those prisons, with names and phone numbers.

When Mr. McCoff saw the list, he immediately recognized one of the names and indicated he would make a phone call and if he received a green light to the letters, that would suffice. We found out that the one name he saw was a friend he met at a national warden's conference a few years ago. When the security staff objected to the sealed letters, the wardens both overrode their objections and approved this important part of the weekend process.

That the letters were sealed made a tremendous impact on these women. So much so that tears flowed like rivers. You see, they never were able to receive a letter from family or friends without them being first read by staff. Now, they had letters of encouragement from people who didn't know them. Not a letter condemning them. A letter letting them know they were loved and were being prayed for *by name* by people who didn't even know them. Wounds were healed and the Glory of God abounded for the remainder of the weekend. The women immediately recognized that the staff were aware of the letters and yet allowed such a thing. The offenders looked at the staff differently. As the ladies exited that night, hugs were happening everywhere. The ladies were given a big bag of cookies and a small white bag of cookies as well. They were instructed to give that white bag to the person — inmate or staff — they disliked the most. Pray before you give that bag, pray for God to release you from that bondage of hatred. Free to experience more of the presence of God in their lives and the lives of the inmates and staff around them.

CHAPTER 12

"In Him you also trusted, after you heard the Word of Truth, the gospel of your salvation."

- Ephesians 1:13 (NKJ)

A wise man once said Jesus died for all of us. That means ALL! Jesus came so that none of us would perish. So that we all had a choice to accept His offer or not. Jesus wants us, all of us, to be part of His Glorious Church. He took on all our sins at the cross so that there would not be even a spot of blemish when He presented us to the Father. What a gift! Freely given. The choice is ours. That is the question presented to the candidates – "Choose life or …."

Sunday morning, I was up at dawn. What a great sunrise. This is the day the Lord has made, let us rejoice and be glad in it. There was an air of excitement abounding as the team prepared to leave the abbey. Some were singing, others praying.

The night before we gathered to share the joy of the Lord and to discuss concerns regarding the candidates. Items that were needed for Sunday were ready: the hand-made wood name tags, the crosses and any other incidentals that have been overlooked. What a blessing to feel so close to God. Right from the start of the weekend there was air of excitement yet also fear and trepidation. The presence of the Holy Spirit was very evident. Though problems did arise over the weekend, Tammy, the facility volunteer coordinator, was able to handle them to the satisfaction of all.

The way potential problems were handled shocked the inmates. They had never experienced such a willingness of the staff to accommodate a volunteer group. The Light of Christ was shining there in the prison. Maybe it was just a flickering light, but always there. The team had a marvelous opportunity by combining each one's light to create a brightness that not only honored God, but through Christ's light the brightness was almost blinding. All encompassing, consuming the evil that was in that place. At least for the weekend. Many events in my life had provided an "after-glow" of some sort, but usually short lived and eventually all but forgotten. I can unequivocally say that the warmth of the presence of God, once truly experienced, you will never forget, nor will it never leave you. Each time you take the time to reflect on the special presence of God you are consumed by the awesome presence of the Lord. "But they have not seen anything yet."

The time for the closing was rapidly approaching. The candidates were not fully aware of the people coming to be part of the service. The excitement of the presence of God was having a tremendous impact on the team and stressing out the staff. The whole revelation of the presence of God was sensed by most, if not all by this time. There may have been one or two what I would call "hold outs." The ones that still could not believe that God would or could forgive them for their indiscretions. If their family would not forgive, how could strangers, let alone God, forgive? That deepest innermost unforgiveness that they held in their own heart. The hurt they have caused their family was so deeply engrained within them, they could not forgive themselves. All the love letters from perfect strangers, the love of the team members, all the homemade meals, and I must not forget the cookies. The cookie monsters became the cookie angels.

There was a brief discussion about the location of the closing. The gym was the area used for most of the weekend as the place where the talks took place, the "chapel" visits happened elsewhere in the classrooms. Except for meals, that were served in the dining hall, virtually all the weekend activities took place in the gym. But for the closing service, the candidates had to move to a smaller room. Crowded though it was, the closeness made the giving of the crosses and name tags all the more meaningful.

While the candidates were there, the attendees for the closing were arriving. They were ushered into the dining hall and asked that they remain quiet. Refreshments such as iced tea, coffee, water (and, of course, cookies) were made available to all the guests. All this to allow the rest of the inmates access to the gym for a period of time over the weekend.

As with any group that size (210), it was difficult to keep them quiet. Fortunately, the candidates were not to be able to hear the noise rising from the crowd. A crowd that size had previously never entered the prison, which meant additional staffing was needed to handle searches necessary to clear the closing guests into the facility.

The moment had finally arrived. The candidates were approaching the dining hall. We could hear them singing the song "Surely the Presence of the Lord." One of the team members had already coached the guests to join in with the candidates when they were entering the dining hall. The song echoed throughout the prison walls. What an awesome presence of God in that place!

The warden and his entire executive and security staff were all present. They were astonished that all but 15 people that registered for closing were in attendance. Tears flowed from the candidates as they entered the dining hall, which now became transformed into a place of worship that none of them would forget.

Many had never received a visit from a family member, but 210 people were here to visit them. Prior to the closing service in the classroom, they received their crosses. Then, each were given a series of three questions to personally respond to: 1. How did you feel on the first night of the KAIROS? 2. What were your feelings as the weekend progressed? 3. What are you leaving/taking with you?

When they had finished their own responses, they were told to select one person to represent the group. That individual would share that composite synopsis with the others at the closing service.

After all were in their places, there was what seemed to be an unending shout and applause from the crowd. I have attended many major league sporting events, but never had I experienced such an overwhelming cheer from a crowd in all my life. It was as if all of Heaven were present and cheering along with us. The presence of God was bringing many to tears.

When all had settled down, Sandy, the leader of the weekend approached the podium and, after a few pleasantries, again introduced the new graduates of KAIROS #1 at CWCF. Another roar from the crowd erupted. The warden was asked to say a few words, as was Tammy. Sandy returned to the podium and announced that it is time to share the table summaries of the weekend with all of us. A hush and then a bit of laughter came from the graduates. Each group seemed to be looking at the selected person to speak for them and many were glad it was not them.

As each table representative approached the podium, the same impressions echoed from each. Here are some of the remarks as I best recollect:

How did you feel on the first night of the KAIROS?

- "We came empty, not really expecting anything."
- "Feeling unlovable"
- "I thought everyone had given up or forgotten me."
- "Helpless"
- "I was without any feelings."
- "Lost, searching"
- "Wounded, empty"
- "Hoping for a glimmer of hope"
- "Not knowing where to turn"
- "For the food!" (no offense to the kitchen)

What were your feelings as the weekend progressed?
"Friendship, love, healing, hope, God's love, peace, happiness"
"Joy of the Lord"
"I felt freedom for the first time since I came to prison."
"A peace that I have never felt before, newfound friends in Christ"
"I also found 10 pounds, thanks to all those homemade cookies."
"Peace of God. Freedom. Expressions of love I never knew existed."
These are just a few of the comments from the KAIROS graduates.

There were many signs in the crowd of the emotion spilling over. Tears flowed freely that day. Applause abounded after every remark. Release of the suppression the devil had filled in the hearts of these women. A true sense of a future filled with a presence of God. These women were given a new potential that comes only from God through His promises.

The teaching of the truths of the Bible truly touched the hearts of all (team members included) in attendance during the weekend encounter with Christ.

Daniel Webster once said: "the Bible is a book of faith, and a book of doctrine, and a book of morals, and a book of religion, of special revelation from God; but it is also a book which teaches man has to own individual responsibility, his own dignity, and his equality with his fellow man."

The revelation of the weekend to the candidates helped them realize that the mistakes they made in the past do not make them second class citizens. But by the shed blood of Christ they were free, free indeed. The taking of responsibility for their actions was the first step in a process of forgiving self, accepting God's forgiveness and praying for the forgiveness of others. Seeking a closer relationship with God through fellowshipping with like-minded others is a positive step in accepting and receiving the grace of God.

The impact on the facility was almost instantaneous. But this was only a new beginning for these ladies. The fullness of the power of God was yet to come. With some, communication with family and friends would be restored. For others, it meant reaching out to a loved one who had abandoned them upon incarceration. And for others it meant a chance to re-start their lives upon release. Now would be the time for them to prepare to follow that which God had prepared for them.

The overall acceptance of the weekend (from a correctional perspective) would ultimately rest in the hands of the warden and staff. The "KAIROS experiment" for Colorado rested in their hands, as well as the permission to proceed in other facilities as well.

"... Let your conduct be without covetousness; be content with such things as you have. For He Himself has said, 'I will never leave you or forsake you.'" (Hebrews 13:5)

It's a beautiful fall morning driving down to Cañon City. The Aspens are turning a fantastic fall color of bright orange. I am meeting Bill Fay at the prison at 9:45 a.m. for a 10 a.m. meeting to critique the KAIROS seminar with Warden Mills and his administrative staff. It's been 10 days since the weekend event. The prison staff has had time to review and discuss the program. However, the members of the KAIROS team had yet to gather to discuss the results of the weekend.

I arrived about 15 minutes ahead of our appointment and found out that Bill Fay was not going to be able to be there. Oh boy, was I almost in a panic. I shot an "arrow prayer" to the Lord to please give me the words, His Words, to represent Him and His people in a God-like, humble, respectful manner.

As I waited outside the warden's office, one by one I watched the senior staff members file into the office. Some gave a smile, shook my hand, while others didn't acknowledge me. I was a little perplexed, concerned, even anxious. I was wondering what was going on in that office. I started to sweat. Then I heard a small whisper calling to me, "You may go in the office now." I had my eyes closed at this point. Again, I heard that voice, "You may go in the office now." Then I felt a hand tapping on my shoulder. "Mr. Potter, are you alright?" I immediately opened my eyes to see the warden's receptionist standing there, saying, "You may go in the office now."

As I opened the door, it was like I was entering a courtroom. Approximately 15 people were in there. I thought, *this is no courtroom. This is a "kangaroo court." Oh Lord, HELP!* Help He did. I felt a warmth, a peace, and the presence of God going before me into that room. I was smiling — almost to laughing. Tammy, the facility volunteer coordinator, got up from her chair and came over to me and gave me a hug and whispered, "everything is good." I breathed a sigh of relief and said a big, "Thank You Jesus!"

After exchanging a few pleasantries, the warden asked each of the department heads to give a report on their observations of the program. The first to give a report was the security manager. From that standpoint, all was within prison guidelines. No issues. With only one exception, to which he deferred to the food service captain. The rest of the department heads, including case management, visiting room sergeants, plus maintenance, and then it was time for the food service captain to give her report.

"This program is the most organized form of pandemonium I have ever seen." Not a problem occurred that interfered with the overall food service prep and the serving line distribution. "It was as if these people have worked together for years. The most effective, organized confusion I have experienced — but don't ever do that to me again!" We all laughed at that, and the warden thanked her (as well as me), for the outstanding cooperation of the food service team.

The warden then asked me for my input concerning the overview of the weekend from the standpoint of the volunteers and visitors. I said: "On the behalf of KAIROS, I would like to thank the entire staff for their professionalism in helping the team negotiate our way through the process of entering and exiting each day. How courteous they were in greeting us into an environment we truly were not familiar with at all. From our kitchen team leader, and I quote: "the entire weekend was a first-time experience for all of us in a prison setting. But to put everything in a nutshell: it was a kick!"

Within the acceptable prison security guidelines. The warden said that he would send a formal written report in approximately a week with copies to the department executive director and all of the other facility wardens with a firm recommendation stating that they should welcome future KAIROS events throughout the prison system. The warden concluded the meeting with an invitation that would relate to the many years of cooperation between the facility and KAIROS of Colorado. He added, "I would pass along his wholehearted recommendation to the warden at Fremont Correctional Facility to move ahead with the program there."

What I felt as I drove back to Colorado Springs was pure joy and celebration with what the Lord had done. Upon arriving home and sharing the outcome of the meeting with Joan, she smiled and said confidently, "I told you it was going to be alright."

I then tried to contact Bill Fay and was not able to, so I left a message with his secretary for him to call me at his convenience and tell him this: "Praise the Lord." I had to tell somebody else, I was bursting at the seams with the joy of the Lord. I called Sandy Browning, the leader of the weekend, and shared with her the report from the warden and his staff.

Two weeks after the KAIROS there was a meeting scheduled to give the team an opportunity to share their own impressions of the seminar. Most of the team attended the meeting, which was supposed to be no longer than two hours. It lasted almost three and a half hours. Once again, the joy of the Lord was ever so present. The excitement of what each had experienced overflowed the meeting room. Each team member expressed their feelings and emotions, and all were still on a "spiritual high!"

The ministry leaders, in particular the treasurer (Joan), was so overwhelmed she nearly neglected her financial report. Once she collected her thoughts, she shared how she was initially concerned about the ministry being able to meet its financial obligations. The team members were each asked to contribute $100 to defer the weekend costs, if they were able. "God will provide" was the ministry's mantra. All were told to bring their offering with them when they came to the meeting and turn it in. Joan recalled that some brought cash, some brought checks. Joan did not have time to open any of the envelopes until the following Monday. I was watching her when she started to open the envelopes and it seemed as if all was going well.

I asked her if she would like me to make her a cup of tea as I was going to make myself a cup of coffee. She said, "that would be great." When I returned to the table, she was crying. I immediately asked what was wrong. She proceeded to show me a letter that was in one of the envelopes which read as follows: "I give my heart to the Lord and give my all that I have." Enclosed was $3 and change.

I must confess that "my eyeballs began to sweat." Wow, what an overwhelming expression of love to God! Let me say this about the funds needed for the weekend expenses: they were met! We started out with $45.52 in the treasury and after all expenses were paid, we still had exactly $45.52 left in the bank. Now if that isn't God, I do not know what is!

"Then it shall be to Me a name of joy, a praise, and an honor before all nations of the earth, who shall hear all the good that I do to them; they shall fear and tremble for all the goodness and all the prosperity that I provide for it." (Jeremiah 33:9) (NKJ)

Chuck Colson, founder of Prison Fellowship, once said, "The most remarkable thing, though, is the difference Scripture makes in the lives

SENIOR CHAPLAIN BILL POTTER

of those who sincerely follow it. I've never heard anyone who said, 'I've studied the Bible; I've lived it for years and it doesn't work for me.'"

These women, like most of us, knew of the Bible but did not really study God's Word. The world pressures us to get things done and get it done NOW!" Time is too valuable to spare for the Bible. Besides, in all probability there is nothing in it that can help me. How I have heard these comments over and over through the years. I tell offenders that God had to put them in prison to get their attention. "God wants you to see His plan for you and this may be your last or only chance to do so." A few would listen, but most needed to be hit over the head with a baseball bat (figurative, not literally) in order for the Lord to get their attention. KAIROS is that spiritual baseball bat. The impact this program has on all who attend is beyond words. If you look over the manual, there isn't anything earth-shattering. There isn't anything that most if not all have not heard before either. The difference — the shock of KAIROS — is that it brings the presence of the Holy Spirit to each individual PERSONALLY.

The candidates have no idea of who they will come in contact with, I mean "in their face" contact. It is hard to imagine such an experience in life, but it happens when you least expect it. Being open in your mind and your heart is the prerequisite, calling out to God and expecting an answer is the other. Far too many people are ready to blame God for their troubles rather than seeking God for answers to situations that occur in their lives. GOD WILL ANSWER YOU. You may not like the answer, but He will answer. For those who hear the answer, the question then remains: How will you respond? That is the reason why some of the inmates are inmates. They did not like the answer from God and therefore decided to do it "my way."

CHAPTER 13

"Unless we form the habit of going to the Bible in bright moments as well as in trouble, we cannot fully respond to its consolations because we lack equilibrium between light and darkness."

\- Helen Keller (APB)

The more I pray, the more I understand God's Word and purpose for not only me, but for all mankind. While this may sound a bit altruistic, it is nevertheless self-evident. As a basic reference for my service to the Lord, I keep this understanding of God's Word close to me. Although there will be times of stress down this wonderous journey called life and where you will find that I slipped and fell, the Word of God is forever deeply engrained in my spirit. The need to continually return to it, however humbling the experience – it must be done.

God brought me out of the jungle I call New Jersey to a place called Colorado. He provided me with a time to work with a Christian company and more than an adequate salary. I did make an effort to do the work expected of me by my company and received periodic monthly bonuses. However, after two years of service to the company, they terminated me.

Over the next five years, my work setting changed several times, from trying to set up a local candy company with a new marketing branch, to going back to cutting meat, to attempting to start the "KAIROS of Colorado" aftercare ministry. All the while proceeding through the Episcopal Church to an ordination to the position of deacon. Some of my "spiritual" journey I will unveil later in this book.

Always keep in mind, God had given me the greatest helpmate, my wife Joan. Words cannot express the many blessings she has been to me throughout our marriage. I could fill another book with all that she has meant to me along this journey. She has helped me refocus, get back on track serving the Lord with all my heart, soul, mind, and strength. Reminding me of the prophet Jeremiah, 33:3, God says, "Call to me and I will answer you and show you great and mighty things which you do not know." Every time I would try to do things on my own, Joan would say to me: "Hon, seek God..." That was all she had to say, and I knew I was falling off track. What a helpmate God used to keep my eyes, heart, and mind going in the right direction. With all the curves and bumps along the way, focus, focus, focus.

Over the next 18 months or so I worked toward ordination with the Episcopal Church as a deacon serving under a local parish church in Loveland. While I pursued my studies, I became increasingly unsettled. Conflict after conflict arose. The more I looked for a solution in the Bible, the more conflict I discovered. Issues over homosexuality, women in the priesthood, to the inerrancy of the Word of God. I was anguishing over these issues ... what the church was saying, and what the Bible stated. Which way was I to go? I honestly did not know.

I spent many a night in prayer over these matters, with no definitive answer. Why couldn't I find the answer? Why must I struggle with these issues? The church was decisive. God's Word was precise. Some would say it was a debate lost in translation. Answers coming from the church made sense, but were they in line with God's Word? After a while, nothing was making sense. I must stop looking to man for answers and depend on the Holy Spirit speaking to me through the Word of God.

Living in a world like we do, so cluttered with distractions, it becomes hard to figure out life for yourself, through prayer and meditation. I needed time to truly seek God and His righteousness. Trying to find time to do this seems almost impossible. Where to turn? What direction to go? The church? The Bible? The people? Yet, the pressures of life — work, my children, the ministry, and church — were endless pressures of life closing in on all sides. I could hardly breathe. "What comes next, Lord? What else are you going to put or throw at me? Come on, I can take it, I have big shoulders, come on, pile it on. I have a few more minutes left in the day... I am waiting." Then I just wept and wept and wept some more. I cried out for help, direction, and peace.

"Seek Me through My Word." Of course, the answers are there! But I have been reading and reading, Lord. Then I heard within my spirit from the Lord: "Now study My Word!" THAT'S IT! STUDY THE WORD. What a revelation. I knew that but did not want to see it. Of course, the obvious answer is study. Sometimes we just read the Word and do not take the time to study it. That was my mistake all along. I now made a critical decision to take the time to do exactly that. Stop listening to others. Take the time to hear from the Lord. Through prayer, God showed me the things that were important and the things that were clutter.

How foolish I was to rely on myself to clear up my life. The Scripture that came to mind was, "Seek ye first the kingdom of God and His righteousness and all these things will be added unto you." (Mathew 6:33) God knows all, sees all, and will provide for His own. While, at times it may seem that I am preaching, in all reality, I am talking to myself in order to bring me back into the focus and purpose of God's call on my life. May each of us reflect on our basic purpose in life: To love one another as God loves us. Now wouldn't that be something!

So, I began by reading commentaries from various Christian authors. But something just did not feel right. I was more unsure of myself than ever. One would say this, another would say that, and still a third would say something different. I was more confused than ever. I prayed and prayed some more. I was not making the connection. *God, I thought You said, "study My Word?"* After endless nights of continued frustration, I just said "Lord, I give up! I am just going to do things the way I think You would want me to do them. Maybe that is the way it should have been done in the first place. You gave us free will to do things our way.

Wait a minute, Bill, I thought. *That does not sound right either.* Then I prayed. I waited. I prayed some more. I waited some more. I waited again, time and time again, I waited. Still nothing. Has God turned me off? Does He not hear me, is He too busy to hear my cry? *I want to believe in you, Lord.* I was holding on, but I was losing my grip. *I need your help, Lord.*

In that moment, I cried. For how long, I do not know, but when I did stop weeping, I sat still for so long. The time, I do not remember, but then I heard that still small voice say, "Now you have come to that place of inner peace that prepares you to hear from Me." I prostrated before the Lord and just let all of me empty out. Pouring out the hurts of over 40-plus years. As I recalled those hurts and melted them out of my mind, not out of my memory, I truly felt a peace, a peace that passes all understanding. I was hearing from the Lord.

I had gotten rid of all the distractions of the world and the junk that was cluttering my life and was listening to God through His Word. He was not discounting the authors of the various commentaries I had read but helping me better understand His Word directly from the source. As other writers had done (study, listen, then write so that those who read them would better comprehend), I was, in all reality, doing as they did.

It is in seeking Him first that we come to the right place at the right time to encounter the God of the universe. Most fall short of this mark, but the ones that succeed have that awesome responsibility to lead others to that same place. Whether in church, on a street corner, or in prison, we are all called to share His Word with others, to be filled with the Holy Spirit, and to proclaim the gospel of our Lord Jesus Christ. There I go preaching again. I make no excuse for that, just stating the facts.

Now that my "spiritual gas tank" was filled, I could start my engine and get rolling in the right direction, knowing that when my tank gets near empty, I know what "filling station" to pull into. Don't need to get my oil checked because the oil I have is the oil of the Spirit, and that always stays full, even though my gas tank may head toward empty every once in a while, against worldly pressures, the oil of the Spirit is always there. I must conclude with an aberration: Some thought we were out of our minds doing things the way we did. Joan and I knew it was God's plan we were following. You see, my wife was and is my spiritual partner, and if I do not seek her help, I know I would be in trouble not only with her but with the Lord.

The day was approaching quickly for the presentation of the program at Fremont Correctional Facility. Bill Fay and I were more than ready to do this. I called Bill with a renewed sense of urgency and hoped that I would be able to pass that enthusiasm along to him. I was excited and wanted Bill to jump on board with me and enjoy the ride. Bill laughed when we talked and said to me, "This is not my train ride." The Lord said to him that he was to help get the "foot in the door" with me for KAIROS then get off the train (to use my terminology), for God had something different for him.

I was surprised at his remark of going in a different direction once KAIROS was started at Fremont. That surprise turned into a renewed sense of God's work within me and Bill as well. Bill knew "his way" around the CDOC, and God was using him to show me that way in order to be able to work within that system as he did.

Before we could move ahead, however, there were certain conditions that the KAIROS national office wanted set up in order to continue to use their materials and name. We did have an ad hoc committee in place to keep some sense of formality, but we needed something more in order to continue functioning in an appropriate businesslike format that was acceptable to the CDOC and to the national office.

Yes, that is the way to go. Establish a permanent panel of people with a directional guideline for each section. Executive, legislative, and judicial. Something like the way our country is set up. That being said, KAIROS national office, in actual implementation, did all three. The implementation or the hands-on work was to be done by a grassroots group of people who were not involved in the decision-making process of the ministry.

Fremont Prison - The day had come to return to FCF and meet with the warden and his staff for a second time in order to answer questions or concerns and hopefully schedule a weekend for the following spring. As I approached the entrance to the east prison complex in Cañon City, I had a sudden chill that almost made me stop in my tracks. In fact, I did stop for a moment and prayed: "Dear God, help me take away this sudden 'spirit of fear' that is present, in Jesus' name."

As quickly as I said that prayer, God's Spirit engulfed me and I started to weep. With tears flowing down my face, I approached the complex checkpoint. I clumsily wiped away the tears, rolled down my window, displayed my driver's license to the guard, and told her of my intent to head toward FCF for my appointment with Warden McGoff. The officer checked her notes, asked me if I knew where to go, and I replied with a simple "yes."

There at that time were five separate prisons at the east complex with one additional facility planned in the not-too-distant future pending legislative funding: Colorado State Prison (CSP). This one would be a "supermax," equipped with and providing space for administering the death penalty. FCF is a medium security, 500-bed men's prison. There were convicted criminals from all walks of life, guilty of all kinds of acts, serving their time. An inmate once told me that "no one" can do his time but him. A lonely, empty position to be caught up in. I have come to find out that many of the staff were similarly laboring, "doing time."

As I parked my car, I spotted a truck pulling up behind me. Another officer came out of that vehicle and approached me. He asked me where I was going, and I responded FCF. Spotting my briefcase, he asked if I would like him to check it out for unintentional contraband before I entered the facility. I was thinking, what might I have put into my briefcase that could be considered contraband? I quickly responded, "sure." Then as I opened it, he almost immediately spotted my letter opener. He told to leave that item in my car, so I did.

"Do you know where to go?" he asked.

"Sort of," I responded.

He told me to wait there, and he would be right back. He parked his truck and spoke on the radio for a moment. I later found out that he contacted the control center at Shadow Mountain Correctional Facility (SMCF) for clearance for us to approach. As we entered SMCF, I noticed a big foyer with several rows of lockers. This was where visitors on the weekend would store their belongings: purses, keys, etc. He then escorted me through a series of two locked sliding metal doors. There was a walkway, about 50 yards of open grassy area between SMCF and FCF. As we were walking, he pointed out to me that there were two guard towers within easy sight. He then said: "Don't ever think you or anyone else could run across this area without being shot. You see, those officers stationed in those towers are expert marksmen. They sure shoot straight."

I then said, "Understood."

The officer left me as we neared the entrance to FCF and told me to report to the control center inside the prison. As the control center officer cleared me, I noticed that immediately behind there was a large room, which I later found out was that facility's visiting room. I was asked to sit down in the waiting area and told someone would be with me shortly. It was "deja vu all over again" (a quote of Larry 'Yogi' Berra.) Staff members filed past me giving me uncertain looks. Admittedly, I was perspiring, nervous and intimidated. This was not a women's prison.

Finally, after what seemed an enormous amount of time (only 10 minutes to be exact), I was asked to go into the warden's conference room. Mr. McGoff came and greeted me and assured me this was not a "kangaroo court" session. I nervously let out a small laugh and sat down. Associate Warden Benny Johnson took over the meeting. Remember, he had participated in a "street weekend" earlier that year to understand the similar weekend we proposed at FCF. Much to my surprise, Mr. Johnson was the one asking me all the questions, from security to food service to janitorial.

Not that we cannot do this or that, but how will we be able to do this or that. Those questions were aimed at the staff to do all they could do to make these things happen without too much interference with prison operations. That was a big WOW for me. Oh, how God was using a crusty prison official to open the door and pave the way for this ministry to move forward with cooperation from staff. This was truly awesome. I enjoyed the rest of the meeting.

As the meeting concluded, Mr. Johnson asked me to wait for him outside. He wanted to discuss the logistics in preparation for the weekend and the selection process for the inmates that would participate. Mr. Johnson and Warden McGoff came out 10 minutes later. Warden McGoff said, "Let's go to lunch in town. We will meet at the Cañon Inn, just follow us out in your car." Okay with me. I hoped they were buying, as I was cash poor.

At lunch, we went over a few things, but overall they just wanted to get to know me better. Relationship, that is the key to this luncheon, relationship. These two insightful men wanted to get to know Bill Potter, the man. What makes me tick, what are my likes and dislikes. They wanted to know all about my family. I told them that my wife and I had a blended family of 10 kids, six boys and four girls. She had six, and I had four, some of which have lived with us and others not.

I noticed Benny glancing a few times at his watch and after about the third glance Warden McGoff said: "Ben do we need to start to head back about now?"

"Yes," was his answer.

I gulped as I started to reach for my wallet when McGoff said, "This meal is on me."

CHAPTER 14

"Because He has set His love upon me, therefore, I will deliver him."

- Psalm 91:14a (NKJ)

F CF KAIROS #1 began on the third Thursday in October 1983. After the weekend concluded, the various shift commanders commented that this was the most organized chaos they had ever experienced. In all that chaos was the presence of the Holy Spirit, sensed by all who participated in the weekend encounter, team and candidates alike. The security staff, food service people, and case management personnel certainly felt the presence of God in that room.

The meeting area where the seminar took place was rather large, about 30 by 50 feet. There was another area where we were cooking on skillets and portable electric cooking ovens. We did pop a few breakers during the course of the weekend. Eventually, the shift captain assigned a maintenance person to help us for the duration of the weekend.

While every weekend has its own personality, the pattern of each weekend has the same meaning and strength, and that is to establish an ongoing relationship with God the Father through His Son Jesus Christ. How we steer the men in that direction is the goal of the weekend. Through personal experiences of team members and the guidance through each talk leads to the altar where they surrender all to Christ.

Some see the goal quickly, while others struggle to relinquish the hold that the world has on them. A few, unfortunately, refuse to let go. As a result, they remain in the grasp of the enemy. But they know that they had an encounter with a power higher than themselves. Their refusal to accept the fact that they came face to face with the Spirit of God, they do not want to recognize that Jesus Christ took upon Himself their sin. On the other hand, those men who believe through the testimonies of team members recognize that that they have been given another chance to step into a world where there they are welcome with forgiveness and acceptance as they witness the explosion of God's love at the closing service.

Some men have been known to surrender to the Living God at the last minute. As they enter the closing service, the overwhelming power of the Holy Spirit just will not let go, Praise God. The weeping, yes, weeping of the men almost overwhelms everyone. A momentary pause, the silence becomes almost deafening, and the place erupts with shouts of joy and celebration, letting the men know that it is okay for a man to cry.

The logistics or the "nuts and bolts" of the weekend are unique. This includes finding equipment such as tables and chairs, partitions (homemade), notebooks for the candidates (inmates), and the meals we serve. This is an enormous undertaking with insufficient time to accomplish all that needs to be done. The home-cooked meals — yes, that's right, home-cooked meals — are served to the participants and all prison staff who want a meal.

The catch is that if they want to eat, they have to do so in the room where the seminar is being held. They are to be served by inmate staff, and the inmate staff clean up after them. Although some of the uniform staff could not leave their locations due to security reasons, we found a way to deliver the meals to them. To the prison staff, this can become a nightmare. The format for a KAIROS is so unique that it creates limitless security issues. Thus, a complete inventory of all supplies is presented to security staff upon arrival at the prison and checked by both staff and the volunteer person in charge of the setup. Both the staff person and the volunteer have a copy of their own, and both sign off on each other's form. Upon completion of the weekend, all unused items are again inventoried as they are removed.

Now there is the matter of cookies, homemade cookies, about 2,200 dozen of them, on average, per weekend. All kinds and flavors you can think of and then some. Sometimes it is through a cookie that a man opens up. I have seen men just stare at a cookie for a long time before taking a bite, commenting that this is "just like my grandma used to make!" They take one bite and say, "Oh, yeah."

Some hoard as many as they can. The team leader ensures that each candidate gets a bag of cookies to take back to their living unit to share with other inmates. This simple sharing of a few cookies does wonders to make a friend, rare in prisons these days. It is amazing how God uses a cookie to make a friend. This is the principle of making a friend, being a friend, and bringing that friend to Christ.

One of the most interesting aspects of the program is that ecumenical side of this ministry. Christians from all walks of life are involved. Doctors, nurses, architects, blue collar workers of all kinds. From Roman Catholics to Episcopalians, Presbyterians, Baptists, non-denominational — all putting aside what has separated us and looking to what unites us, Jesus Christ. This makes a mighty impact right from the start. While initially the majority of the team members were either Catholic or Episcopalian, over the years the event has become more non-denominational. KAIROS requires that seven ordained clergy act as the spiritual backbone of the seven table families. They are responsible for spiritual direction as needed by the candidates. The clergy conduct individual counseling and there is a godly presence during the weekend and long after.

Fremont Correctional Facility would become the benchmark facility for the Colorado prison system. When another facility in the state would request KAIROS to make a presentation at that facility, a team from the ministry would ensure the ministry could handle the event. They needed to determine if there was a sufficient number of team members. The turnover ratio of available volunteers was an ongoing problem. While every team member wished they could be on a weekend each month, that was practicality impossible. Family, church, and work always had to be a priority, so new team members always had to be recruited. However, the baking of the homemade cookies is never a problem. The ladies that made them were always eager to do so, praise God. So the logistics for KAIROS weekend is a challenge.

Another challenge is materials, delivery, and setup for weekend seminars. Participating prisons became aware of the peace a KAIROS weekend brings to a facility, which lasts far beyond the actual date of the seminar, so the demand for the seminars grew.

My optimism was running high after the weekend at CWCF and FCF. The joy of the explosion of the ministry of Jesus Christ to those souls who were almost forgotten by society but not by God. How humbling it is to realize that God through Christ is present, even in the jails and prisons. Team members are consumed by God's presence as they walk through a prison door and hear it slam and the lock clicks behind them. Most first-time team members stop for a moment and take a deep breath and know from here on in that they are in God's presence.

References from other facility wardens, prior to a meeting, are forwarded to the warden to allow adequate time to research before a meeting is scheduled. I thank God for the short period of time I served as a member of the KAIROS national board in Winter Park, Florida. It was there that I began to understand the purpose of KAIROS' stringent rules. They have a proven track record, based on experience. If any deviation from roles occurs, a local group subjects themselves to sanctions up to suspension from the national office. However, the official manual was, as years would prove true, a living document subject to review and editing.

At the heart of this ministry is the Holy Spirit of God. The joy of this ministry has been, and I believe ever so strongly must be, service. It is in service to God that I am closest to His presence. Walking into a prison is the most exciting experience I have ever had. Once, when I was walking into a prison, an officer who most always greeted me asked, "Why are you so cheerful and always smiling?"

I responded: "Don't you see my best friend walking with me?"

Looking rather quizzical: "I don't see anyone with you."

I replied, "It's Jesus Christ."

He just turned and walked away shaking his head. About a year later, that same officer came up to me and asked if I had a minute to talk with him. Of course, I took some time with him. We rode together in his truck around the perimeter, and as we talked, he asked me, "who is the Jesus you say is always walking with you?" Joy filled my heart as I introduced him to the Lord.

Once I was just a little late getting into a facility, and I was chewed out by the facility chaplain as he was leaving for the day. I thought, *What was bugging him?* Then God spoke to me and said: "stop bellyaching and pray for him." Wow, that only could have come from God. Before God prompted me, the furthest thought from my mind was to pray for him. Humbling. Then I thought, *Bill, how many times have you wished people would just pray for you?* How many did just that and I never knew it? Or was that the time the Spirit of God came over me when I was having a temper tantrum? Then I thanked God for those that were praying for me even though I did not know it. Think about that. How many may be praying for you! That is awesome.

You never know what opportunities God has in store for you. Many team members would say they served wanting to give something to inmates, but they received more in return. God's Spirit works in mysterious ways, more than we can imagine.

The following Thursday at 10 a.m. a critique of the seminar took place at FCF. What an entirely different atmosphere that conference room was compared to CWCF. It was cordial and heartwarming to hear all of the kudos, from the housing officers to the security personnel. There was never such a smooth religious program ever presented in that facility. Everything went off like clockwork. The setup people from KAIROS showed up when expected, the setup of the equipment went as scheduled, and the food delivery showed up on time and everything went without a hitch. Comments included: "What a well-oiled machine is this KAIROS." "If that is how this program is run, bring it on any time."

How little did they know as to what actually took place behind the scenes! From meals being made in Denver and transported to FCF 112 miles away and arriving within a 15-minute window was a feat in and of itself. All the team members were praying that no one would become ill and all the food would be piping hot. Achieving this was nothing short of a miracle. If there was a star rating for this event, I believe it would be 5-star!

This weekend was the benchmark for others to come. Some would reach that mark, some would not. After a year had passed, the Spirit of God was gaining a foothold in satan's den, the Colorado prison system. The word of this ministry spread, not like wildfire, but gradually through regularly scheduled wardens' meetings. Some were sincerely interested; others were not so enthusiastic. Only upon a facility's request does KAIROS consider expansion into that particular facility. It does not actively seek out facilities.

The ad hoc committee for KAIROS of Colorado met in September 1983 and, after a brief discussion, decided to schedule a meeting for all team members to formally elect a board to supervise the overall ministry and draw up a constitution, bylaws, etc., for October next. Letters were sent out to all members with a ballot with names on it and with space for write-ins. While this seemed a little clumsy at first, it proved to be the best approach. Surprisingly 92% of the team members (138 of the 150 members) voted in person or mailed in their ballots.

The elected members, all of whom were present, met briefly after the meeting to select a treasurer, an executive director, and a representative to the national board. They also established a meeting calendar for the next year for the board. They gave the executive director the authority to call for an emergency meeting should one become necessary. Plans were drawn up to incorporate in the state of Colorado as soon as possible, with application for 501c3 status with the IRS.

Dates were selected for KAIROS #2 and #3 at CWCF and KAIROS #2 and #3 at FCF to be submitted by the director for each facility's approval as soon as possible. Once the dates were approved, the state board would notify the team leaders for those weekends and send them an active list of prospective team members and then schedule meetings.

One aspect of the program sought to establish small group reunions. The purpose was to have inmates praying to God, asking God's forgiveness for their sins and praying for the needs of others. This small group of inmates would share their individual concerns and needs. This was unheard of in such an environment, let alone between inmates. But as this ministry grew and expanded to other facilities throughout Colorado, prison staff realized the authenticity of the program.

I continued to be the leader of KAIROS of Colorado for the next seven years, establishing the program in two other facilities: Colorado Territorial Correctional Facility (CTCF) and Arkansas Valley Correctional Facility (AVCF.) What a joy it was serving this ministry. Then one day after a KAIROS team meeting, I was approached by one of the team members and asked if I would like to work in his meat market in Loveland, even manage it if I so desired. I said that I would pray about it and let him know by Monday next.

When I arrived home, I told Joan about the offer from Dave. She expressed some concern about doing that, but I said "nothing ventured, nothing gained." We agreed, and after some time spent in prayer, we decided to look into the possibility of making the move. Joan reminded me of my commitment to FCF and that I may not be able to travel down to Cañon City if we moved to Loveland.

I argued, "it's just 90 minutes farther. I can handle that 90 minutes in a heartbeat." I was also holding a Bible study on Saturday nights and a service on Sunday. All these things to think about, pray about, and decide.

My prayer time was focused on finding what God was up to. My stress level was almost overwhelming. The demands of family, Joan was working in a sandwich shop in The Springs, the kids were settled in their schools and did not want to relocate. Not easy to uproot a family once again. We had moved three different times in The Springs, to a new school each time. Now even a farther move up north to Loveland. Oh God, what more can there be. All I heard was, "with God, there is always more." WOW! Isn't that the truth. What will there be next? Only God knows.

On Monday I called Dave and said I would like to give it a shot, but there were a few things that needed to happen first. If it worked out, we would need to relocate to Loveland and get the kids registered in school.

When I met Dave at the shop in Loveland on Monday morning, I was surprised at the shop itself. Rather small in comparison to the supermarkets I was used to working at. But much to my surprise, there was a good volume of business generated. He had a custom slaughter business that entailed going out to the local farms to kill and dress out the cattle, custom cut to customer specifications, and other livestock customers wanted dressed out.

Dave also wanted to do more custom cutting for hunters. He needed someone who knew how to make sausage and other types of smoked meats. He had heard me talk about my butcher experience during break times at team meetings. Was he calling my bluff, or so I thought? I found out he was concerned about my health, with all the issues I had in the past with my back. In just a few days, I put all of Dave's concerns to rest.

Dave, who served as a deacon in the Episcopal church, was a great guide to help me through the same process. He was open to giving specific days off, as needed, in order to accommodate my training toward being ordained. At one point, he gave me a car, a Volkswagen Rabbit, when one of our cars died. This vehicle was ever-so important as my transportation to deacon preparatory training and other necessary classes to meet the requirements for ordination.

As I was studying, I also was going down to Cañon City every other week for ministry "on-the-job training." FCF offered me the opportunity to counsel requesting offenders.

That VW Rabbit was great on gas. Until one Sunday morning, while traveling down to Cañon City, as I got off of I-25 onto South Nevada Ave., it decided to quit running. I was able to roll into a motel parking lot and right there was a phone booth. Thank you, Lord! Hallelujah! It was just about 9 a.m. when this all happened. I had change enough to call down to the prison and tell them I was not able to make it that day, and then I called Joan to come and get me. She brought a strong rope so we could tow the car back to Loveland.

"I will be right there," she said.

As I was hanging up the phone, I turned around and an attractive woman all dressed up propositioned me: "want to go on a date?" I was kind of caught by surprise at first … on a Sunday morning!

I then responded, "No, thank you. But if you need some help, let me tell you about someone who can get you out of this mess, and His name is Jesus."

For a moment she just stared at me. I thought she was going to kick me or smack me, one or the other, when right there in that parking lot she fell to her knees and cried. We prayed together for a while and then I led her in the sinner's prayer, and she accepted Jesus into her life. She then left. Just across the street was a Dunkin' Donuts Shop. So, I went across the street for coffee and a donut. It was just a short time thereafter that Joan showed up and she towed the car and me home.

I worked for Dave for approximately two years before the business unexpectedly closed. Thank God Joan had a job that kept the family afloat while I went looking for work.

CHAPTER 15

"I will lift up my eyes to the hills, from whence comes my help? My help comes from the Lord who made heaven and earth."

- Psalm 121:1-2 (NKJ)

Things were not looking up for me, as God would have it. There was just not enough money coming in our household. We were about to be evicted from our home that we were renting in Berthoud. We had rented a U-Haul truck and had it all loaded up except for our kitchen table and a few chairs. We had to be out by noon that day. As we sat with Jennifer, the only child who was still living with us at that time, we prayed for God to tell us what we should do and where we should go. Joan and I were assured that God would provide. Jennifer needed to know how, through prayer, God's timing is always perfect. I thought He was pushing us to the limit. I was on the brink of chaos. Panic was about to overcome me. "GOD," I cried out, "HELP."

Then, at about 10 a.m. there came a knock on the door. I thought it was the landlord asking us to get out. But instead, it was a dear friend, Andrew Kaminski. He said to me, "When Patsy and I were praying this morning, God told us to ask you and your family to come and live with us for a while. I do not know why, but we both knew that God was telling us to offer our basement apartment to your family until you get back on your feet."

Another wow, God? Of course, we accepted ever so gladly. The only requirement was that every day we would gather for a Bible study for one-hour max, and one day a week for a dinner get together. That would be great. What a great time we had with the Kaminski's, where we lived for almost six months. After a short period of time, Andrew offered me employment at a local radio station in Loveland selling radio advertising. This was a great opportunity for me because this was a Monday-through-Friday job. That meant that I could continue to go to FCF twice a month and continue to prepare for the office of deacon in the Episcopal Church.

From time to time, as work would permit, I would go down to FCF on Friday evenings. On one of these trips, I was walking into FCF to the chaplain's office. The office in front of the chaplain's office was always closed by the time I arrived. This night, the door was open and there was a man sitting in there and he called to me to, "Come on in sit down for a minute." He introduced himself as Bob Hickox, the new program director, and he asked me if I had any questions.

"No, not really, Mr. Johnson, the assistant warden, pretty much filled me in on what my parameters were," I responded. He then said he would be "riding herd" over the programs from now on at FCF. As I sat there, I had developed a habit of attempting to "pigeonhole" people. Looking at Mr. Hickox, with his big cowboy boots up on his desk, a type of sailor's beard, nice western suit on a rather gruff voice, I really could not pinpoint or fit him into a stereotype role.

"Hey, where are you at? I want to know more about this KAIROS ministry you head up."

I quickly refocused and said, "Excuse me, sir. I was thinking about something else. What was it you were asking?"

"I want to know more about KAIROS," he repeated. Appearing to be somewhat agitated with me, I quickly apologized and told him I would bring him a leader's handbook next week so that he could look it over. He agreed and I then went into the chow hall which was right across the corridor from these two offices. As I did, I thought, *You blew this one, Bill. What must he think of me?* I recalled the adage that you only have one chance to make a first impression, Oh, boy, did I goof this one up royally.

The chow hall food was not great, but I made a habit of going to the chow hall to meet the men and get to know them and them to know me. This method of meeting the offenders would prove invaluable to me over the next 35 years or so of prison ministry. At least the coffee was always hot.

During this time of getting acquainted with the men, I would tell them my schedule. This became a valuable tool of communicating, if they wanted to talk in a more private setting. It did not take long for the men to seek me out. After the first few weeks of my visits to the prison, I had to finally establish appointment times. Otherwise, there would be a lineup of men waiting outside the office to see me. During this time, Bob Hickox was observing these "goings on," as he would refer to them. He was trying to figure me out. But with God on my side, it always seemed to work. Prayer does work, especially in crucial moments.

Mr. Hickox called me in one day and asked me "if I had ever heard of the American Correctional Association (ACA) or read their recommended qualifications for prison chaplains."

"No, not really," I replied.

He then handed me a copy of the requirements set down by ACA. If I ever hoped to be a chaplain in the CDOC, I needed to read them. At this time the CDOC was not imposing these requirements. But it appeared the department might soon adopt the ACA standards in order to avoid presumable future problems, such as lawsuits by offenders. The state attorneys general were requesting that CDOC adopt such standards. I told him I would look at them and see what was required of chaplains. I thanked him and left.

As I reviewed these requirements, I was pretty confident I qualified until I got to the last item. There was a potential showstopper. There was a phrase I was not familiar with, "Clinical Pastoral Education" (CPE.) What in the world is that all about? As I went deeper into the CPE question, I found out that this is a full year of study in order to earn the certificate of certification so as to meet the ACA standard for a chaplain.

Another boulder, Lord. Why, why, why? I cried out. I was not getting any younger. I was almost 50, as if He didn't already know. Oh, I forgot to mention the cost: $2000. That might as well have been a million. Things were tight already, now this? I was just about to give up. I was driving home from Cañon City feeling depressed, so much so that, I stopped at

McDonald's in Colorado Springs and got me a Happy Meal, but that did not help. Still down in the dumps.

When I arrived home and told Joan about this CPE and how upset I was and feeling down, she said, "Hon, pray. God has the answer."

Well, I was not in the mood to hear that. *Pray, yeah, He knows what's going on. So why do I need to pray all the time?* Arguing with myself, grumbling, growling, mumbling, sometimes almost in tears, I went to pray. Inevitably, as I prayed, God let me know it would all work out. All I needed to do was trust and obey. *Easy to say God, you are not in my shoes. Besides, it's hard to do at times like these.* Then I heard, "Put yourself in my shoes and see how that feels!" (my interpretation of Matthew 27:35-39).

Sure enough, things got to be harder. Still, I prayed and prayed some more. When I looked into CPE training, I found out that there was a CPE program at the Colorado Institute for the Mentally Ill in Pueblo. Aha, sounds like a place for me! Anyway, I contacted the hospital and was connected to the chaplain's office. I spoke with one of the chaplains and he said yes, there is a program about to start and that they had an opening if I was interested. It was starting that up-coming weekend, and it was for just one quarter, in other words, 13 weeks. I would need to get a few documents to them before it started, and, by the way, the hospital offers full scholarships for all qualified attendees. Wait a minute, a full scholarship, Thank you, Lord!

I stuttered, "Wha, wha, what did you say?"

He repeated "a full scholarship provided by the hospital." I was glad I was seated when I was talking to him. Otherwise, I might have fallen on the floor. As it was, I almost slipped out of my chair. What do I need in order to join the class? When Chaplain Hardy informed me of what was needed, I said it would not be an issue for me to meet those requirements but just might take a little more time. He asked me if I could come down to his office and meet with him to discuss the particulars of the program and fill out paperwork for acceptance into the program.

"What time do you want to meet? I will be there." Another WOW moment! The next obstacle was going to be the gas. Our budget was almost at its bursting point, but as God would have it, another wow moment was about to happen. But, before I get to that, the next morning was Friday, I received permission from Andrew so that I could take the day off in order to get to the meeting with Chaplain Hardy. He said okay, but I did not have money for gas. I needed an advance on my pay so that I could get gas.

Andrew's wife was the bookkeeper at the station and also did the payroll and had some petty cash on hand as well. Should I ask her for an advance on my pay and she could take it out of my paycheck? A dilemma. Maybe Andrew would lend me 10 dollars till Monday? *Pray, Bill, Pray.* So, I shot a quick prayer up to the heavens. Had no idea nor did any come to mind. But maybe, just this one time, ask Andrew for that 10 dollars. I still was a little skeptical, but here goes. Well, here is that wow moment from God once again, like I was talking about earlier. Andrew did not lend me 10 dollars, instead he handed me one of his personal gasoline credit cards and said, "Fill your tank and keep the card for as long as you are going to Pueblo." Now that is a wow moment. Thank you, Lord!

> *"Ask and it will be given to you, seek and you will find; knock and it will be opened to you. For everyone who asks receives, and he who seeks finds, and to him who knocks it will be opened."* (Matthew 7:7-8) (NKJ)

Sometimes the road ahead seems like an insurmountable mountain. Pray and that mountain is just a short hill to climb!

My work at the radio station was going well. I sold some advertising, wrote some ads for my clients, and finances were improving. So much so that Joan and I went looking for a place of our own. Fortunately, we did not have to look too far. Found a place just a few blocks from where we lived with the Kaminski's, a nice three-bedroom home on Eisenhower Blvd. just down the street from the radio station. The rent was within our budget, so we moved in on the first of September 1987.

By the time Christmas rolled around that year, we were doing okay. Joan found a job with a computer hardware company in Boulder as a security guard. Prison ministry was going full blast at the time. Three prisons in Cañon City. Oh my, only with God at the helm was this possible. Nearly 400 people were needed to provide the necessary staff to fulfill the demands of the ministry. People not only serving in the prison itself, but also providing the home-cooked meals as well as others who supported the ministry financially. Out of this miraculous group of godly people, 150 to 200 people would travel on a Sunday afternoon to go to a prison in Cañon City to visit inmates, criminals, offenders.

These people believed in the awesome power of God. A God who not only changed their heart, but who can change the hearts of hardened criminals. Unthinkable. Impossible. At the absolute best, jailhouse Christians. No one changed lives in just three and a half days. Not possible. As they prayed for God to give them a peace about serving in this ministry, God recalled to the mind of each Matthew 25:36b: *"I was in prison, and you came to Me" (NKJ)*. That in and of itself was no minor miracle. God does move in mysterious ways.

I must digress at this point, so that you may understand my feelings as I began my CPE experience. This was not my first time entering a mental institution. When I was just eight years old, my mother told me about my twin brothers who died shortly after they were born. After the twins were approximately 10 weeks old, my mother needed surgery and was hospitalized. During that time of hospitalization, my mother left the twins in the care of a neighbor who had a 16-year-old daughter who could help with the boys. Mom agreed and left them in their care.

One day, while the twins were in the neighbors' care, the daughter asked if she could take the twins out in the carriage for a walk. We lived in Union City, New Jersey, a suburb of New York City, with a population of 55,000, a busy city with public transportation, buses, and trolley cars, too. While out with the boys, the girl met up with some friends and stopped to talk to them. As she stopped at a corner, she neglected to put the break on the carriage. Turning and talking to her friends, the carriage began to roll off the sidewalk and into the street. Just at that moment, a trolley car was turning and hit the carriage and instantly killed the twins.

The girl became hysterical to the point that she eventually wound up in a mental hospital in Secaucus and remained there until her death in 1958. At eight years of age, I was exposed to what was then a state-of-the-art mental institution. It was archaic by the standards in 1987 at the state hospital in Colorado. My childhood memory of that time returned to mind when I entered this CPE training program. Much to my surprise, I did find an entirely different atmosphere. I am glad times change for the better. Praise God.

As I was progressing through CPE training, the CDOC implemented its new requirements for chaplains. To my surprise, they were requiring only one quarter of CPE training. It seems that the ACA standard was a minimum of only one quarter of CPE. There was a caveat to this minimum requirement. Although the minimum suggestion was in the requirement, it was strongly recommended that candidates complete two quarters and a four-quarter completion would be best.

I learned that the CDOC would implement a one-quarter requirement for chaplaincy. Another wow moment — thanks, God. As CPE training continued, our finances were getting even tighter. Although I had Andrew's gas card, I needed additional funds for meals. A diet of eating either hospital food or prison food just wasn't cutting it anymore. With no chance of using family funds for even another $25 per week, it was just not going to work. Reluctantly I meet with my CPE instructor, Chaplain Hardy. I explained my dilemma to him. He gave me some sound advice to follow, all of which I did not listen to at all.

During my time at the hospital, another one of the students was going through a similar predicament. He lived in Colorado Springs and would go home every night while in training. He was also married and a Baptist minister of a small missionary church in Fountain. He told me that occasionally he would go to the blood bank in Pueblo and donate blood and get paid $25. He said all they did was take the plasma out and return the rest of the blood to him. He could go there twice a month. That held him over for that period of time.

I prayed about that and rather quickly decided to go for it. I almost felt bad doing that until I went to the blood bank and got paid for giving blood. However, it satisfied my stomach, and all was well in Mudville. I hit a homerun and won the game. I did not strike out! (Sorry, Casey). I went a total of three times during my training at the state hospital. I learned for the first time in my life to pray standing against a wall with my eyes open and my hand on the doorknob!

Joan never knew about my blood donations. I would always tell her that the food was not bad. That was not a lie in and of itself; the food was good, I just did not tell her where I ate my meals. The hospital did provide housing for students in what was formally the nurses' residence. An old brick building built in the 1950s, the hallways were wide but dimly lit. The rooms looked more like those in the psych ward in *One Flew Over The Cuckoo's Nest*. This CPE was an experience that I would truly never forget. There are stories I am saving for another book, should I live long enough!

Another Colorado chaplaincy requirement was to provide an ecclesiastical agency endorsement. Since I was planning to be ordained through the Episcopal Church, that would not be a problem. Time would prove different. Boy, this was getting rough. I did not have much family time and was missing that. I was letting things pile up. Long days at work. Things were getting even tighter with finances, but the Lord blessed me with a wonderful wife who was holding things together on the home front. She always had a smile and a big hug for me when I arrived home. She truly is my best friend.

As CPE was about to finish, the class was informed of opportunities for the advanced quarters of the program, none of which were in Colorado. There was an interesting option for a full year CPE program in Texas, one in Austin at a mental hospital, and the other in Amarillo at a general hospital. There was a full scholarship available for both, which included a stipend and family housing. Sounded interesting. Joan and I spoke about applying for these positions and decided that Austin might be the one to look into.

The next time that I went to class, I asked Chaplain Hardy what the application process entailed. He gave me the phone number of the hospital and who to contact. The first chance I had to call, I did so. The switchboard operator connected to the chaplain's office. When I spoke to the chaplain, I was encouraged. He said that he would mail me the application, and that I should return it as soon as possible. The decision on the candidates was going to be made over the next 10 days. When I received the 10 pages of forms, I filled them out and sent them back the next day, priority mail. A week later, I received a call and was asked to visit Austin for a face-to-face interview the next week. Of course, I accepted. Remember that Baptist minister I mentioned? He applied to Austin as well and received an invitation, too. We agreed to carpool and go down together. That following week, as we drove down to Austin, we were both excited, encouraging each other, knowing that there was only one position, yet excited with the prospect of one of us being offered the scholarship.

Upon arrival at the hospital front gate, we were asked for identification. After the officer verified our appointments, she directed us to the administration building, handed us temporary badges, opened the gate, and let us in. Almost as bad as getting into a prison. On the inside, however, this facility seemed almost like a college campus. The grounds were well-manicured and the buildings were of gothic style architecture. All in all, a genuinely nice first impression. As we met with the chaplain and exchanged pleasantries, he called in a nurse and told her to give us a tour of the facility. The nurse said, "Follow me, everyone." She advised us as we toured the campus to not talk to any of the patients.

As we were walking around, we happened to see a group of others touring. They were just ahead of us. I did notice that one of the group ahead of us stopped for a moment and talked to a person sitting on the bench.

As we continued on our tour, we were approaching the area where that individual that I saw earlier was sitting on the bench, and he was still there smoking a cigar. When we were passing by, this person motioned to me. I thought this person was a staff member taking a break and wanted to ask me a question. As I stopped, the nurse escorting us turned and hollered for me to get back with the group. I just waved her off and thought to myself that she seemed rather bossy. Then I noticed that this gentleman's badge was yellow. This meant that he was a patient. Clearly, I goofed and never should have stopped in the first place. Was I in trouble.

I quickly caught up with the group back at the administration building. I was a little out of breath as we were told to sit and wait for the committee interviews. Jack, the Baptist pastor was hoping that we would be close to being the first ones called. Much to my surprise, we were the first called. Both of us at the same time. During this process we were told that there were only two positions open and four applicants. That meant we had a fifty-fifty chance to obtain one of the slots. Now I was getting excited. I thought it was going to be a shoo-in for at least one, maybe both of us.

One of the senior staff physician interviewers asked me a direct question: "Do you think you can save any of the patients?" I thought for a moment and replied, "No, I cannot, but the God I serve can!" then there was a brief moan from the committee and then a pregnant pause that seemed to last forever. The same person that asked me that question asked Jack, "What do you think about Bill's comment?" Jack glanced at me for moment and then looking directly at the panel said, "I agree with Bill, I surely cannot but our God most assuredly can!"

Another WOW moment — thank you, God. What a surprised look not only on the senior physician but from me, too, and a frown from all the interviewers. It was at that moment that I knew this was not the place for me to continue my CPE program studies. Then Jack looked at me with a frown as well, as if to say, "We are out of here!"

We were right about that. Very quickly the discussion ended and we were told that there would be a letter in the mail about their decision. We shook hands and left the room. We had already packed our bags and the car was loaded and ready to go. As Jack and I left and headed back to Colorado, we both were quiet. Then Jack broke the air of heaviness and asked me how I felt about the interview. What a relief! I thought this was going to be a long ride home.

This was definitely not the environment I wanted to be in for a year. There just seemed to be a cloud of doubt surrounding the entire hospital. A doubt that these folks were not going to be healed ... ever! Jack agreed with me. That breaking of the "ice" made the rest of our trip home a celebration of not getting a job, as funny as that may seem.

It was about 8 p.m. when I dropped of Jack in Colorado Springs. I was feeling very tired and didn't feel able to drive the rest of the way home, so I pulled into a Denny's and called Joan. I told her that she did not have to worry about packing and moving to Texas. Even if the position was offered, I was going to decline it anyway. I would explain it more when I get home. I was too tired to drive the rest of the way home and told her I would park at the truck stop just north of The Springs and catch a few hours' sleep. She said, "Okay, see you in the morning."

When I got to the truck stop and tried to sleep, I just could not. The constant noise of the truck motors running kept me awake. After an hour or so, I called Joan, woke her up, and told her I would be home in a couple of hours. Just leave a light on for me. Go back to bed. I would be alright. It was about 3 a.m. when I arrived home. What a nice feeling to be back into my own bed. The next morning, I explained to Joan what had happened and why I would not consider taking a position there. She most assuredly agreed.

A few days later as the CPE class was drawing to an end, Chaplain Hardy called me into his office. He asked me if I had any plans to proceed with another quarter of CPE. Not really, I said. The prison system was not requiring any more than one quarter of CPE to meet their qualifications for chaplain. He seemed somewhat disappointed as the hospital was going to offer a second quarter of CPE this summer. But I was sure further CPE training was not what God wanted next from me.

CHAPTER 16

"The Lord shall preserve your going out and your coming in. From this time forth, and even forevermore."

- Psalm 121:8

It was a crisp, cool Saturday in October 1988 when Joan and Andrew's wife Patsy were on a KAIROS weekend in Cañon City. Andrew and I were having breakfast at a nearby restaurant in Loveland. As we discussed going to the closing at CWCF, Andrew asked if I would like to go church with him tomorrow. Now the church Andrew went to did have a reputation of being a "holy roller" type church. Speaking in tongues, dancing in the aisles, waving flags and all those different shenanigans going on.

I must admit that my wife and I had been to that church once or twice in the past and were not too impressed by the music and all that stuff. Now the message was spot on, top notch. The pastor of that church could preach and preach and then preach some more. I could listen to him all day and night. That's how good he was, a great minister of the gospel of Jesus Christ. I loved to hear him preach. He almost always left me feeling challenged. But wait, I was an Episcopalian. I was on the brink of ordination in the Episcopal church. I do not need such distractions from my call. I must hold on to my church's doctrinal position.

How do I wrangle out of this situation? I remembered that I was scheduled to preach at All Saints Episcopal Church that Sunday. No better excuse than that. Or is there? Wait a minute, Andrew always went to the late service at 11 o'clock. That's the exact time I was to preach. Oh, thank you Lord for this small blessing. Andrew would not even think about going to the early service, or would he? No, not even if I asked him to. So, I did just that.

"Andrew, if you would go to the early service, I would be delighted to go with you to church."

Nonchalantly, he replied, "Okay."

What did I just hear? I said, "Excuse me! You hardly ever go to that service, why now?" "I do not know why. Just okay, let's do this for a change of pace."

The reason why, as I found out later on the drive down to the closing, was that Patsy liked to sleep in on Sundays. Andrew was glad to go to this service for a change. Now I was backed into a corner. I suggested going to the early service in the first place. I couldn't back out now. So, somewhat half-heartedly, I said, "Great."

"I will pick you up in the morning," Andrew said.

The rest of the day and into the night I struggled with how I could get out of this church service. Maybe tell Andrew I need to prepare my sermon? No, that would be an outright lie. That is not right. There was no way around it, I'd just have to man up and go. By 2 a.m. or so I finally went to sleep. At 6:30 a.m. the alarm woke me up and I was really groggy. I hit the snooze alarm, which I thought would give me another 10 minutes of rest.

I did wake up — half an hour later, with music coming from the radio and the phone ringing. It was Andrew and he asked if he could pick me up in 10 minutes and we could get coffee and donuts at the church before the service. I thanked him for calling and told him I overslept. Just come over and I would get ready as fast as I can. It was a good thing that I showered the night before, so all I had to do was shave, comb my hair and get dressed.

We arrived at the church just before the music started, the dancing began, and the flags were unfurled. I grabbed Andrew ever so tightly by the hand and prayed: "God, help me understand if these people are worshipping You in spirit and truth." Then the Holy Spirit came over me like a gush of wind and I started to speak in tongues! Initially, not knowing what was happening, I was just celebrating this worship service. Out of the corner of my eye I could see Andrew turning his head toward me with his mouth wide-open and shouting, "Hallelujah!" This was not what I was asking God about, He, in His awesome, mighty, convincing way always hits a homerun.

Sometimes we need to leave our battles to the Lord. When we think we are strong enough to handle it on our own, that is when the devil jumps into action. Prayer brings God into action. For a long period of time I was not a believer in the fullness of the gifts of the Spirit. This time, God touched me through His Spirit, which was nothing short of amazing to me. I was fully on board with this provoking of the Holy Spirit. Andrew gave me the biggest hug of my life! What joy filled my whole being, I felt stronger in my spirit and armed with the "sword of the Spirit, which is the Word of God." (Ephesians 6:17 NKJ) Not only was I feeling stronger in my faith, which was instantaneous, now I could go forth with a renewed power from God to become the chaplain God was calling me five years ago to become. I now had my toolbox filled and the complete knowledge on how to use my gifts.

This Sunday was Pentecost, and what a day for God to touch me this way. I was extremely excited as I walked into All Saints Episcopal Church that Sunday. The message I had prepared prior to being overcome by the Holy Spirit was a distant memory now. I was fired up. Ready to say whatever God was wanting me to say. I felt like I had a grin on my face from ear to ear. That moment, as I was telling the pastor, he said to me: "Better not say anything to anyone. You just might get thrown out. While I, myself, speak as you say you do, I do not tell anyone about that. Be careful. Do not be too open about what happened to you at Resurrection Fellowship (Rez)."

If this was an attempt to burst my bubble, it just was not going to work. God, through His Holy Spirit, would not let me give in to this temptation. This day was a day to speak with all the power of God that was within me.

We put on our vestments and process into the sanctuary. The church was almost full, the hymn was "Holy Spirit, Thou Art Welcome." Is this another wow moment, God? A wow moment of a different sort. As the service came to the logical point where the sermon was to be given, I stepped up to the podium, opened my Bible to the second chapter of Acts, and was about to read the part where the apostles were filled with the Holy Spirit and God said to me, "Look up, look up and see the people."

As I picked my head up to see the people and what was going on out there in the pews, almost in utter shock I started to cry. What I saw was skeletons draped in black. I just could not mutter a word. I cried. I walked off the altar area and into the back of the church, sat down, and cried some more. After the service was over and the people were leaving, strangely enough, not one of the congregants stopped to speak to me. Instead, they left with their heads down low. As the pastor approached me, he motioned to me to follow him into his office. It was there that he chastised me for my actions during the service. He then told me to go tomorrow morning to see the bishop and explain to him what exactly happened to me that day. Feeling rejected, I left the church, never to return.

I went into prayer mode as soon as I got home. "What was God trying to say to me? Was the Episcopal church not for me? That can't be, as I was only three months from my ordination day. It could not be that — right, God? What was the place He is sending me to going to be like? A place of darkness? Prisons are the devil's stomping grounds. I would have a fight on my hands every day. Wait a minute, God. I have been doing prison ministry for over six years, and I was no stranger to this setting. I know what things are like. I have CPE training under my belt. I was in a prison five days a month right now. I was no stranger to what you are trying to show me."

I did not know what to do. Then I remembered what my wife would always tell me: Go and ask God. Pray about it. So, I did all that. Stopped talking and listened to what else God had to say. As I listened for a long time, I heard Him say, "I have plans for you, my son. Plans that will take you beyond the Episcopal church. Just follow Me and My Spirit. Look beyond the Episcopal church and look at the Church universal."

This cannot be from God, could it? "Keep praying, Bill." So, I prayed and prayed, and then I paused and listened ... I listened, I felt as secure as I ever had before. I knew at that moment in time, it was right to go see the bishop.

Andrew picked me up about 2 p.m. to go to the closing at CWCF.

The ride down was filled with laughter and singing praises to the Lord. It seemed like such a short ride down (actually, it took 2 hours). When we sing to the Lord, time seems distant. It's a wonder we did not get a ticket for flying with the Holy Spirit. Maybe that was why we did not get stopped?

The closing was awesome! God made His presence known to one and all. On the drive home, when I told Joan about what happened that morning, and the atmosphere got just a little cold. You married men know what I mean. The LOOK you get when a certain topic of conversation you were pursuing was a no-no. I then became quiet, but Andrew wanted Patsy to hear it all! Joan just stared out the window as I shared what happened at Rez and at All Saints.

We no sooner got in the house and Joan turned to me and said, "We are not going to Rez. If you think I would go there, you have another thing coming."

I always wondered what that "other thing coming" meant. "Calm down sweetheart. I was going to speak with the Bishop in the morning." She was okay with that information. By this time, it was late, so we went to bed.

On Monday morning, I was up bright and early. I wanted to be in the bishop's office right when it opened. Sure enough, he was not in yet, and I sat and waited for about an hour. Thank God, there was coffee, and I took full advantage. The secretary had to make a second and almost a third pot by the time the bishop arrived. He went directly into his office without any acknowledgement of my presence. His secretary followed him in and closed the door. It was about a half-an- hour later when she came out of the office and said the bishop would be with me shortly. He was on an important phone call, and she assured me that as soon as he finished the call, he would see me.

Another 15-minute wait. By now it was going on 11 o'clock. I began to think that I may not see him until after lunch. I know he is a busy man, but I have been waiting. Even though I did not have a scheduled appointment, I guess if I needed to wait I would. After all, I was not told to schedule an appointment time for another day.

At 11:15 a.m. the bishop's door opened and he smiled at me and invited me into his office. He asked if I wanted coffee, I smiled and said, "No thanks, my tank is full." He chuckled as we sat down. He told me that he had spoken with Father Bunyan and he was aware of what happened yesterday. He took a positive stance about the Holy Spirit and the speaking in tongues. He also said he had his "prayer language."

He then replied, "This type of message is not widely accepted in the Episcopal church, nor is it encouraged as a practice. I have spoken with chaplain at CTCF and he is expecting you this afternoon to go over your future candidacy for ordination. I knew then that my future with the Episcopal church would be shortened.

I was driving to Cañon City singing praises to God with not a worry in the world. I had Jesus, and that was all I needed. Why shouldn't I be happy? I just had stopped singing "Amazing Grace" when I arrived at CTCF. Went through the entrance and entered into the prison proper. As I was walking over to the chaplain's office, I was cordially greeted by several offenders. With a smile on my face, I walked into the office and there, sitting at his desk with his back to me, was the chaplain. With a rather loud voice he said, "Sit down, Potter. I will be right with you."

After a minute or two he turned around and looked at me. Well, if ever there was fire in someone's eyes, it was in his. "What in the world were you thinking?" he shouted. "How do you expect to even think about being ordained in a few weeks?"

"Wait a minute!" I recoiled. "I did nothing biblically wrong."

"BIBLICALLY WRONG?" he responded. "That was not the time or the place to do such a thing."

"Where else is there to do such a thing? If not in the church, then where?"

He stared at me and then said with a profoundly loud voice: "I will see to it that you are not ordained, ever, in the Episcopal church or any other church. You will never be a chaplain in a prison in this state or any other. What do you have to say about that, Potter?"

Without hesitation, and with the Spirit of God swelling up within me, pointing a finger at him I said, "I will follow God where He leads me, and neither you, the Episcopal church, this state, or any other state will stop me! Put that in your pipe and smoke that!" I abruptly got up and left his office and the prison.

By the time I got to my car, my knees were shaking. I opened the door and almost fell in. I was shaking ever so badly. What came over me I do not know. But I was physically drained. I went to the nearest coffee shop I could find and regrouped. I called Andrew and told him what had happened. We prayed and cried and prayed some more. On the drive home I was singing to the Lord and I had to pull over for a while and cried once again. When I finally got back on the road, it was almost 6 p.m. I called Joan and told her I would not be home till around 8 o'clock. Feed the kids and keep a plate warm for me.

As I was driving home, a thought came upon me and I had to pull over to write it down. Did you ever have something in your mind that you wanted to write down, but never did? That would probably happen here if I did not stop right then and there. I got a pen and paper out of my briefcase and wrote the following down: "Our battle is not just for the strong alone, it is for the people who pray, believe in God's Word, and stand strong in its defense."

I had calmed down by the time that I got home. I shared with Joan the goings on of the day. She smiled, came over to me and gave me and hug, and said "It's all going to be okay. We are still not going to Rez." I laughed. We watched a little TV and went to bed.

There was a church of similar beliefs and practices in Greely that Andrew told me about, so we looked into it the following Sunday. While they did not dance in the aisles, nor have banners or flag dancers either, they were a fully spirit-filled congregation. The pastor Dave was the lead pastor with several others on staff. They, along with other members of the church, made us feel welcome. We were off to a good start.

It was about three or four weeks later that an evangelist and very astute trumpet player came to the church. That sounded good. We were excited about this person appearing at what came to be known as "our church." When the evangelist, Phil Driscoll, came to the church, the sanctuary was packed. The service was extraordinary insofar as this was the first time that as the service was ending, Pastor Dave had an altar call for people who needed prayer. I looked at Joan and she looked at me, we nodded, took each other's hand and were about to go down for prayer. Our 13-year-old daughter Jennifer grabbed my hand and went down with us to the altar for prayer.

There were so many people that came down for prayer that day. When pastor Dave came to us, there was an awesome presence of God with him. I could feel it. The power of God. He went first to Jennifer and prophesied over her that she would become a nurse. That had to be from God. Even though it took over 30 years to happen, she became a nurse. Glory to God.

Then he approached me. Putting his hands on my head, at first he prayed in tongues, then he said that I would be, and I quote: "chief of Chaplains here in Colorado." I was thinking, "he's got this one wrong." I just got thrown out of ministry from the Episcopal church and by a chaplain to boot. But then I remembered that "I can do all things through Christ who strengthens me." (Philippians 4:13) There it is again. I must remember who is in control: God. For the time being, I will focus on being a good volunteer at FCF. That is first on the agenda. *Strengthen me, Oh, God.*

The week at K-Love Loveland went by rather quickly. Sold some advertising. Wrote the promos for them and, lo and behold, it was Friday when business day usually ended by noon or 1 p.m. at the latest. I stopped home and picked up a change of clothes for the weekend, gave Joan a hug and kiss, asked if there were any last minute "honey do's" for me, and she said no. I know she let me off the hook and I got off easy. I headed toward Cañon City.

The drive down through The Springs went fast. I was an hour earlier than usual. When the prisoners were counted (count time) is not the greatest time to arrive at the prison. I soon found out the control center sergeant was not a happy camper at count time and did not like to be disturbed. I knocked on the window because he was either avoiding me or just did not hear me. He turned around very abruptly and looked at me and gave me a big smile and asked me to pray for him because the numbers were not matching up. There was a re-count in progress. I asked him if he could take a minute and allow me to pray for him right now. His jaw dropped, his eyes welled up, and in a rather penitent voice said yes.

I put my hand on the glass of the control center window and began to pray. A rather short prayer for me, but nonetheless I called upon the Lord to help in whatever was happening and allow this matter to pass. As I concluded this prayer and opened my eyes, I saw this big, burly sergeant holding his hand up to the glass as if we could touch. With a tear in his eye he said, "Amen." He told me that the chaplain had left already and gave me the keys to the chaplain's office. He opened the gate and let me into the prison hallway. As I entered the office corridor, I saw Mr. Hickox seated in his office.

He motioned to me to come into his office. As I did, he waved to me to sit down. This was not good, or so I thought. I had never had a one-on-one with him before. He said to me, "Bill, my name is Bob. That's what you can call me when we are not in a formal setting." That was a relief — that broke the barrier for the both of us. We would have many good years working together.

He asked me if I would be interested in a position at the prison working as an assistant to the chaplain. Another God WOW moment! I was overcome with joy. Wait a minute, just a few weeks ago I left the Episcopal church. Now there was a position for me at the prison.

I do not understand all this, God. So many things are flying through my mind. Bob said it is not a CDOC job, per se, but a contract position. There would be a contract through my church as a chaplain's assistant. The contract would be renewable the next year, pending available funding. Would I be interested in such a position?

I would have jumped for joy but that would not have been advisable. I asked Bob what the chaplain thought about this? "I have not told him yet," Bob replied. He said that he would handle him and not to worry about it. I indicated that I was attending a church in Greely and would have to talk to the pastor. Bob then handed me a copy of the contract offer. If all parties were agreeable, get it back to him next week.

"Have a good weekend, Bill." He was getting up, putting his coat on, and was leaving. I guess that was my indication to leave his office as well. Shaking a bit, I went into the chaplain's office and closed the blinds, sat down, and cried tears of joy. Thanking God for all He was doing.

"But how is this going to work, Lord?" All I heard — "follow me." Where is all this going? Follow me. Trust and obey. *I trust you, Lord, but ....*

I do not know what happened the rest of the weekend. I called the church as soon as I could and set up an appointment to meet with Pastor Dave at 10 a.m. Tuesday. That day could not come soon enough. I was excited, to say the least, but I was intimidated, too. Confused, not fully understanding the implications of the contract. How would the chaplain receive this news? Does he even know about it? I would think he would. What about the words of chaplain at CTCF? How much, if anything, did he share with the other chaplains? Trust and obey, follow me. The anxiety of it all was overwhelming.

I called Joan and told her all about this, and she was as excited as me. What about my job at the radio station? I know Andrew, as a friend, would be extremely excited, too. He knows my heart is in prison ministry. But as my employer he might feel different. I was doing fairly well selling radio ads. Had a few good months, but nothing like being the number one salesperson. I did not think I would be missed that much.

This job was great for me. They would give me the time off I needed to go to the prison. Andrew gave me his credit card for gas when I went down to Cañon City. He had invested a lot of time and money in me. I prayed he would understand. I figured I would not say anything to Andrew until after I spoke with Pastor Dave. When I told Joan about this, she agreed that was the best way to handle matters. Tuesday morning could not come quick enough.

Finally, Tuesday arrived. My waiting was over. Pastor Dave was waiting for me and ushered me into his office. We prayed together for a moment. Then I told him what was going on and, with a smile on his face, he said: "Let's do it." He took the copy of the contract and said he would take it to their legal counsel and get back to me on Sunday. Great! Then we talked about ordination and ecclesiastical endorsement. I had heard about this requirement but never paid much attention up until now. Not to worry, Dave said. He would put me in contact with the proper organizations that handle these matters. Another WOW moment, God. He's got a million of them.

Sunday service was simply marvelous. After the service, I caught up with Pastor Dave and he said, "See you first thing tomorrow morning at the office."

"Okay?" I said with a quizzical look, "What is up now?" I did not like the way he abruptly shook me off. The trying times we put ourselves through, many of which are unnecessary, weigh us down. I had a rough night's sleep.

What obstacles will there be now, Lord? "Trust and obey." *Alright, I get it.*

Bright and early, I arrived at the church, so early that nobody was there yet. I waited about 30 minutes before his administrative assistant arrived. We greeted one another as we got out of our cars, and she told me that Pastor Dave was not coming this morning!

"But he told me to meet him here bright and early today?"

She, in a rather curt way, repeated, "He told me he was not coming in today."

Okay, I get it. I said thank you to her. Then just as she was entering the church, Pastor Dave pulled up.

He jumped out of his car and said, "Hi, I am glad that you are still here. I totally forgot about meeting with you today, let's talk in my office."

"Everything looked good. Here is your copy of the contract, signed and ready to go."

What a sigh of relief this was for me. I left there singing praises to the Lord. I could not wait for Friday to come to hand Bob the signed contract. Needles and pins all week. I did call Bob and told him that I had a signed contract. He replied: "great." He then told me that the chaplain did not like the idea of hiring me. Although he did favor an assistant, not particularly me. Bob said, "Don't worry, we will get over this hurdle."

I would find out soon enough that this was not to be. Another lesson learned along God's path. Sometimes things go a different way than you thought they would. God had a plan that was a learning experience. Trust God in every detail of life, even when things are not be going according to plan. Whose plan? Yours or God's? That is when "trust and obey" comes into play. We may not want to hear this, but we need to take to heart what God said in the Bible. We need to realize what happens to those who did not listen to the Lord. I did not want anything like that to fall upon me.

CHAPTER 17

"Be anxious for nothing, but in everything by prayer and supplication, with thanksgiving, let your requests be made known to God, and the peace of God, which surpasses all understanding, will guard your hearts and minds through Christ Jesus."

- Philippians 4:6-7(NKJ)

These Scriptures have been difficult for me to fully understand. Anxiety is part of human nature, isn't it? Anxiety was ingrained in me from childhood. At the age of six I had my appendix removed. Anxiety began when I heard I was going to have an operation and that I was going to be in the hospital for a few days. I did not want to be away from my parents. I cried and cried over that first brush with anxiety. Many more times throughout my life anxiety would show its ugly face.

Robert E. Lee was a great Confederate general during the Civil War period. In a prayer he circulated amongst his soldiers one Christmas, in part it went like this: *"Let us pray for ourselves, that we may not lose the* word 'concern' for those who have never known Jesus Christ and redeeming love, for moral forces everywhere, for our national leaders. Let prayer be our passion. Let prayer be our practice." (APB)

What an inspiring prayer. Ever so appropriate today.

In early November, I was waiting to hear about this chaplain's assistant position for which I had applied. Bob Hickox called and told me that he had been promoted to warden at the Delta Correctional Center (DCC). I congratulated him. I never will forget his next words: "You might just as well forget about that contract position. The chaplain already indicated that he was not in favor of you, let alone an assistant."

For the first time I heard the expression "vacancy savings." The chaplain also indicated that he needed new office equipment and the money might be better spent there.

Another setback. On a brighter note, I was formally ordained in November as a Minister of the Gospel of Jesus Christ. This was a marvelous, spirit-filled service. Ecumenical from beginning to end. There was a Presbyterian minister, Episcopalian deacon, Methodist minister, and a Roman Catholic deacon. My CPE chaplain, Reverend James Hardy, also participated in the service. Many of our friends and KAIROS team members attended as well. Even though Bob delivered some disappointing news, I was proceeding according to God's plan. I was only slightly discouraged that Thanksgiving Day.

December in Colorado can be a snowy, icy, and slippery month. Being careful when you drive is paramount. Plans were made to have a Christmas celebration at FCF in Cañon City. The radio station hooked up with the Marine Corps Reserve Toys for Tots program. The station agreed to take the barrels for collection around to the different businesses in Loveland, collect the toys, and keep them at the station until the Marines came to collect them.

A big snowstorm hit Loveland and caused hazardous driving conditions in the area. While I was at the station, a call came from one of the collection sites, a King Soopers Market. I was asked by the station manager to stop by and pick up the toys that afternoon. Sure, I would be glad to do that. It is Christmas and it's all about the kids, Santa, and presents. Upon arrival at the store I found a barrel of toys filled to overflowing with stuffed animals. I felt like a kid again.

The parking lot had a myriad of ice ruts throughout. I parked right in front of the store but could not avoid the rut. As I was bringing out the toys, I opened the back-seat door, started to put the toys and stuffed animals in, I slipped on the ice and hit my right knee on the edge of the door. For a moment I saw stars. I was on the ground. Several people came over and helped me get up and put the rest of the toys in the car. By the time I reached the station, my knee was quite swollen. Upon entering the radio station, Patsy was the only one there. She saw me limping and asked what happened.

"Oh, it's nothing." I told her what happened, and she insisted that I fill out an accident report, to be on the safe side. Reluctantly, I sat down and filled out the form. After I completed the form, I headed home. I had hoped that Joan would give me TLC. She did. She brought me an icepack, made me a cup of coffee, and helped me put my feet up. She is just the greatest. I cannot say enough about her.

When I woke the next morning, my knee was throbbing, swollen and hurt like the dickens. I showed Joan and she first called the radio station and told them that she was going to call the doctor. Joan called and the doctor's receptionist and asked if she bring me the next day. When the doctor looked at my knee and took an x-ray, he said nothing appeared to be broken. He gave a shot in the knee to control the swelling, gave me a prescription for pain and sent me on my ho-ho-ho Merry Christmas way.

I fell on Thursday. By Monday, the knee was twice as swollen. I went to the doctor's office and he sent me right over to the hospital to be prepped for a procedure. He extracted some 60 ccs of an ugly yellow liquid from my knee. He told me that I had a staph infection. He gave me some strong antibiotics intravenously and told me I would be hospitalized for a few days. Suffice to say, I eventually would need a knee replacement. This recovery would take months.

In July of 1988, Bob Hickox called me and said that he was now the warden at the Delta Correctional Center. He then proceeded to ask me if I would be interested in a position there as a religious programs' coordinator.

I said, "Yes, sir, I am greatly interested. How soon do you need me?"

Without hesitation, he responded, "now."

My heart immediately sunk. I said I couldn't do that now. I was having knee surgery next week and I would not be available, because the doctor told me I would not be able to return to work until January. I said "thank you," hung up, and thanked God for this opportunity. I knew His plan was still at work: a chaplain's position in the CDOC.

About an hour later, my phone rang, and it was Bob calling me. He told me he was praying about this need at DCC and he decided that I was the man for the position and that he was willing to wait until January. Then we both heard: "October 1 I will be there."

I said, "who said that?"

Bob responded: "I sure didn't."

Then I said, "standing on God's Word and will be there October 1."

"Don't rush anything, I was willing to wait." Bob replied.

"No, October 1."

The next day I had an appointment in Denver with the orthopedic surgeon, Dr. Carne. I told him about my conversation with Warden Hickox and going to Delta October 1 as the religious programs' coordinator.

He said that he did not know who my "God" was. All he knew was that on August 24th he was doing a total knee replacement and that I would be hospitalized for the week following. I would need months of therapy, possibly two or three months, then he would see If I was able to return to work. All I said was, "Jesus is my God and if I heard October 1, I would be able to go to work October 1st."

The surgery went as scheduled that Friday. The nurses kept asking me over the weekend if I needed any pain meds. I said, "no, no!" The only way this knee could move was with God helping me. When I went to see Dr. on Monday and saw how well I was doing, he decided to discharge me and ordered that I could do my therapy as an outpatient in Loveland. I said to him: "Jesus," as I pointed my finger to heaven.

On September 28th when I went back to see Dr. Crane, he discharged me, and I was able to report for work October 1st. He would say this is extra-ordinary. I shouted, "hallelujah, thank you, Jesus." As quickly as I could, I called Warden Hickox and told him of being able to start on October 1st. He was amazed. You have to go to through a three-week training program at the CDOC Training Academy in Cañon City. Something or someone

(Jesus), told Bob to put me on the Training Academy schedule just in case there was an outside chance I would be there on October 1.

Jump ahead with me to November: The Training Academy was finished. My initial move to Delta was only me and some luggage. Joan had challenged me to find a suitable home, to which I did rather quickly. During this time, I was staying in a local motel. The first Saturday I was at the facility, the local Roman Catholic priest conducted Mass at the small facility chapel, a building that held about 45 to 50 people, max.

Father Nathaniel seemed like a genuinely nice, personable individual. After the Mass, I asked him if he would like to join me for lunch in the chow hall. While he declined, he said that he would like to chat we me for a few minutes before he had to leave. Sure, that sounded good to me. As we talked, he asked me where I was staying. I mentioned: "one of the local motels."

He replied, "No way, you come stay in town with me. I live all by myself in what used to be a convent for nuns. I have a housekeeper that comes in a few days a week and cleans and cooks."

"Sounds great to me. Starting next week, I'm in." Father Nathaniel and I would become good friends over the next six years.

Sunday morning came I was ready to give my first sermon at DCC. I was prepared and ready to go. I had flyers posted all over the prison. In the living units, the chow hall, and all the day rooms. As many places as I was allowed, or so I thought.

Warden Hickox informed me that he would not be present the first day I arrived at the prison. He was going to be on a hunting trip. He also said all of the shift commanders, case managers, and support staff were informed about my impending arrival and that I was to report to the control center first thing. The officer in the control center would give me keys to the chapel. Bob indicated he would not return until the following Monday.

As I parked my car, the perimeter security officer approached and asked me to identify myself. The officer, being satisfied, asked me if I wanted a lift to the control center. What an opportunity to get to know this man. After I arrived at the control center, I met the shift commander. He handed me some papers, which contained memos. In it was a memo from the warden identifying those areas where I could go throughout the facility. He particularly stated: "Reverend Potter may go into any area that the warden is allowed."

Another WOW moment, God? However, the shift commander had a different opinion about where I would be permitted to go. He directly said in a very crass voice: "You may go up to the chapel and stay there. Nowhere else! Do you hear me?"

"Yes, sir!" I almost was brought to attention by the tone of his voice. He sounded more like a drill sergeant than a shift commander. I said I had a copy of the memo Warden Hickox posted. Isn't it on the roll call board?

The shift commander stated, "I am in charge now, and what I say goes!"

Again, I replied, "Yes sir." Back to the chapel I went. Now to get to that first Sunday service.

I sat in the chapel and prayed for the shift commander. It was approaching 10 a.m. so I called to the control center and asked them to announce Protestant chapel service. They did. Ten o'clock — nobody showed up. I called again to the control center and asked for another announcement. They did so, still nobody. So, I proceeded to preach to myself. As I did, I started to cry. I cried out to the Lord: "Why God, where are the men? I was not able to go out of this chapel. No one to preach to, God."

Then as I was sobbing, God said to me: "Your ministry is not in the chapel. Your ministry is out there with the men. Go among them and preach the Word. That is where you belong, out there among my people."

But I thought the shift commander said … ?

Shortly thereafter, I left the facility and headed home to Loveland and my family. My work schedule was Thursday through Sunday. On Monday, I prayed about circumstances surrounding my first week at DCC. Should I call Warden Hickox to tell him of the incident with the shift commander? On the other hand, there was nothing that could not wait until Thursday. On the bright side, I told Joan of some of the places that were for rent in Delta. In particular, there was two places of interest that I thought would be great for us.

Joan said, "You pick it and that will be the one that I will make work." The rest of the week would be spent packing and getting ready to move.

The next six years or so would be filled with excitement, joy, and tragedy before God moved us again. I will share highlights of that tremendous period of time of embracing prison ministry. I will do my best to be as close to a chronological order as I remember.

Per the shift commander, I stayed in the chapel, the first weekend I was at DCC. He was very precise, clear, and insistent that I know my place and was to stay there — period! I spent most of my time praying, reading the Word, cleaning, sweeping, singing, and mopping the chapel. A special time for me to be with the Lord.

I was reading in Philippians from Paul's understanding about being content. 'I have learned the secret of being content — whether well fed or hungry, whether in abundance or in need. I can do all things through Christ who strengthens me. (Philippians 4:12, HCB)

I must admit, at first I was a bit miffed at and with the shift commander. Then I prayed and meditated on God's Word. I was more interested in having shift commander receive more than just a verbal reprimand. There were two activities that took place in the chapel on Saturday. As I mentioned previously, first was the Roman Catholic service at 10 a.m. with Father Nathaniel. In the afternoon, Pastor Darryl Proffit of the Delta First Assembly of God conducted a Protestant service.

Pastor Proffit and I first met about two months prior, when Warden Hickox asked me to take a ride out to Delta and "check it out." In what part of Colorado is Delta? He said hang a right on I-70 and drive almost to the end (259 miles or so) and hang a left. Drive another 40 miles south on Highway 50 and there you will find Delta.

He also told me just before you get into Delta, look for a sign on the right that will indicate a right turn to get to DCC. He was right: Four hours later, I was approaching Delta. I saw the sign for DCC, made the right turn, and drove for another eight miles or so, arriving at a series of buildings in a valley. Did not look much like a prison, though.

Years later, I would be ever so thankful about the assignment that God gave me at DCC. It was at that time that I met Pastor Proffit. A burly man, about 6'3," pleasant and friendly. As he tells of his first encounter with me: "I tried to pigeonhole you because that is what I like to do." After knowing

SENIOR CHAPLAIN BILL POTTER

me for 30-some odd years, we are still best of friends and he still cannot figure me out.

Pastor Proffit commented to others and myself that he considered Joan and I an anomaly. As both being divorced before we met, he at first did not know how God could use us in an ordained ministry. We proved him wrong, glory to God. Our friendship with the Proffit's flourishes to this day. Praise the Lord.

The rest of the weekend I labored on how to deal with the shift commander. How could I work with this man day in and day out? What will his staff think of me as a result of my actions? That was why I prayed on Saturday and Sunday. If this was the place God wanted me to be planted and grow in Him and spread the Good News of Jesus Christ to the lost, that included shift commander, too, didn't it? Now I get it, I need to pray for him as well. Make a friend of him and then I could minister not only to him, but to all of the staff. Let this beginning be a sign of the joy of the Lord upon this place. There is good news coming.

Thanks, Lord. I get it now. Your love is what is most important, and You have challenged me to be a reflection of that love to one and all here at DCC.

My heart was filled with joy come Thursday when I returned to DCC. I went directly to Warden Hickox's office and asked to see him. I was told to go in. Mr. Hickox was sitting at his desk, and he was ever-so-cordial as he greeted me

"How did it go your first week here?"

I replied, "not so good." As he questioned me about the events of the week, I could see that he was starting to do a slow burn. Before I could finish, he interrupted me and shouted "Barbara, get me my copy of the memo about Reverend Potter's coming on board that was signed by all the shift commanders." In short order Mr. Hickox had that memo and asked me if I showed it to the shift commander.

"Yes, Sir." I quickly replied.

Bob said, "I will get this straightened out today. Barbara, get the shift commander up here NOW!"

"Wait a minute," I interrupted. "I would prefer you handle things a little differently. When you speak to the shift commander, be more subtle. Affirmative, but subtle. Let him know that we talked and together we arrived at the conclusion that he did not handle the situation in a professional manner. "Please do not take a punitive action," I asked.

He pondered that for a minute or two and agreed that this was the correct way to handle the situation. Warden Hickox did handle this matter quickly. As I was leaving his office, the shift commander was sitting outside waiting "his turn" with warden. So, the next shift change I was there and was introduced by the shift commander in question as the Religious Programs Coordinator and was to be trusted and given access to the facility just as the warden has full access. Another WOW moment!

I was elated at this introduction by the shift commander. I found out shortly thereafter that this rather hard-crusted man was not the most liked either. He was not most likely to be a winner of a popularity contest in the near future. From that point on, I would make him a target, showing him more and more of how God loves him and so do I. We became good friends.

The inmates had free access to telephones, which were directly outside the control center. They were permitted to call most times during the day. The calls were made either from a prepaid account or collect. This would be a good place for me to hang out, by the phones. Exclusive of the chow hall, this was the best place to see the inmates. Unless it was raining, I could meet them, talk to them, in other words, be a friend. Friendship is important to anyone, especially a prisoner. There are no friends in prison. Only the ones who are users or used. Everybody wants or is wanted by someone.

There certainly were gangs, cliques, and Christians. People want to be part of something or someplace, even inmates. Come next Sunday, there were about a dozen or so that showed up. The so called "Bible-thumpers" and one or two just wanting something to do before a football game on their TV. Most had their own TVs. Some color ones, but most black and white. I didn't think they even made black and white TVs anymore, but the inmates had them.

On Friday of that week, Mr. Hickox paid me a visit at the chapel office to see how well I was getting settled in. Moreover, he wanted me to step outside for a moment to show me a tract of land in front of and just west of his office. The facility at that time only had 96 beds for inmates. But there was a big expansion getting started. A 500-bed facility was in the planning stages for DCC. Most of the current buildings were going to be torn down or re-modeled, a more modern facility would replace this one.

Part of this master plan was an expanded religious program facility to be used by all faiths. The problem was that there was not any funding for this building included in the budget. Warden Hickox said, matter-of-factly, that the funding should come from private sources. How was he going to find such funding? He was planning on me being an integral part of the fundraising process, through the Delta County Ministerial Fellowship (DCMF.)

That was a shocker! This was not in my job description. I don't have the influence to even suggest such a plan to DCMF at its next meeting. I didn't know anyone!

Warden Hickox was a strategist. He was always thinking one step ahead of everyone. He was attempting to instill in me the same skill. I was a quick thinker, so I quickly caught the concept of his way of accomplishing or getting things done. He also convinced me to join the Delta Rotary Club. This was a group of the community's most influential businessmen and women. He wanted me to get to know them through this organization.

This was to prove an especially important piece of the puzzle. Learning from these men was instrumental in making contact with the rest of the business community. Bob always told me to think "outside the box." But remember, do not do anything unless I know about it first. My one-word response was: "Understood."

The Rotary Club met every Wednesday for lunch. At those luncheons, most of us liked to talk shop. I overheard the president of one of the banks talking about the newly installed carpet, which was wearing out. He had contacted the carpet company and they came and assessed the situation and agreed there was a defect in the carpet and that he would make arrangements with the manufacturer to replace the carpet. My mind quickly kicked into gear and thought, *Ask what they are going to do with the carpet they are removing.* That carpet would look nice in the chapel. It would certainly brighten things up.

After the meeting adjourned, I spoke with Warren the bank president, and asked about the carpet. He told me that was in the hands of the manufacturer's rep as to how they would dispose of the carpet. He was willing to give me the phone number, which he had at his office. I was excited! Free carpet, Free, almost-new carpet. *Another WOW moment, Lord?* The Scripture that came to mind was: "But Jesus looked at them and said to them, with men this is impossible, but with God all things are possible." (Matthew 19:26NKJ.)

Somehow, this was going to happen, I knew it. Upon return to DCC I immediately went to the warden's office to speak with Bob. I told him about the potential of getting this carpet from the bank through the manufacturer's rep. Did I have his permission to proceed? "Go for it," he said. Just keep him posted.

When Steve called me with the phone number, he wanted to give me a heads up because the rep said there would a stipulation. Now Steve would not tell me exactly what that was, but he sounded skeptical. As soon as he gave me the rep's number, I called him, and got an answering machine. I left a message for him to call me back. Admittedly, I was somewhat nervous. Then I reflected back on Matthew 19:26. I prayed about the matter and felt a calmness overcome me, a feeling that it would all work out.

That Friday, Dave, the carpet rep, called me and said, "There is good news and there is bad news. Which do you want to hear first?"

"Give me the good news first," I said, "then we will figure how to work out the bad news after that."

Dave said the good news was that we could have the carpet. The bad news was that we not only had to take the carpet out ourselves, but we would need to help install the new carpet. That did not sound too bad.

"I need to talk this over with my boss and get back with you next week, okay?" He said yes, but you need to call me by next Wednesday at the latest. We said our goodbyes and hung up.

I called Mr. Hickox and told him what the requirements were in order to get the carpet. "We will handle it," he told me. The WOWs just kept coming. In a little over two weeks, we had carpet in the chapel and the facility had some carpet for other areas in the prison. The whole process was somewhat of a circus. Two or three inmate work crews were in the bank on a Friday night and all day Saturday over two weekends. The first weekend was to remove the carpet, the second weekend was to help to install the new carpet. After all was said and done, only one chair was out of place. Now to the almost impossible task of a new chapel. Notice the word "almost." That might take many years to happen. But read on. God's timing is always right on.

147

"Now faith is the substance of things hoped for, the evidence of things not seen."

- Hebrews 11:1 (NKJ)

I have not, up until now, mentioned Mr. Granzella, the assistant warden at DCC. I would call him "old school," a hard, crusty manager. He had been at DCC long before it was a prison. This "camp" was used as a summer site for minimum-security offenders to help the state parks with maintenance crews, building new trails and cleaning up various sites that suffered some damage over the winter.

In my brief conversations with Mr. G, he was less than cordial. He did not initially want to meet at the chapel, but I insisted. Partly because I wanted to show off the carpet. Mainly because there was the issue of the old, mostly broken, wooden auditorium-type seating. However, the method to my madness was to show him how badly we needed new chairs. Also, to let him know I had someone who was going to buy the chairs we needed. Because of the price break on the chairs, we could get 100 chairs for just a few dollars more, which the donor was willing to cover the cost, if the facility would pick up the cost of shipping.

The chapel did not have any available storage space but would be willing to allow the facility to use these 35 or so chairs in the academic department, which needed some new seating badly. When Mr. G made it up to the chapel, I gestured that we sit down in the front of the sanctuary.

He timidly approached me. I have never seen him look so apprehensive. Nonetheless, he came forward and sat down by my side.

I said, "Mr. G, before we start, I would like to pray."

I heard a gulp, and reply, "okay."

As I finished the prayer, I explained my plan about obtaining the chairs. I had paperwork to show price comparisons. In so little convincing, he agreed. Another WOW, Lord! The rest of the story is that when the chairs arrived, Mr. G was fuming over the shipping cost. After much grumbling, he did pay the shipping, but informed me that any further discussions would be held only in his office.

During this time period, about six months, the Lord was encouraging me to start an inmate choir. I kept saying no. *Lord, I cannot read any music, let alone lead a choir. I do not want to hear any more about it. Period.* But, the Lord is persistent.

"Start a choir," He said.

"All right, I will!" The response was so surprising. The quality of good voices was astounding. The selection of music was more difficult than I thought it would be. I went to my church and asked the music team leader where and how she selected the music for the church. Thank God that I made this request. She pointed me to a Christian music company, Brentwood Music of Nashville, Tennessee.

What a place to start. This music group had everything I needed to get a choir started. The sheet music, the split track tapes to listen to and to use during a performance. I was able to purchase a boom box for a reasonable price. This was really (bottom-line) grassroots work. We were thankful for what we had at that time.

There was a need for some kind of choir attire in lieu of inmate uniforms. I was told by the music team leader from our church that there were choir robes at our church that were not being used. I thought, *Why not ask Pastor Proffit if we could borrow them for the inmate choir? We could even arrange for their first use be at a church service at the Delta First Assembly.*

"Sure, why not? But I have to get the board approval first." He said that there was going to be a meeting that Tuesday night. He did not see a problem, so we scheduled the Chapel of Hope Choir to sing the following Sunday.

The board did approve lending the robes to the Chapel of Hope Choir. Here we go: robes, music, a great program, and a great choir. "God you are good all the time and Your mercy endures forever." (My version of a condensed Psalm 136.)

Over the next few years, God moved mysteriously at DCC. The choir was going out almost weekly. The programs at the chapel began to increase with a daily Bible study, an Islamic volunteer program, and a Native American Indian Sweat Lodge Program. While all this was under my purview, I did not have to participate in nor directly supervise any of the actual activities. Although I was somewhat interested in their procedures but not as a participant. Thanks be to God.

I must interject some things that need some further explanation. Some of the churches that the choir performed at wished to make a monetary contribution to the ministry. Because these were CDOC and DCC authorized program, we could not accept any donations for the chaplain, instead to the DCMF that was supplying sound equipment, music, and robes. The funds that came in for the choir exceeded expectations. The choir became quite a ministry.

On one occasion, the inmate choir built a float for the Annual Deltarado Days Parade and on several other occasions won a trophy for the best parade float. The men who participated in the choir had to go through a screening process in order to be part of the choir. The standards were high. The men had to regularly attend church and not have any write-ups for a year. Some who applied made it and some did not. One of the men who made the cut, Wesley, quoted a Scripture from 1 Timothy 1:12: NKJ"... *and I thank Christ Jesus our Lord who has enabled me because He counted me faithful, putting me into the ministry."*

Wesley was in the choir for a long time and was a strong warrior for the cause. He helped lead many inmates to Christ. He was a blessing to one and all. Always smiling, always ready to share the Good News of Jesus Christ with anyone, whether or not they were interested. Always celebrating, always with the joy of the Lord in his heart.

One of the reasons Warden Hickox called me to DCC was that while he was at FCF he noticed how much of an impact that KAIROS had within that facility, and he wanted that program to be at DCC. When he first discussed this with me, I told him that this particular program was designed for maximum- and medium-custody facilities, not at a minimum facility. He insisted that he wanted this program at DCC. So much so that he and I went to Winter Park, Florida to present his case.

Even though the national board of KAIROS was not in favor of doing this in minimum security prisons, they were willing to set it up at Delta as a pilot program and invited Mr. Hickox to become a board member, which he gracefully accepted. This program became the backbone of the religious programs at DCC. This program blazed the trail for other large group ministries such as Prison Fellowship and Freedom Fellowship, groups centered on introducing men to Jesus Christ.

The local programs that came from the churches played an equally important role in rehabilitating offenders. DCMF introduced programs that impacted not only the individual offender but his entire family as well. On Christmas weekend there was a special program for inmates. This program allowed the offender to pick out a toy and clothing gift for his children who could visit him on Christmas weekend. On the Thursday before Christmas, my wife would have a small group of volunteers come in with her to help the inmates wrap gifts. In addition, Russell Stover Candy Company donated a box of candy for each inmate to wrap and give to his spouse.

There would always be enough to go around, even if someone came unexpectedly. There would also be a complete turkey dinner for all who came to visit that weekend. We even fed most of the staff on duty at that time. "The joy of the Lord ... all things are possible." These words are always with me. What a true joy it is to serve the King of Kings. My wife has often said "that I retired from work the day I started in prison ministry."

There have been days when I left the Delta prison mad, upset, frustrated and disappointed, when I have said "No more ... I quit!"

Joan tells me: "Calm down. Go and pray. The Lord will give you the strength to carry on."

I always knew the outcome. I would cry a little, maybe at times a lot, but I relied on that *"peace that passes all understanding"* (Philippians 4:7 NKJ). Enough said.

During this time period, mid-1993, the Delta First Assembly of God was in the process of searching for a pastor. My dear friend Darryl Proffit had left the church in Delta to pastor a church in the Denver area. It was at this time one of the elders of the church requested that we return the choir robes. Ok God, what do we do now? "Pray" was what I heard. So, I gathered the choir members and asked them to join me in prayer for new choir robes. As we prayed, the Lord told me get some catalogs for choir robes.

Why? We do not have the funds to buy robes.

"Get the catalogs, Bill."

I went on the internet and found some businesses that sell robes and contacted them and they sent their catalog. Meanwhile, unknown to me, some of the inmate choir members mentioned to some of the study groups to join them in prayer about the robes.

All this was taking place during the summer months of 1993 when the choir did not have any programs scheduled. The catalogs had some beautiful choir robes in them. As I skimmed through the catalogs and saw the pricing, I thought this was not going to happen any time soon. I better inform the inmates to get their best greens out and keep them clean and pressed.

I did inquire of other local churches if they had any choir robes that we could borrow for a season. But there were none available, or so I was told. Around Labor Day weekend 1993, some of the local churches were calling to schedule the choir Christmas program. One church just outside of Montrose in Colona wanted the choir to sing at their Fall Harvest Celebration. I said sure, we will be there pending the Warden's approval. I would let them know as soon as I get the paperwork approved.

On that Tuesday after Labor Day, I received a phone call from one of our Prison Fellowship Volunteers, a gentleman who wanted to remain anonymous and asked if we were still in the market for choir robes. Yes, I replied. He indicated that he would like to donate the necessary funds to buy new robes, if I was interested. Another WOW moment, God. Thank you, Lord.

When I informed the warden that I had found appropriate robes, I received approval and was waiting for the phone call from the donor. I said, "I knew the moment you called that God was going to answer our prayer about the robes." The next day was the absolute "drop-dead" day to submit an order for delivery of our robes to have them in time for the Colona Church program.

Some of these "God incidents," as I call them, may seem of little importance in light of the bigger picture, but they were essential in the groundwork of dealing of God's Bigger Plans for the Chapel of Hope.

The local city of Delta Ministerial Alliance (DMA) is not to be confused with the Delta County Ministerial Fellowship DCMF. I was a member of both groups focused on feeding those in need and helping with rent and utilities. But DMA did not control what was distributed by each individual church to persons in need. They were looking for a way to control "double dipping."

I often discussed ministry issues with Joan, who had a profound thought: "Why don't they combine their efforts and have one church handle the food bank, another handle the utilities, and another handle the rent. All of them combining the other's financial aid proportionally in all of the areas of concern. This way no one was overly burdened." I asked her to put that in a formal proposal and speak with them at the next ministerial alliance meeting. She not only did that, but she spoke to each of the pastors in advance to "feel them out," to see if they were open to the concept. All were in favor of the plan she put together.

The church handling most of the utility gifts would like to continue doing so, provided the others would help financially. The same process was arranged with the rent and gifts. Interestingly enough, none wanted to handle the food bank because of the labor required. At the meeting, Joan presented her plan, with a unique way to establish a community food bank. Joan worked at a local store that had plenty of backroom space to house a food pantry, and the store-owner was willing to allow a food bank in that location. One central location in the heart of town, easy to find for the churches to bring their food supplies, and an inmate crew to help with the stocking of the shelves (which were already in the back of the store.) Also, an inmate crew was permitted to help out with the food supplies two days a week. The ministers all agreed and would put the plan into effect within 60 days.

This plan was in effect until I took a position in 1996 at the CDOC central office Colorado Springs. All areas of the ministry inside and outside the prison were working on "all cylinders." I was always thinking of new programs to start at the facility. I remember the words of Warden Hickox that kept echoing in my head: "Think outside the box."

There were some programs that Prison Fellowship (PF) started many years ago and were still going strong, like the Angel Tree program. This program allowed inmates to select two gifts (one clothing and one toy) for the offender's children. Then a church that was in the area of where the family lived would buy, wrap, and deliver those items before Christmas.

I thought, *What if we could duplicate this program and do it in the facility when a family visited DCC on Christmas weekend?* That would involve more of the inmate population. Wouldn't that be something! I put together a proposal for Warden Hickox to approve, and much to my surprise he said YES! There would be stipulations: No battery-operated toys and no guns of any kind. That was something that would be overcome by putting the batteries in a clear plastic bag with the family name taped to it and then giving it to the families as they were leaving the prison. Simple enough.

Bob instructed me to file the necessary paperwork for approval. I now had the task of recruiting local churches to sponsor the gifts. What I thought would be somewhat difficult to accomplish was really easy. The local churches were eager to get involved with us. Glory to God.

I contacted some of the local retail stores to donate stocking stuffer items and wrapping paper. This was more arduous and time-consuming than planned, but not insurmountable. Soliciting from the inmate population a list of potential visitors and the children that would be visiting them on this holiday also was not as difficult as first thought. The only stipulation was that if a child or children could not attend, then their gifts would be turned over to one of the local charities. Lots of planning with some disappointments, but many a joyous event.

Initially, the biggest objections came from the visiting room staff. They perceived a security "nightmare." Warden Hickox assured them that the chaplain is confident things will go on without a hitch. Thanks, Warden Hickox! I most assuredly understood the security risks and took every opportunity to train the volunteers that would be assisting with the program and the security risks involved.

There were other obstacles for God to overcome. There was an overwhelming response to the program, potentially more people than the visiting room could handle. There was a capacity of around one hundred people maximum at any one time. What a great problem to have, so many people to visit in a prison on Christmas! Imagine that! As most prison visiting rooms are almost empty on this holiday, here we potentially would not have enough room to handle all the visitors that weekend.

How do we deal with this one, God? Make a morning and an afternoon shift. In other words, two shifts? This would accommodate all of the visitors. But how will the visiting room officers receive this? A celebration of the birth of Christ. All in attendance discovered the generosity of the Christian community of Delta County.

Warden Hickox said, "We will provide more security staff that day. Not increase the amount of staff, but to move the staff on duty around in such a manner that there should not be a problem handling the load on that weekend."

The visiting room staff reluctantly agreed. "So it was written, so let it be done." The critical point here is to remember Christmas Day did not fall on a weekend every year, but the Lord is in control and the author of all this fun stuff. This is to His Glory!

God was glorified. Yes, the toys and the clothing items were important. But the program showed a criminal and his family the forgiveness of a loving God as exhibited through His people. John 15:12 says, "This is my commandment: that you love one another as I have loved you."

The Spirit of Christ shone through the churches that supported the program to the Christians who purchased the gifts to the volunteers that helped the offenders wrap them to the prison officials who supported the program and finally to the visiting room personnel who facilitated the whole event without incident. Glory to God on high.

The impact of this program could not be measured in a temporal way. How far reaching, not only throughout the prison itself but also within the line staff. As for the gifts for the no-shows, officers who knew of a needy family were permitted to take from the gifts unclaimed. The love of Christ was shown throughout that community through the sharing of that love. Joy to the world, the Lord is here!

One story I must relate, a request from an offender was for his four-year-old son who wanted a rocking horse. There was none to be found on the Western Slope of Colorado that Christmas season. The only item that closely resembled it was a stick horse, the type where you squeeze the ear and it whinnies and makes a galloping sound.

One of the volunteers who went shopping with my wife for that rocking horse was, I must say, in a fully joyful frame of mind. She was seen "riding that stick horse" down the aisle in Wal-Mart late one night. I leave her name out for obvious reasons.

As I mentioned, the Russell Stover Candy Company graciously donated Christmas candy for the program. On that day in the visiting room, I was walking around the room handing out the candy when this four-year-old boy came up to my wife and tugged at her dress and asked: "Excuse me, ma'am, but do you see that man over there?"

Joan said "yes I do."

"Well as I was riding on my horse, I did not get any candy."

My wife smiled and responded, "I bet if you go up to him and ask, he will give you some candy."

"Thank you, ma'am," and he galloped off to the side and got his candy. As he was riding away on his horse, he was overheard saying: "This is such a nice place, I just might come back." This was the first time this little boy visited his dad in prison. Shine Jesus, shine!

There were other activities where God's blessing was revealed to one and all. On this Christmas weekend, one particular Christmas Eve, small gift bags were assembled for each inmate and every staff person. These bags contained three homemade cookies, two candy bars, a pair of socks (for the inmates only), and a candy cane. The socks were provided by the Salvation Army and the rest of the items came from the local churches. Another outpouring of God's love.

During these Christmas programs, a group of 15 to 20 volunteers at 8 o'clock on Christmas Eve would come in and sing Christmas carols throughout each of the living units while distributing these bags, which had been decorated by Sunday school children with a Christmas greeting. Oh my God, how sweet You are!

The desire the Lord put on my heart was to reach out to all of the flock at DCC, from the inmate right up to the warden. What seemed to me to be almost impossible was possible through God. Without my daily prayers to the Lord, none of these things could have ever happened. The more I remained in prayer, the more miracles happened at DCC. Jesus must reign in our lives if we are to show the world who He really is. The joy of the Lord must truly be our strength. Period. Jesus taught His disciples to first love one another, as He has loved them. Then to love others in the same fashion, passing on the love of God as shown to them by Jesus Himself. This is the mission statement for each and every Christian today. This was and is my mantra.

Another "down" time in the prison was New Year's Eve. Lots of "homemade brew" hooch, fights, and tensions would run high. I prayed: "God, how could we celebrate this less-than-Christian event in a way that honors you? Tell me, Lord, what can be done?"

Then it came to me: Have a party! A party? Really, a party? In chapel, have a party? Have the worship team band sing Christian praise songs, serve food, and make sure the staff gets fed, too?

Then, I thought, *Let the men eat all they wish with the understanding that they may NOT take or sneak any item back with them to the living units.* I presented the idea to the warden, and he said it might work.

"Put the request in writing, and we will see."

I helped the warden recall his days at FCF where they had such a New Year's Eve program. He smiled just a little and said, "you guys put the fear of God in the shift commander that night." The first thing he saw as the group came in was the champagne-like bottles. He could not see beyond that. He summoned the security team and as they inspected these "champagne" bottles, they were pleasantly surprised to see the bottles contained sparkling apple cider. Mr. Hickox warned not to bring in anything like that here!

CHAPTER 19

"I will lift up my eyes to the hills, from whence comes my help? My help comes from the Lord, who made heaven and earth."

- Psalm121:1-2 (NKJ)

There is a common expression "If life serves up lemons, it is our/my responsibility to turn it into lemonade." If life comes with lemons, we don't have to drink the juice without sweetening it up with the sweetness of God's love. Sometimes it is hard to find the sugar. We just forgot where we put it! For me, the sugar in my life comes from and through prayer and searching through the Bible where the sugar never runs out.

The Word of God was and is the sweetest, truest words I've ever found. The sugar comes from His love for me and you. He gave His life for me and you so that we may have life everlasting. What kind of man is this? In essence He was man and God — God incarnate. A God who came to live amongst us in order to demonstrate how much He loves us. The influence He has had on the world is immeasurable. No one but God would have or could have designed a better plan for His creation. He shows each of us the way to spend eternity with Him in His kingdom. Just imagine, He tells us that He has "… prepared a place for you." (John 14:2b NKJ)

Daniel Webster (1782-1852), American statesman during our country's antebellum period, declared: "The gospel is either true history or a consummate fraud. It is either a reality or an imposition. Christ was what

He professed to be or He was an imposter. There is no other alternative."
(APB)

This simple statement undergirds my profession of Christ as my Lord and Savior. There is no other alternative that gets us through this life and into God's presence. I do recall the first time I was put to the "test" regarding my belief in Christ. It was at FCF, on the first day I went in to recruit candidates for the initial KAIROS seminar scheduled for April 1983. It was a brisk spring Saturday in March. I arrived around lunchtime, after checking in at the control center. An officer escorted me to a meeting room that would hold about 50 or so people. It had no windows except a small window in the door. I was told to wait there, the sergeant in control, after the inmate count cleared, announced that the inmates could sign up for the seminar. So, I found a table and brought it to the door along with two chairs.

About 45 minutes passed before the announcement was made and then about another 30 minutes went by before the door slowly started to open ... I almost was going to shout for help as this big black dude (6'9" while I was 5'8") came in with what I presumed was the meanest stare and look on his face. With the fear of God giving me all the strength I could muster, I invited him in to sit down. Then, all of a sudden, with the biggest smile and brightest white teeth I had ever seen, in came Wayne Hudson. His first words to me were "Praise the Lord, brother!" That was a great icebreaker. My knees stopped shaking as I sat down with a plop.

I interject this story because I had lots of fear about facing real hardened criminals. Through my 32 years of ministry (volunteering, contracting, full-time CDOC employee, and Good News Chaplain), there was always the knowledge that these people are not incarcerated for missing Sunday school. I tried to instill that reality into the minds of the hundreds of volunteers that I worked with during that ministry.

In actuality, there was a threefold ministry that encompassed my chaplaincy work. Holding this all together was Jesus Christ. Without Him, I was no more than a loud clanging gong making little or no sense of what I was doing. With the Bible as my training manual, I was a winner from start to finish. Keeping focus is what is most important. The years spent serving the Lord in the Cañon City prison system was the most informative, humble days of studying, learning, and growing in God's Word, but they were ever so rewarding!

This ministry I was called to was joyful but stretched my very being. Showing my family I love them meant so much to me and kept me focused on Jesus and growing in relationship with God, family, and friends. The example that Joan and I showed the children would touch them for the rest of their lives.

The move to Delta was interesting, to say the least. We could not afford a moving company to move us, so, we had to be somewhat creative. I shared with Pastor Proffit our dilemma. He made a few phone calls to some church members and found one that would lend us his truck (Jerry Hines), which was used to transport onions from the field to the packing plant. The harvest season was over, so we could use that truck. What a blessing that was for us. Although it took a little over a month to get the smell of onions off our furniture, all things were good.

Our attendance at the Delta First Assembly of God was a wonderful opportunity for the family to worship together. Although this did not happen as often as we liked, it was a true blessing for us. It was my firm belief that anyone who is a volunteer, chaplain, or staff must have a regular connection with a local church outside the prison, to maintain sanity, sense, and stability. The joy of the Spirit of God is the source of the refreshment and recharges the soul.

As I said earlier, the Lord's vision of the church behind the walls was to truly be a church to the fullest, yet within the CDOC regulations. That's why the off-site inmate choir activities were so important to the inmates' re-introduction back into society as productive citizens.

One of those activities involved visiting several nursing homes during the course of a month for a sing-along and Bible study. This allowed offenders to interact, under supervision, with the residents of the nursing home during the Bible study time. Of course, the warden and staff had to approve the program. This was a lesson in trust, that took training the offender how to interact with the residents and their responses to them, to God, and to our singing.

The songs were all from a traditional old hymn book. Most of the men recognized them from their youth, but it took some refreshing practice.

Some of the men asked to be excused from this type of outreach. But, as the others returned and shared their joyous experiences, they eventually asked again to be part of this program. In particular, we went to a nursing home in Cedaredge, and on the way back to the facility one of the choir members shared this encounter with a resident: "During the time of discussion on the Bible reading, the woman that I was sitting alongside asked me, 'tell me, sonny, what was your crime that got you into prison?' I was a little taken back when she asked me that, and I just said, 'that is not who I am now, ma'am.' Then she asked me how much time I had to do before I went home. I told her that I was expecting to be home by this time next year, ma'am. Then in a very stern voice she told me that she did not commit any crime but getting old! 'The only way I was getting out of this place is feet first, sonny! I was given a death sentence for just getting old!'" There were a lot of tears that evening as we headed back to the facility that night.

On our trips to visit other nursing homes, we would arrive around dinnertime and have a meal with the residents. After a few meals, the men asked if they could eat before they left the facility instead of at the nursing homes. I asked them, "You mean to tell me, the food is better at the prison than at the nursing home?"

"YES!"

Well, that was a first since these men never refused food before at any other place. As part of the prisoner ministry, these men often had to interact with elderly residents. Never was there a complaint about improper remarks or suggestions.

These men were handpicked because they were men who made a mistake and were truly repentant. Men who wanted to return to their family and be productive citizens. There were those who were what could be called "career criminals." Some of these men may have re-offended several times. They testified that they had enough of the criminal life and genuinely wanted to go straight. But they did not know how or where to start. They were looking for God in all the wrong places — until now! They needed the love of God as shown through His church and His people. Love was the hallmark of this small community of Delta. The outpouring of love shown to one and all, staff included, was nothing short of phenomenal.

That steadfast love of God shone ever so brightly for our many years there and continues today.

One offender comes to mind. While at FCF, Stan (lifer) was never getting out of prison, nor did he have any hope of moving to a lower- or minimum-security facility such as DCC. Somehow, he did come to DCC and attended KAIROS #1. From all outward signs, he had nothing to live for. He had already served over 21 years. No one had visited him in five years. He thought that God had even forgotten him!

With little to no hope, death would be his only consolation. How open would he be to hear what God has for him? He had a heavy heart as one who was hurting and in need of healing from the Great Physician. Little did he know what the Lord prepared for him. He found people who would be friends. They came back and visited him once a month and kept him in their prayers. Commitment was made by the KAIROS team members to continue the primary focus of the ministry with offenders– make a friend, be a friend, bring that friend to Christ!

Stan had a talent he learned in prison: playing the guitar. This would be a great advantage at the monthly meetings. Just in case there was a need for a musician for the meetings, Stan was the go-to guy. Stan found his best friend, Jesus Christ, He was always with him, even during his darkest of times. He made a commitment to Christ to always call Him first when trouble was in sight. He became the "Mister Inside" recruiter for the program. A man that had never shown any emotion and always had a stoic daze upon his face, suddenly, he became a man with a perpetual smile. His nickname soon changed from Monster to Smiley. He became a strong believer in Jesus. Stan obtained approval to go off grounds with the choir. What a miracle! There are many stories like Stan's.

These men make a powerful witness for Christ. They are unknown to the world but known to the King of kings and the Lord of lords. Their testimonies are at the grassroots level, right at the heart of men, by men, who once thought that God had forgotten them and that God had given them their final death sentence. Imagine inmates bringing the good news of Jesus Christ to inmates who felt forgotten by God. Who better than one of the peers to tell them "the rest of the story." The Scripture became their mantra: *"Stand fast, therefore, in the liberty by which Christ has made us free, and do not be entangled with a yoke of bondage."* (Galatians 5:1 NKJ)

Throughout my 32 years of ministry, I encountered many such men who became warriors for Christ.

Back to the story: As plans continued to expand the facility to a 500-bed prison, plans were also moving forward for the new chapel. I had contacted several architectural firms in order to get a building design. I consulted the DCMF and the Delta City Alliance pastors. It was Pastor Proffit who referred me to the Assembly of God headquarters in Springfield, Missouri. They were very cordial and sent me several designs of churches that their architects developed.

Of the designs that they sent me, I selected two. I went to DCMF for their input and approval. They told me that the facility security issue had to be considered. They indicated that I was the closest to the issues and therefore the best situated to make that decision. I thanked them, made a selection, and asked to proceed with a presentation to the facility. I made an appointment with Warden Hickox for the next day.

When I met with Warden Hickox, he immediately said: "No, I was not going to let you build your 'Starship Enterprise.'" (I am an avid Star Trek enthusiast.) I was somewhat taken aback. As I took another look at the drawings and understood what he was saying, I tried to explain that this was not my motive for this particular design. All I was doing was trying to look at the designs from a security perspective. He chuckled and responded, "Sure." Well, on to plan/design "B."

Bob was more receptive and gave an immediate thumbs up. "Go get blueprints of this design and I will put them through the hoops."

The next day, I made phone calls to the Assembly of God national office in Springfield, Missouri to get these blueprints, and they indicated that I should consult local firms in order to get the necessary prints. That sounded reasonable. I soon found out that this would be more difficult than I first thought. The cost of such prints was out of sight. Many more thousands of dollars than had been appropriated. At this point, we had less than $10,000 in the chapel building fund. I called to ministerial churches to seek prayer with regard to funds needed. I also called upon the volunteers to join in this prayer need.

On a Tuesday night in August I was chaperoning/supervising a PF meeting. At 8 o'clock, the facility always had a formal count of all offenders. One of the volunteers, Lucille, asked me how the new chapel was coming along. Slow, I responded. I told her of the hurdles. There always seemed to be a need for money. But the bottom line was not money but time spent on our knees seeking the Lord's guidance. I asked her to join me in prayer about this matter. In fact, we prayed right then and there. She then informed me of a couple who lived in Cedaredge. She told me that this couple was philanthropic and that they gave to a local nursing home, and funds to complete a wetlands project. They might be interested in helping the chapel project with a few dollars. The following day I met with Warden Hickox and mentioned to him this lead for funding since he lived in Cedaredge. He said that he was aware of this retired couple and the help they have given to various local projects in Cedaredge. We found a phone number and called them. I left a message on their machine and asked them to please call me back. I wasn't sure I would hear back from them.

Tuesday of the following week I did get a return call. This couple was interested in coming out to the facility to see firsthand what the plans were all about. I planned for them to come out on Friday morning and meet with the warden and me at 10 o'clock. I was on pins and needles until Friday. When they arrived, Bob and I met them at his office. After a few formalities, Bob showed them the master plan and how important the chapel was in that planning. We then took them up to the old chapel and showed them the architect's model of the proposed 5,000 square foot chapel.

They seemed interested in the project. While in the old chapel, they met a couple of offenders and spoke briefly with them. Then Mr. Petersen looked me square in the eye and asked: "How much money do you want from me? What is the bottom line here?"

At that moment, the Lord told me to shut up. I have already given him the amount! Well, that was a first for me, being speechless. Then I said to Mr. Petersen: "God has already given you an amount, so who am I to question that." He then said: "how about fifty?" I looked at Bob and he looked quizzically at me and gave me an affirmative nod.

"Whatever your heart leads you to do is a blessing."

Mr. Petersen opened his checkbook and took out a check that he had already written. I was thinking, maybe $50 . Well, that check was for $50,000! My jaw dropped, and when I showed that to Bob; his jaw dropped as well.

Bob and I made a quick recovery, and humbly thanked the couple. Mr. Petersen said, "This is the first installment. Keep us in the loop as you progress." They committed to matching funds-dollar-for-dollar until completion. That final contribution wound up to be a whopping $186,500 of matching funds. Another WOW God! The community support was overwhelming as well-as the Petersen's contribution.

The search now began for an architectural firm to give us the building plans. I by no means wish to say that architects are not worth every penny they earn, but blueprints were expensive, beyond our budgeted funds. But as God helped me to be persistent in my search, I was blessed to find a Christian firm in Grand Junction that was willing to work with the ministry in reaching our goal.

"... speaking to one another in psalms and hymns and spiritual songs ..."

-Ephesians 5:19 (NKJ)

We are underway! With blueprints in hand, I proudly walked into Warden Hickox's office with the biggest smile on my face since my wedding day — soon only to have my bubble burst! With the warden was Garth Yorgensen, physical plant manager, who had to first approve the blueprints. I was informed that the physical plant manager's approval was a key factor in the overall approval process. Garth assured me that he would move it along as soon as possible. His responsibility was to make sure that all the specs were in line with the CDOC rules. Once he gave his approval, I would be notified. This somewhat eased my concerns. I was not aware of how many hurdles we would have to jump through before construction could begin.

Alongside the fundraising for the new chapel, I had to manage the ongoing daily operations of the chapel programs. My responsibilities included more than attending to the religious needs of the Christians. I had to recruit representatives from other faith groups, including but not limited to Mormons, Muslims, American Indians, and Jehovah's Witnesses.

With a population of under 30,000 people in the county and 8,455 in the town of Delta, this seemed like an almost impossible task. In my due diligence, by God's grace, I was able to locate representatives for all of the religious needs of the inmate population.

The Delta Rotary Club was a starting point. In speaking to the members, I was able to locate a Muslim volunteer who was a Colorado State University professor at an agricultural research center located in nearby Hotchkiss. An American Indian group in Durango also agreed to come up to the facility to establish a sweat lodge for our Indian population. The ministry seemed to be functioning on all cylinders. For the building project, there were so many stipulations of the building structure standards in order to have the chapel (which later was called an all-purpose worship center) that would be in compliance.

There is always something that gets in the way. There was a call from CDOC headquarters for a wardens' meeting to discuss the upcoming budget and the cuts necessary to meet the next fiscal years' budget requirements. At this meeting, the department executive director asked the question: "If there was one position that you must eliminate at your facility, which one would that be?" Ten of the 12 wardens said, "the chaplain." But Warden Hickox was adamant of how critical the chaplain was to DCC. Unfortunately, he was overruled by the others. A disappointment on his part but a blow to the overall morale at the facility.

The following day, Warden Hickox informed me of the department's decision to eliminate the chaplains' position throughout the entire system and to implement a volunteer chaplains' program to meet the religious needs of the offenders. Did that take the wind out of my sail! I cried out to God: WHAT IS *HAPPENING?* We are just getting things rolling, the plans for the new chapel, funding was coming in place, other faith groups coming on board, *.programs expanding.* I was at a total loss. What would I tell the almost 200 volunteers at DCC?

I talked to my wife about all this and Joan counseled me to "keep praying. God will provide all the answers you, we need." Easy for her to say. But where is our paycheck coming from two months from now? There I go again, God, worrying about money. I have obligations. I have children to feed.

In the quiet of the day, as I prayed, an overwhelming calmness filled me. I feel your peace, God, yes, I know you own the cattle on a thousand hills (Psalm 50:10). It is hard not to worry when you know you will lose your job in a few months. Then, as I prayed, it came to me: I work for the Lord! He will sustain me; *I do believe Your Word, Lord.*

In a day or so I received a call from Mr. Gasko asking me to come to HQ in The Springs for a meeting two days later. He wanted to discuss the future plans of the department with regard to religious services/programs. *Is this another WOW moment, God?* I most assuredly agreed. He set the meeting for 10 a.m., which meant that I would need to leave at 6 a.m. in order to make that meeting or go the night before and get a motel room there in The Springs. I opted for the latter. All kinds of thoughts went through my mind the next day. *What is going on, Lord?* I went to pray and seek the Lord's guidance and all I heard was "go."

"Maybe this is a job offer, maybe not. Anyhow, away I went, and Joan came with me. That was a blessing to have her by my side. She was going to drop me off and do some shopping. Our hotel was just across the street from the CDOC office. I could have walked there, but I did not. I told Joan I would call her when we finished the meeting. It should not take too long, about an hour or so. Little did I know what was in store for me at the meeting.

At the stoke of 10 o'clock Mr. Gasko welcomed me into his office. He was a retired U.S. Army Colonel, straight forward and to the point. He was cordial yet decisive in his ways. He asked me to assist him in drawing up a profile of what a Religious Program Administrator's position would look like. As we talked, he asked me if I would be interested in applying for the position. My initial reaction was, of course, yes.

This would mean another move for the family. Changing schools for the girls. *God, if this is your way of providing for us, thank you, Jesus.* What an opportunity for me to help design a religious program for an entire prison system. I asked Mr. Gasko if I would be able to call my wife and tell her I would be a little longer in this meeting. He said, "No, have her pick you up as scheduled, and we will meet next week at Buena Vista prison. Get your thoughts together in a formal proposal, and we will discuss it at that time."

We talked about what he envisioned for the department, what I should use as a "baseline" for my job description. Make sure that you qualify for that position. However, this position would be competitive and anyone who met the qualifications could apply before the published closing date. That meant that this was open to the chaplains that were being terminated as well. For this reason, they should have a "favorite son" advantage over a contract employee such as me.

These chaplains, although ordained through their respective denominations, in reality some did and some did not do much in the area of ministry to the offenders that were not of their denominational persuasion. (My personal observation). I was looked down upon by many of them because of the activities taking place in Delta. When there were chaplain meetings, they would ask me questions like, how did you get this or that? I would tell them, "you do not have because you do not ask." (James 4:2b) They seemed not to appreciate that approach. As I thought, prayed, and prayed some more, I began to see a plan of ministry coming together. An outreach effort across Colorado to impact prisoners for Christ.

First things first. I had to put together an outline proposing the qualifications necessary for the administrator of volunteer services and the six accompanying positions assigned to the office. In later years the program departed from the original intent of the Office of Volunteer Services (OVS) to the point of dissolution. I proposed that the administrator must hold a degree in either theology or biblical studies. In addition, the candidate must be recognized/ordained to a formal office of his/her faith group for a minimum of three years and of good standing in such a group. The ideal candidate should preferably have a minimum of three years criminal justice experience such as a chaplain, volunteer, or CDOC employee with the aforementioned qualifications/experience as well as at least one quarter of CPE. This covered the necessary bases. I would let the "powers that be" finalize the formal job description before posting.

The next item on the agenda was to design the position for the rest of the team. There would be need for clerical support at HQ. There would also be a need for a second person in the office to process/screen volunteer applications and other general office responsibilities. That left four remaining positions. I envisioned that those positions would be in the field with an office in one of the prisons they would support with an active volunteer corps. These volunteers would be fully trained according to the (yet to be) developed CDOC training for volunteers. A fifth position would be responsible for the training of the volunteers with the OVS, doing the necessary background checks for final approval. The remaining positions of regional volunteer coordinators would have training/certification from their preferred group/denomination with a minimum of three years' experience in either prison/military/church work.

I was asked to write a proposed five-year plan for the OVS. First and foremost would be the hiring of the support staff. Then, developing the initial training course for volunteers. The politics involved within the department were amazing. I had never encountered such positioning. The aforementioned CDOC director and the region directors under the department executive director were not so receptive to my position proposals. They not only wanted to play a role in the selection process for these positions, but they also wanted to appoint their own people.

Unfortunately, they had the power! I had little to say, but people who know me, knew that I was going to say it. When I finished my "dream team" selection process, I forwarded it to HQ for their review and for them to develop a final position description hopefully along the guidelines I had proposed.

As the selection process was drawing to a close for the administrator's position, there were over 120 applicants, but it came down to three, of which I was one. The selection was narrowed down by an autonomous hiring committee which was part of the CDOC personnel department. I received a call from Mr. Gasko who expressed a desire to meet with me once again at the Buena Vista prison. I was a bit nervous as we met. He assured me that I was a serious contender for the position, although I was not on the top of the list. No worry he said. The final selection would be made via an oral test. A meeting would be set up the following week at HQ for the interview. There would be a three-member committee of which he will not be one. And by the way, the meeting is next week.

HOLD EVERYTHING! There was a building program for a new chapel that was far from complete. What happens with that Lord? Do I just drop everything and jump ship before the ship is even built? I was confused. Back on my knees I went, seeking direction from God. All I heard was "Go." My heart was with this Delta ministry. What do I say to

DCMF and the DMA pastors if I was selected for the position? It was all confusing, but You, Lord, are not a God of confusion. When I prayed, all I heard was go? Why just that. Was obedience and trust the message I was to bring to the churches? Would God provide for the future of the new chapel? The rumor around the department was that Hickox and Potter were building their "shrine" at Delta. What would my reputation be when I leave?

Then God, spoke clearly as if He had physically slapped me on the back of my head:

"This is not your house, it is mine!" Oh boy, I was getting out in front of God. What a wakeup call! Then, in the midst of all this confusion, I sought counsel from a dear pastor friend, Buddy Bishop. When we met and prayed, Buddy looked at me and said: "you will be back." I was taken aback by that remark. Buddy said "that was a spontaneous remark." That must have been God! What does all this mean? "I COME TO YOU Lord and all I hear is go... go where? Do what? Do I just let the pieces drop where they may?" There was fifty thousand dollars in the chapel building fund, the slab had been poured, and the CDOC engineers had approved the project plans. There always seemed to be one last hurdle to jump over.

Warden Hickox and I had to speak before a Colorado legislative committee and explain to them why they should approve a Christian chapel on state property. When Bob went and spoke to them, he explained that this was an all-faith worship center to be used by all faith groups, Christian, Jewish, Muslim, Mormons, etc. He further explained that if the alumni association were permitted to build a field house on state college property that would be used for all sports activities, why then would there be any question about a ministerial association building an all-faiths worship center on state property? No further questions were asked, and the committee approved the request.

"What about the rest of the ministry? How would it survive? I was not going to leave everyone high and dry. *Okay, God, I understand, but who will come forth and take over?* Then I heard once again, "GO!"

"Trust in the Lord with all your heart and lean not on your own understanding; in all your ways acknowledge Him and He shall direct your path." (Proverbs 3:7) There was nothing else I could or would say to that.

When I arrived at HQ, the other two candidates were already there. One was a woman volunteer chaplain from Denver and the other a volunteer chaplain from the women's prison in Cañon City. I was just a little nervous as my turn came. Not sweaty, just nervous. The interview was noticeably short, about 15 minutes. I was really nervous on the way home, thinking, *Where do I go from here, Lord?*

"Are you trying to be in control, Potter?"

Okay, Lord, set me right. Let me recognize that my strength comes from You, my hope lies within You and I must lean on You at all times.

I pulled off the road at a rest stop and prayed. I don't know for how long, but the Lord once again gave me that *"and the peace which surpasses all understanding will guard your hearts and minds through Christ Jesus."* (Philippians 4:7 NKJ) Once again, God's peace overwhelmed me to the point of tears. Why do I let myself get to this point of need? I should know by now where my help comes from.

Recognition of God with us should be first and foremost each and every day. I did not start my day asking for the Lord's help, He was always with me, but sometimes I think, "I need to do this by myself, Lord." I have gone too many days that way, much to my chagrin. As I started on my travel back home, I started to sing praises to the Lord. By the time I arrived home I was feeling G-R-E-A-T!

Joan asked me how things went, and I told her. She looked quizzically at me and I responded with a "praise the Lord!"

She quickly smiled and said, "You have the job, right?" "Not really," I replied. "We will find out next week."

The ensuing week was tense at first. As we prayed together, things were smoothing out. An air of confidence in the Lord was emerging within the family, although we hadn't started to pack yet nor found a place to live somewhere on the other side of the mountain. The time waiting for a call from CDOC was tense. We lived 200-plus miles west of Colorado Springs. Here we did not know whether to put our house up for sale or to look for a place to live on the other side of the mountain. So, we waited, and waited. Finally, in mid-May I got the phone call from Mr. Gasko informing me that I was chosen for the position of administrator of volunteer services. Y-E-S! That was a wonderful call. Now came the stipulation: I had to go through the CDOC Training Academy once again.

Well, I was not a happy camper. I must do this. Why? I did not have any choice in the matter. I was to start July 1, period. Alright, I would be there. We had some friends that lived in Cañon City, Ray and Marilyn Mulay. They both worked at the DCC when I was there and since had transferred to Cañon City shortly prior to my acceptance of the new job. I gave them a call and inquired if they would put me up until I finished the required training academy classes. They were glad to hear from me and wholeheartedly agreed.

I had mentioned earlier about my grandson Paul. I need to interject a personal story here, a blessing that turned into a tragedy within the family. Almost two years prior to this time frame, we had an unexpected blessing. A grandson named Paul arrived. Our daughter Jennifer blessed us with him in July of 1994. What a happy child he was, always smiling. Unknown to us, he had a tumor on his brain. By the time it was discovered, there was not much that could be done. He had surgery to remove it, but that was not enough. We buried him two days before his second birthday.

I put this in here because of two important outcomes. The first being that our faith was severely shaken to the core. Some people from our church were questioning the strength of our faith. Others were asking "where is your God" when this happened? Why didn't He intervene and save Paul? Wait a minute, God did not kill our grandson, He received him with open arms. There are many stories I could tell you about Paul, but I will relate just one.

I had just had knee replacement surgery on my left knee and was recovering at home. I grew up on McDonald's burgers and that was my go-to comfort food. My wife and Jennifer along with Paul went to McDonald's, had lunch, and brought me back my lunch. As I was sitting in the living room eating, I spotted Paul coming in by me. I motioned to the French fries, as if to offer him one. He smiled and came over and took one. As he started to turn away, he glanced at me, looked at my bandaged knee, had a big grin on his face and proceeded to snatch the bag of French fries and ran off. That little stinker stole my fries!

CDOC Training Academy: Here I was on crutches going to the training academy. First day of class they were reluctant to allow me to be part of that class due to my surgery. I assured them by the time the classroom work was complete that I would be able to do the physical part of the training. Little did I know of the upcoming interruption. At the beginning of the second week, actually day two, I received a phone call from my wife that Paul had died. I was in a state of shock.

We thought that all was well after the last surgery. I just told the teacher I had a grandson just die and I had to go home, and I ran out the door with tears in my eyes. Joan told me that they were still at the hospital. I said I would meet them there. She told me to go to the house and meet them there, since by the time I got to Delta they would be home. I said I would see them in Grand Junction. I think I just cried all the way to the hospital. I do not even remember going through any of the mountain towns or going over Monarch Pass.

Somehow, I made that four-hour trip in 2 ½ hours. I felt like the life was drained right out of me. I was mad, but at who? The doctors? The nurses? God? Me? What more could I have done to help save this child's life? He did nothing wrong. I had many questions. I went on my knees and prayed. I cried out to God. "Why God? Why?" I heard in a tender voice: "Be assured that Paul is with me. All is well."

"I am the resurrection and the life. He who believes in Me, though he may die, he shall live. And whoever lives and believes in Me shall never die." (John 11:25-26 NKJ) "Do you believe this?"

Oh, yes, Lord, I believe.

On our way home from the funeral, just atop the Grand Mesa, there was a curious assembly of clouds forming on the mesa. As we were driving home, the clouds seemed to take a particular form. It appeared to both Joan and me, the shape of a boy sitting on a cloud, holding his head in his hands. A valley formed in front of the child and coming over the other side of the formation was the form of a man (Jesus.) He had outstretched arms, picking up the child and then, as if they were heading up into the blue sky to heaven, disappeared. We had to pull off to the side of the road, as both Joan and I were in tears. Tears of joy!

We both saw it; we believe that God was showing us that Paul was in

His hands. When our "friends" continued to question our faith, we told them straight out: "We cannot believe anything more than we saw." Paul was a miracle from God who blessed us with almost two years, two years of joy! If we had any thoughts of seeing him again, it would be in Heaven.

I did not complete the training academy at that time. I needed to spend time with my family to console and be consoled. The CDOC was graceful enough to give me all the time I needed, within reason, of course. About 10 days later, I went to HQ to begin my new assignment.

CHAPTER 21

"... Do you still hold fast to your integrity?"

- Job 2:9

William Bross (1813-1890) was a highly successful American journalist, the co-publisher of the Chicago Tribune. In an interview, he discussed his success. One of the questions asked: "What do you consider essential elements of success for a young man entering upon such a profession as yours? He answered: Sterling, unflinching integrity in all matters, public and private. Let everyone do his whole duty, both to God and man. Let him follow earnestly the teachings of these Scriptures and eschew in fidelity in all its forms." (APB)

The next three years were some of the most rewarding and some of the most frustrating of my life. My version of "the good, the bad, and the ugly," as you will soon discover as you read on.

It was a beautiful day in early August in Colorado Springs. My first day at central office. I reported to Jerry Gasko's office. I had paperwork that I brought with me from DCC. I had a Roladex with some phone numbers that would prove invaluable. Mr. G (as I called him) told me that an office had yet to be prepared for me. In the interim, I would be in a "very small" one-room space for two weeks or so. "Not a problem as long as I have a phone."

Mr. Gasko said "that was not a problem." Sometime later, this would prove to be a problem. In reality, it appeared to be a converted broom closet. Humble beginnings.

Joan and I found a house in Pueblo West, complete with a swimming pool, albeit a 16x34 foot oval, above-ground pool that was in great shape. As we were getting our loan for the house, signing papers with a mortgage company, there developed a hitch. The FHA denied our loan application. The loan company said: "do not worry." That's when I started to worry! I was told that we would receive a letter denying our loan application from FHA, but they have secured for us a "conventional" loan at the same interest rate in place of the FHA. Okay with me. At the time of that call, Joan was not home. When Joan arrived home, I had been really busy and neglected to tell her about my conversation with the lender. Our loan was confirmed, and we will sign those papers at closing, so all is well, not a problem, don't need to worry her. Or so I thought.

Our closing was set for a Monday. I had called the real estate agent to see if we would be able to move in the Saturday before because the house was empty, I worked Monday through Friday, and so did our friends. I would need them to help unload the U-Haul on the weekend. The seller agreed to let us move in the Saturday before the closing. I thought that was great. All during the previous week before the move Joan held a yard sale. There were certain big items I did not want to take with us to Pueblo West. Joan had marked prices on these items which I thought were too high. The day before we were to load up, these items had not sold. Joan had to do something and needed to leave the house and the left yard sale in my hands.

When people came by to look at our stuff and seemed interested in these high-ticket items ($30-$150), I was not going to let them leave without giving them a GREAT DEAL. Joan had $75 on a grill that I did not want to take. I sold it for $5. There was a recliner that we did not want, although I did not sell it — I gave it away! I explained to Joan the reason for giving it away: The people needed it for a family member who had just come home from the hospital. The chair was a full-lift chair that belonged to her uncle who lived with us and recently died. At that time, we did not need such a chair. I thought this was a perfect item to bless people who needed such a chair. Joan then informed me that I was no longer needed at the yard sale.

Here we were moving to Pueblo West. Andrew and a few other friends from KAIROS met us at the house. There was an air of excitement in this move. The opportunity for me to help the CDOC set up this new prison ministry! As we were unloading the truck, Joan went to look in the mailbox to see if we had any mail to new our address. Lo and behold, there was a letter from our mortgage lender that said our loan application was denied. As she read that letter, she cried. Then she shouted STOP! With tears running down her face, she said the letter from the lender that said our loan application was denied. What are we going to do?

With a big gulp, I proceeded to tell her the circumstances surrounding the letter and assured her that all was well. She was definitely happy over that, but not with me for failing to inform her earlier. The following week, all went well with the closing. Mom was happy again (with me, too).

The work at HQ was different than I had expected. I was not yet in with the "in crowd." I was more "apolitical." I was more interested in getting to know my office staff and expediting the location of my permanent office. The following week, all of my staff were together. At the beginning of the process of selecting my staff, I was told it would be up to me. This all turned out to be quite different in the end. Politics came into play. I was informed that my administrative staff has already been approved and I did not have any need to interview either one. That was okay with me. Office staff is office staff. They had CDOC experience and in the long run would prove to be a tremendous asset when moving things along the way.

The process of selecting the four region coordinators was a horse of a different color. The region directors wanted to get into the act. Although this was to be an open competitive exam with a focus on ministerial, ministry background, I was told that I would be actively involved in the selection process of the final 10 candidates. In reality none of this would take place.

There were a few chaplains that were going to be re-assigned within the department that were interested in being a region coordinator. Well, in short, they did not make the cut. There were certain issues I was told that needed to be dealt with. Two region directors had already selected their region volunteer coordinator. I did not have a choice. I was upset to say the least. These people who they were insisting have these positions did not have any of the qualifications described in the position description. I had to take a stand for at least one of the positions. There was a very heated discussion in Mr. Gasko's office with a region director. I did get the person I wanted in the slot for the western region, but that was the only one I had selected. That was okay with me. One is better than none.

Things started to move quickly. Volunteer Services was overwhelmed. We met with all of the wardens to find out how this newly established division could help their prison. I had to draw up the Administrative Regulation for Volunteers and design a training program for volunteers with the help of the Training Academy. Thank God for the Training Academy. They took on this task and did an outstanding job!

One of the hardest tasks was recruiting people from various faith groups who would be willing and able to provide a religious authority for their faith. In short, the Christian faith groups came forward in a heartbeat, but the other faith groups were not so quick to respond. Some never did. In canvasing the faith groups represented in the inmate population, I discovered that there were 38 different inmate faith groups identified. They soon mushroomed to over 100.

My task was to develop a reference manual for these faith groups that would identify the religious items deemed essential for the inmates to practice their faith in prison. But some items that the offenders wanted were not deemed a basic tenet of their faith group and therefore such items would not be considered necessary to practice their faith.

Such a manual, I thought, would not be difficult to write. Was I in for a surprise. Some of the lesser known pagan faith groups that offenders practiced had different kinds of relics/items that their tribe, coven, or group use. Each have differing items for worship that are deemed a basic tenet of their practice of worship. This would be a source of conflict in the coming years. It got to the point where a judge determined that if the offender deemed it necessary for him/her to practice their faith, then he/she had the right to have the item in their possession.

As things were moving forward, most of my meetings with wardens, program managers and facility volunteer coordinators were positive with rare exception. One, maybe two wardens did not want help from this office. I just shook off the dust and left. (Matthew 10:14)

Although most of my staff was not qualified according to their own job description, my hands were tied by the politics of the department. General staff knew what their responsibilities were, they just failed to meet them. They were being led by their region director as to what they wanted them to do rather than doing what the position called for.

At the beginning of the second week at the office, I was told I needed to attend the staff meeting. So as that meeting began, I had my own presumption that I would open the meeting with prayer. I found a Scripture verse that I thought would be appropriate for the meeting:

> "And let us not grow weary while doing good, for in due season we shall reap if we do not lose heart." (Galatians 5:9) (NKJ).

This was a good first meeting with the executive staff and would set the path on which this office would function and cause some to reflect on their own situation. I was not asked to do or say anything. One of the administrative assistants asked me if I brought any cotton for my ears, it gets "rough" in here from time to time. She smiled and seated herself. This meeting, for all purposes, seemed very boring. A lot of statistics, inmate beds that were open, how many inmates were housed out-of-state, things like that. As the discussion progressed, the deputy director expressed his concern about the number of empty beds in Colorado as compared to those inmates that were housed out-of-state. His voice was getting elevated over these numbers.

At this point, it was not involving me, so I decided to quietly leave. I stood up, closed my Bible and Day-Timer, and was asked by the deputy director: "Where are you going?" I replied: I needed to be excused."

He, taking a deep breath, told me to sit and he apologized and then abruptly adjourned the meeting. The next morning, I received a memo from the deputy director that I was not required to attend any future executive staff meetings. I was not disappointed. They did not particularly involve me any way.

One issue that I had with the deputy director I must share with you. I was asked to submit my information as to what I wanted my business cards to say. So, I wrote the information I felt necessary to be on the card. Beginning with Rev. William T. Potter. Sent that information up the ladder and the next day I received the memo back saying: it is not appropriate for an employee of the state to have the title of "Reverend" on their business card. Well, I was just a little perturbed over this and I was going to see the executive director, whose office was one flight up. As I was walking down the corridor, the executive director was coming up in the other direction toward me. He waved his hand and hollered, "Hello, Reverend!"

I had known him for a while before coming to central office and that was what he always called me. I put a little more pep in my step as I approached him and stopped right almost in his face and retorted: "What did you say?" He repeated: "Hello, Reverend?"

I then handed him the memo and asked him to handle this for me. The next day it was approved to use the title Reverend on my business cards. *Hey, God, another WOW moment! Thank you, Lord.* This is such a God incident because the executive director was rarely at HQ. He spent most of his time in Denver at the State Capitol dealing with legislative issues relating to the CDOC. What an assurance knowing that God is always with us, just a prayer away.

There surfaced an immediate need for a Prisoners Faith Group Desk Reference. In addition, there was issue as whether inmates that were satan worshippers could possess the satanic bible. This came in the form of a request from the Colorado Attorney General's (AG) office, and they needed it in 30 days in order to back the department's position on banning such a book. The AG wanted an in-depth explanation as to why banning this book was necessary.

> As I pondered what to do and how to do it, the Lord showed me in 2 Timothy 2:25-26 NKJ: *"In humility correcting those who are in opposition, if God will perhaps grant them repentance, so that they may know the truth, and that they may come to their senses, and escape the snare of the devil, having been taken captive by him to do his will."*

Of the six people on my staff, I called upon two of them to collaborate with me and help draw up a white paper to submit to the AG's office. This was a "priority one" mission for the next several weeks. We read and re-read this satanic bible and wrote an opinion as to why this book should be denied to CDOC offenders.

I immediately called the pastor of my local church and had him put the three of us on the church prayer list, which he did. I encouraged the other two to do the same. What a sickening, heart-wrenching, awful few weeks. Reading page by page the hateful words that were encouraging those who believed this was a valid worship practice. We all had sleepless nights, and when we did sleep, it was a restless sleep. We were tormented. To say our strength through all this horror was in the Lord would not be an exaggeration. The basis for our conclusion was found in the Scriptures, 2 Timothy 2:13-14 NKJ: *"Hold fast the pattern of sound faith which you heard from me, in faith and love which are in Christ Jesus. That good thing, which was committed to you, keep by the Holy Spirit which dwells in you."*

I had two days to put our three opinions into one. On Friday of that week, I was totally lost. I called the AG's office to speak with the Assistant Attorney General (AAG) assigned to the case. He told me just send all three and he would use whatever he thought relative to the case. The pressure was off. That was a big load off my mind. I still wrote my own combined opinion of all three.

When all was said and done, there was a comprehensive brief put together and finished on time, which I hand carried to the AG's Office in Denver. That was my first mistake. I should have just dropped it off. After about a 30-minute wait, the AAG handling the case came out. He invited me to his office as he skimmed through the brief. He said he wanted me to be in attendance with him before the Colorado Supreme Court as reference counsel. I had no choice but to say yes. One week from that day, we had to appear. Wait a minute, in one week we go to court, and you have the only copy of our report? You can prep me, but I do not have any material to refer/study this week. I asked if someone would make me a set of our briefs. He pointed to the copy machine and handed me the originals and said: "go make them yourself and bring me back the original." I made the copies and gave him back the report and left. However, two great blessings came out of this hearing. First, I did not have to say a word, although I did sweat a lot. A representative of the ACLU was there to represent the position of an offender who wanted this horrible book in his possession. The court heard both sides of the argument. The AAG said that within 30 to 60 days the court would render an opinion.

In approximately five weeks the AAG called and congratulated me. He informed me that the court ruled in favor of the CDOC and we did not have to allow such a publication into the hands of offenders nor in a prison library. GLORY hallelujah! In my work as the administrator of volunteer services, nothing was ever more worthwhile than accomplishing this victory.

When it was time for me to visit DCC, I would do all I could to avoid going there. I had to do what I had to do. At first, they were not pleasant visits. I would see the slab for the chapel foundation and nothing else. Oh, there was the red iron for the main support beam which was donated and transported for free by my longtime friend Sam Abeyta. He owned a steel fabricating business in Denver. He also had an ex-felon working for him and he did the necessary fabricating on his own time in order to complete a piece of his parole, community service.

When I would speak to the ministerial fellowship, they would tell me that they were busy trying to recruit a chaplain. The building was secondary at this time. On my second visit, much to my surprise, there was a chaplain on board, hired by the ministerial fellowship. That was a Praise to the Lord, or so I thought. He was not formally ordained. Soon I would find out that things were not all as good as I was first led to believe.

My dear friend, Pastor Buddy, we often met for coffee. He and his wife Cecily were always a solid support to me and Joan. In September 1997, on a visit to Delta, I stopped in to see Pastor Buddy. We spent about an hour talking and praying. He then asked me: "When are you coming back?" I thought that was a strange question to ask me. Then I remembered saying almost two and a half years earlier that I would be back. I responded: "the Lord would have to speak to and through my wife in order for that to happen." I was praying that the Lord would quickly persuade Joan that we needed to return to Delta. Lord, Come quickly.

The Delta situation persuaded me that there needed to be a clearer understanding within the department and with the volunteers as to the definition of "chaplain." This clarification must be along the guidelines set by each faith group. No one should be a designated chaplain without having the title of a religious leader by their faith group. All other faith group volunteers who came into a facility representing their faith group must be considered a "religious volunteer." These changes would prove challenging. Not impossible, but extremely difficult. However, I would not be able to accomplish these changes to the CDOC definition of "chaplain" that in any way satisfies the ACA standard.

I have got to backpedal here now so that you will understand. Sometime in June of 1997 I received a phone call from Deputy Director Larry Trujillo, and he told me to get out to Delta the next day and finish the building of the chapel. I was a little taken back. I asked if it could wait until the following Monday so that I would be able to clear up some tasks I have in front of me.

"Okay, but no later than Monday. That's an order." Larry could make such a demand of me because he was the deputy director of the department. So, I planned to spend a week at Delta to survey the situation and determine how to proceed from there. How do I approach this situation? I hoped at some point in the not-too-distant future I would return to DCC to once again serve as chaplain. How do I complete the building of the chapel without revealing that I might be returning in the future? *Guide me, Lord.*

My first appointment was with Mr. Petersen, the primary donor of funds for the chapel, to confirm his contribution. He agreed to meet with me for lunch. I spoke with the president of DCMF and invited him to join us for lunch. He declined but did inform me that Mr. Petersen's wife died about a year earlier. I knew that because Warden Hickox informed me. At the time, Joan and I went to Cedaredge to pay our respects to the Petersen family.

When I met with Mr. Petersen, he told me that he would not be putting any more funds into this project unless I returned to DCC as chaplain. I thought for a moment or two, then I told him that was in my plan, but I would not be able to return full-time to Delta as chaplain until next June. As I continued, I then said that it is important to re-start the project almost immediately. So that by this time next year the chapel would be complete. He agreed. We shook hands and had a great lunch.

During that conversation, Mr. Petersen said that he was going out on a "date" that night. He laughed, I smiled. He said he was a little out of practice since he hadn't gone on a first date in over 60 years. But he suggested he might in the not-too-distant future be marrying that woman. I offered, "if you need some pre-marital counseling, I would be available." He chuckled and respectfully declined my offer. "I have enough experience in that part of a relationship."

I never understood what it meant to have too many irons in the fire, that is up until now. The issues at HQ, and now the chapel building project. There was 250 miles between the two. I could not manage both without some help. I then scheduled a meeting with Mr. Trujillo and asked him if he would allow me to delegate some of my duties to others under my command so that I could devote most of my time to the chapel project at DCC, but keeping a hand on the operation at HQ. He questioned me as to how I could accomplish my duties while completing the chapel project. On Fridays and each following Monday I would be in the office and the rest of the time at Delta. If needed I would be able to spend an extra day or two at the office when called upon. He thought that was a good plan and agreed.

On my first trip back to Delta I met with the DCMF chaplain at DCC. Mike was never on hand. While he was not formally ordained, when I quizzed him he seemed very knowledgeable. Now, looking into the chapel fund, I have some idea what could or should be purchased to get the project re-booted. When I left Delta, there was approximately $50,000 in the chapel building fund. Now that money was gone, or so I was told. I was furious. Somebody has to pay for this!

I CAN HANDLE THIS ONE, LORD. THIS IS A NO-BRAINER.

That's how mad I was. I knew charges were going to be filed — there had to be. But against who? As I prayed, I felt a need to go to the book of Isaiah to first of all calm down and then be refreshed by His Word.

And lo and behold, there was the answer as to what to do. I did not want to hear this, Lord. Someone is responsible and they will pay. They stole the money! Then it came to me, as if the Lord Himself spoke: "Do not look back." What does that mean? Then I, in my head, heard this: "I own the cattle on a thousand hills." (Psalm 50:10) My storehouses are all full.

I the Lord Your God will deal with this matter; you focus on your part in the building project. Then in Isaiah 58:9 (NKJ) I read this:

> *"Then you shall call, and the Lord will answer; you shall cry, and He will say: 'Here I Am.'"*

That was the answer — healing. Others involved with DCMF knew there was something seriously wrong with the handling of the funds. Just let it go and move on. Do not tell anyone of your initial findings. The Lord your God said move on, do not look back. If the project were to continue, then healing must first take place. Healing needed to start with me. For you see, the person who took the funds, whether he knew it or not, would never be known. As I prayed, the peace of the Lord came over me and I knew it was the right thing to do — move on.

This Scripture came to be my benchmark throughout the rest of my ministry work. *"Rejoice in the Lord always. Again, I say rejoice. Let your gentleness be known to all men. The Lord is at hand. Be anxious for nothing, but in everything by prayer and supplication with thanksgiving, let your requests be made known to God; and the peace of God, which surpasses all understanding, will guard your hearts and minds through Christ Jesus."* (Philippians 4:4-7 NKJ)

CHAPTER 22

Move'n On Up to
the West Side

"For this is the will of God, that by doing good you put to silence the ignorance of foolish men — as free, yet not using liberty as a clock for vice, but as bondservants of God. Honor all people. Love the brotherhood. Fear God. Honor the King." (1 Peter 2:15-17) (NKJ)

D riving to The Springs every day from Pueblo would have been boring, but I always took special notice of the clouds assembling over Pikes Peak as often as I could. One day, there appeared to me the face of Jesus. I pulled over and wanted to get my phone and take a picture. By the time I got my phone out of my briefcase, the cloud formation disappeared. What a vision to see at the start of the week.

I always arrived an hour ahead of time. Every day that I was at the office, I would slowly walk down the corridors of the second and third floor, pausing briefly and praying in front of each door. I would pray a blessing for each person who walked through those doors. Praying that God would be glorified. Just a habit I developed. This morning, I felt really good. I felt the presence of the Lord more and more by my side. Strange feeling, but I knew it was a "good" strange.

This particular day, I received a message from the AAG about the work regarding the satanic bible to call him. What's up now? So I called him. He was very cordial and said he was sending me some information that he recently received about making a presentation to the National Association of Sheriffs regarding how the department was dealing with the recent federal law — the Religious Freedom Restoration Act (RFRA) as it came to be known. The request wanted us to hold a workshop on the matter. I was not shy to share what the CDOC was doing to provide adequate religious services for/to the offenders. But first of all, I had to clear it with my supervisor. He gave me an affirmative and told me to make sure I get enough handouts for all who would attend.

Next, I needed to ascertain the anticipated attendance, including the workshop, and whether they wanted us to repeat that workshop over the course of the convention. After I received that information, I determined how much material I needed to bring/ship to the meeting site. Then the real preparation began. Materials needed to be printed/ordered. It was decided that I would drive to Salt Lake City instead of flying, which was okay with me, I love to drive. Then an outline of the presentation needed to be drawn up and approved by the CDOC before I would be able to present the workshop. All this needed to be done in less than 30 days.

In spite of all the time challenges, we were able to get things done on time. One item I must bring up that could have crushed it all, was that I was told that I would need to share the workshop arena with a man from Taylor University. He was a "legal" resource as to whether the CDOC was properly interpreting the new law. This troubled me. I did not have nor did I understand all of the legal ramifications of this act. I was not going to put myself in harm's way at this workshop with so little interpretation at this point of RFRA. When I found out the information that Taylor University was presenting, then I understood the anticipated results that were expected of me at the workshop. I would develop a relationship with Professor Thomas Beckner that would extend far beyond this convention.

I was glad that Professor Beckner was staying at the same hotel as me. We got together the night before to get acquainted and go over the format that would be used. We had a few laughs and agreed to meet for coffee in the morning. Overall, the workshops went off without any problems. The department's most difficult part was meeting the RFRA requirements as interpreted by the CDOC. The procuring of an adequate cadre of pastors/representatives for all of the faith groups throughout the inmate population. The other main challenge was to recruit a full-time volunteer chaplain who would provide services not only for his faith group inmates, but with equal vigor recruit other faith group representatives, based upon the needs of his assigned facility. This "full-time volunteer chaplain," as he would be initially titled, a non-gratuitous employee for insurance purposes.

The OVS would provide them with non-financial support. In an altruistic world, this would work. In reality, this could never be accomplished. We would not be able to convince any volunteer from a particular faith group to go out in their community and actively seek someone from a different belief to go into a prison. Not going to happen!

When we are in service to and for the Lord, He does not let an opportunity go to waste. After the first workshop was finished, a gentleman, Ralph Self, introduced himself to me and said he was a chaplain with Good News Jail and Prison Ministry (GNJPM) located in Richmond, Virginia. This ministry supplies chaplains to jails and prisons throughout the country. He gave me his card, the phone number of GNJPM HQ and said: "Give the office a call. They might be able to help you out." As if God arranged this Himself (He did), I was scheduled to go to Richmond in two weeks to see how the Virginia DOC handled their religious programs.

Chaplain Self explained that they had full- time volunteer chaplains (they raise their own funds) at all of the jails and prisons they are serving. In addition, the Virginia Council of Churches, which was a separate organization, had chaplains in the state prisons. Isn't God so good to draw all this up for me? I could not have a better game plan even if I tried. The last piece of information that needed to be added here is that of GNJPM. Upon contacting them I discovered that they had just moved to Richmond, Virginia that previous week. In spite of that, they would be glad to meet with me as long as I wouldn't mind stepping over a few boxes. No problem, I replied. The only issue was coordinating a time to meet. Initially, we could not work it out. I had a tight schedule and so did they. So, we left it at "let's see what the Lord has in store for us when the time comes." I liked that approach. "With God all things are possible." (Matthew 19:26 NKJ)

The next two weeks flew by, visiting the prisons under the eastern region director's responsibility. My meetings were with volunteer coordinators, reviewing their programming, scheduling and checking on their religious programs/services made available to offenders. Often their scheduling was poorly designed. They had Catholic and Protestant services and one or two prisons had some kind of Muslim service conducted by an inmate, in violation of the department's regulations. In the not-too-distant future that would change.

I have to digress again. Two weeks had gone by and I was boarding the plane in Denver headed to Washington, D.C. with two members of the Colorado Council of Churches. We flew into Washington, D.C. because it was the cheapest major airport closest to Richmond. We were going to rent a car to drive the rest of the way to Richmond because our meetings did not start until the next day. I love to think of myself as a conversationalist. For the people that know me, they know my bent toward eating hot dogs. My favorite all-time hot dog stand is a place called Callahan's (now closed). I grew up on them. Whenever I came within 200 miles of that place, I had to make a detour to Callahan's. After all, it was just 2½ hours away from Washington, D.C., much to my chagrin, I could not convince them. There were four passengers that were listening that I convinced to go with me, but we could not arrange the diversion.

The following two days we met with the Virginia Council of Churches. They explained their involvement with the state department of corrections. We met at their central office. They had many handouts to share regarding ACA standards and RFRA compliance issues. On the third day, we were scheduled to tour several prisons. Unfortunately, there was a kerfuffle at one of the prisons and the director decided to go on a full, system-wide lock-down. Thus, our tour was cancelled.

I then suggested that since we had the day to ourselves, we should consider going to visit with Good News Jail and Prison Ministry (GNJPM.) I was excited about that. God cleared away when I thought there was not a way. My two colleagues, however, wanted to go sightseeing. Neither one of them had ever been to Richmond before. I wished them well and told them that if there was time for me to meet with GNJPM, I was going to meet. After all, I was there on a mission from CDOC to see how other prison systems and ministries handle serving offenders. We agreed to meet up for dinner. The next morning, we were to head back to Colorado.

This meeting was a revelation. GNJPM was a perfect match for the CDOC. They recruited, trained, and paid for the chaplains. But they only come by invitation. All they needed was a letter inviting them to come to Colorado, to see if it was plausible for them to set up a chaplaincy ministry throughout all the state prisons. After they did their due diligence, GNJPM accepted our invitation with a goal of providing chaplains for 14 prisons.

The CDOC would require each of those chaplains to successfully complete a four-week Training Academy program to meet the CDOC prerequisites. It would be one year after an agreement was reached with GNJPM before one their chaplains came on board. Over the next three year period, 10 chaplains supported by GNJPM were in Colorado prisons. Praise the Lord!

In my job, there was always the politics of a government agency to deal with, and it can bring you down in a hurry. The manipulation of finances, I found out the hard way, was always first and foremost on the mind of the comptroller. From the first day at the office, this man made it his job to befriend me. Much to my chagrin, after my first six-months on the job, I went to make some purchases out of my budget and found out that the funds I thought I had were taken by the treasurer's discretion and put in the general fund to cover budget shortages. Just three months before this incident, I went to see the treasurer to find out if my budget figures were correct and he told me yes. Then he questioned me as to why I was asking. "Oh, nothing," I replied.

Me, being the usual big mouth that I was, told him I wanted to purchase some furniture and a copy machine for the office and laptops for my region volunteer coordinators. He said, "why don't you wait until mid-January, you can usually find sales on furniture?" He deliberately deceived me in order to take those funds from the account. I was furious. I would remember this, so it would not happen again.

Grinding things out over the next two years was difficult, especially knowing that my days were numbered at CDOC. God had plans to move us back to Delta in a rather short period of time. But He would have to speak to my wife first and tell her it's time. I was not touching that subject with a 10-foot pole. Fortunately, Joan has always been open to moving our home when the Lord called.

Our dear friend Pastor Buddy was talking to my wife in November of 1997 and asked her, "Are you packing yet?"

"What are you talking about?" she responded. He quickly surmised she did not get a word from God yet concerning the move back to Delta. Pastors have a unique way of picking up on things like this.

In January 1998 while sitting at the kitchen table having breakfast, Joan said to me: "It's time."

I just said quizzically, "time for what?"

Now she knew I was back at Delta for a few days each week, working at getting the chapel built. She now suggested we move back to Delta as chaplain. I almost choked on my oatmeal. I was shocked but at the same time thanking God for answered prayer. Joan commented that God told her in a dream the night before that it was time to return.

Now I had some decisions to make. Do I now notify the department of my resignation to be effective June 1 or not? There were a lot of irons in the fire. I needed to finish certain projects before I left. How do I support my family? Where are the funds to come from? We need to find a place to live. We need to sell our home.

Then it came to me as I prayed: "Trust in the Lord with all your heart and lean not on your own understanding; in all your ways acknowledge Him, and He shall direct your paths." (Proverbs 3:5-6 NKJ)

At times, it so hard to trust you, Lord.

"Lean not on your own thinking but trust Me."

I know — I get it — but sometimes … Trust? … Acknowledge? … He shall direct. I know all these things will happen, but how will you direct us? Then it all came to me! "Let go and let God," that's what Proverbs 3 means. It is one of the most difficult of things to do. But those days would prove to be the most exciting and miraculous times of my life. With God, it is quite a ride!

Just before I was to hand in my resignation to my superior, my scheduled annual review was discussed with me. Most of it was a fair evaluation, but the projected expectations were not. They included as part of my workload for the coming year to plan and schedule chapel building programs at other facilities. I was furious. No way was this future expectation to be part of my responsibility. After my flare-up, Mr. Trujillo removed that part of my evaluation. Then I handed him my resignation. Was he surprised!

There were others surprised by my resignation. Why would you leave a tenured position for one that didn't even have a guaranteed paycheck? This is where Proverbs 3 comes into play. Remember Good News? I did, so I contacted that ministry and asked if could apply for a chaplain's position with them for a position be at the DCC. Although this came as a complete surprise to them, they were happy to accept my application. What a relief that was for Joan and me.

When I explained my plan for Delta and the support I needed, they were somewhat reluctant. But we finally came to terms. They realized that my priority was to finish building the chapel even though finances were not yet available. But "… lean not…" You know what I mean. At the end of my first year with Good News, my complete budget was met and the building fund was on target. What an awesome, wonderful God we serve!

Prior to my return to DCC, Warden Hickox issued a memo stating that I was to be considered the senior chaplain and have signature authority over all religious/chapel issues. This did not set well with Chaplain Mike. He would become an adversary instead of a colleague. As much as I would try to convince him otherwise, he was, in his mind, second fiddle.

Unfortunately, all this friction resulted in Mike being removed from the prison as a chaplain. But God has a plan for us all, if we just take the time to pray and listen. Mike moved on to become a great leader, establishing Christian training schools for pastors in Africa. (Isaiah 58: 8-9) What joy it brought to me that Mike went unto the Lord for direction in his life. He met a wonderful woman, married her and they both became blessed missionaries to the African people.

"To Him be the glory forever and ever. Amen."
(2 Timothy 4:18b)

Back to Delta. Here we are still having services in the old chapel. Crowded as it may be, it was still a blessing to have them there. There were times of strength and times of trials. Strength in Christ through the Holy Spirit is a humbling yet awesome experience. One particular Sunday, an offender stood up and said he was "coming out of the closet." He expressed his desire to say he was gay. The Holy Spirit just rose up in me to declare: "unless you change your ways, you are going to be bad!" This offender looked at me and said: " I would sue you for all you have, chaplain." I was almost shaking in my boots, but I do not wear boots! I knew I was speaking from the Word of God on this subject, so I felt that whatever action, if any he took, I was covered. (Mark 13:11b-14a NKJ)

The offender filed a "level 2 grievance" against me, which meant that the warden would handle this issue and resolve it or move it up to a step three. Upon questioning the offender, the warden dismissed his case on the grounds he was not held against his free will and could leave the service at any time, and I was not misrepresenting the Bible or the general rules of my faith group affiliation.

CHAPTER 23

"Oh, sing to the Lord a new song! Sing to the Lord all the earth. Sing to the Lord, bless His name. Proclaim the good news of His salvation from day to day. Declare His glory among the nations, His wonders among all peoples."

- Psalm 96:1-3 (NKJ)

April 30, 1999 was set for the celebration of the opening of the new chapel at DCC. Invitations were being printed and mailed out to supporters, local churches, and businesses that supported the building fund as well as CDOC executives and local government officials. So many marvelous works of God were happening and blessings by the dozens. I wish to share what brought us to this expected time of celebration. The following (in all likelihood) may not be in proper chronological order. It is as best this mind is able to remember.

First and foremost, the offenders had to have some "buy-in" in the building. So, all the general construction work was performed by skilled inmate volunteers. One offender in particular took an 8x16 foot mirror and etched the various Christian symbols on the mirror. This was to be the altar-front centerpiece. Facility staff supervised all the offender work to make sure everything was up to code. The electric work was all done in-house, as there was a licensed master journeyman electrician on staff. With the exception of the transformers needed to supply the power to the chapel, he supervised all the electrical work. All in all, this was a labor of love from the facility staff, the inmates, all of the supporters, Wardens' Hickox and Green, and most of all, the Petersen's.

DCMF approached the power company for a grant application to seek a donation for the power transformers. The process included a presentation in front of the power company's community project board. This was a benevolent branch of the power supplier. All seemed to go well at this presentation but they were non-committal at that time. All they indicated was a letter would follow shortly. Shortly? What does that mean? A week? A month? What? So, we waited and then we waited some more. After three long weeks of waiting, the letter of approval came through for the project to be funded by the company's community project board. Praise God!

The next big-ticket item was the plywood/particle board. There was a plant that manufactured these items in the next town over from Delta. I inquired of my colleagues at Rotary if they knew anyone from the plant that I could contact about donating these items. Sure enough, there was a contact person that went to one of the local churches that was the plant manager. Could this be another WOW moment, God? We would soon find out!

After contact was made with this individual, he indicated that the company normally does not make such contributions to churches/religious organizations. I asked if we could meet to further discuss the project and he said: "Sure, any excuse to get out of the plant for a few minutes is always appreciated." At this meeting, when I filled him in on the background of the building program at DCC, he said to me, "submit in writing what you explained," and he would forward the information to his central office. He did not seem very hopeful that this would get approval.

We all prayed about this one. About two weeks later, he called me and indicated that his company would not be able to donate all of the boards we were looking for, but if we would be willing to purchase a portion of them, then the company would donate the rest. I had a big gulp and paused for a moment and asked: "How many do we need to buy to fulfill the order requested?" I asked. (Now, we had requested 208 sheets.)

He chuckled a little at my reaction and said, "If you are willing to purchase eight sheets, the company would donate the other 200." Now, that is a BIG WOW, LORD! I said I would be over the following morning with a check! He laughed and said he'd have the coffee pot on.

The rest of the story here is that they delivered all those sheets of plywood to the facility in their own truck and ensured that all sheets were properly placed! How about that!

When we started with the groundwork, we were told that we would need gravel for fill and cement piers (32) of varying sizes for the foundation. I was told it would take about 18 truckloads of gravel. I do not remember how many yards of cement we needed, but God provided that, too. Now listen to this one: another God incident happens here. One of our near and dear volunteers, Greg Fedler, just happened to own a gravel pit. I went and asked him about helping us with some of the gravel and he said he would supply all the gravel we needed at no cost. WOW!

Another one of the big-ticket items was the plumbing. There were offenders that claimed they could do the work, but the facility did not have a licensed plumber and therefore could not pull a permit. I inquired around but had no luck locating anyone that would or could help us. Then I was informed that there was a Plumbers and Pipe-fitters Union Headquarters in Grand Junction. I gave them a call and much to my surprise, the business agent agreed to meet with me and talk over how they could help! Another WOW moment God! Thank you, Jesus.

When the representative came out, I took him over to the warden's office and introduced him to Warden Hickox. Bob and I explained the project goals and asked how the union could help. Here was another "God incident." The business agent said that they did not get such "big" projects often enough for their apprenticeship program and that he thought this project would fit right in with their plans for their apprenticeship training program. So, as we supplied all the materials, they would take care of the rest. Offenders would assist where needed. Another WOW moment God! How does all this happen?

"Oh, *give thanks to the Lord, for He is Good! For His mercy endures forever." (Psalm 107:1 NKJ)*

In the little town on the western slope of the beautiful Rocky Mountains in the state of Colorado, God was composing His opus, as all of this was being orchestrated by God. Only an Awesome God, through Jesus Christ, could complete such a work.

When the Muslim clerics in Denver were approached about participating in the project with a specific, separate area in the eastern section of the chapel set aside just for their worship and study, they were excited. They indicated that they would contribute the funds necessary for that "dedicated" area of the chapel. When informed about the square footage cost, they indicated at that time all was fine. They never did fulfill their commitment. That area became an all-faith study room, but Muslim inmates were permitted to use the area for their Friday worship.

In the initial planning, there were windows that were to be used for decorative inserts. In addition, there was to be a circular window atop the outside wall, five feet in diameter in the universal symbol of a dove, which would be seen by all offenders upon arrival at DCC. Stained glass windows are expensive. There were a few qualified artists for such an undertaking. Artists who would donate their talent to the project are rare. Artists who would donate all of the material, talent, and installation — well that would be impossible to find. Yes, you guessed it, only God would send such an artist, and He did send Madeline! Glory to God!

The next great blessing came from a man I have known for years. We had met early on in the Delta ministry. Dave and his wife Elaine were involved with Prison Fellowship, which sent out their quarterly newsletter. There was an article about a new program, Marriage Seminars, a weekend encounter with inmates and their spouse. What a concept. What a way to help unite a family before the offender leaves prison. Building a bridge, help fixing what was once broken. That's what PF is all about.

The PF newsletter came through the warden's office, which means (at least I thought it did) that the warden read it, then it was sent out as a read-and-initial document for others to read and then return back to the warden's office to be filed. I was excited with the possibility that the warden may have some interest in this cutting-edge program. This was a stretch at best. But it gave me a foot in the door to explore the issue.

I jumped at the chance, the opportunity to further present, this family healing process before the offender is released. In two other states (Virginia and Texas), it was helping re-unite inmates with their family, healing buried feelings and deep wounds. At these seminars, all of these issues are openly dealt with.

Warden Hickox was somewhat surprised that I was willing to jump on the PF bandwagon and be so positive for the program. Now I had a stipulation or two of my own. First, we would limit the attendance to 10 couples. Second, this would take place in the chapel. Third, there would be no security staff present except for verifying count time issues. Fourth, there would be meals served in the chapel for the couples (provided by PF and home-cooked), with a candle-light dinner served on Saturday night. Fifth, and last, on Sunday the couples would renew their wedding vows, if they so desired.

Mr. Hickox looked at me and said: you want to do what!" " I just want to help these offenders make it when they leave DCC," I replied. He hesitated for a moment and then said: "Heads will roll if this does not work."

Without a moment's hesitation on my part, I firmly replied, "Yes, sir."

He then instructed me to draw up the necessary paperwork with the names of the PF volunteers that would be conducting the seminar as well as a detailed list of the offenders and their spouses to ensure we had approved applications on all in our file before the weekend began. Lastly, we needed a detailed list of the meals, right down to the last spoon and fork, and NO sharp tools of any kind.

"Yes, sir!" Then I hightailed out of his office before he had a chance to ask any more questions. But he did later anyway.

The seminar was approved for the following February. That was great. It gave me enough time to get the logistics all planned out and the local church community on onboard insofar as providing places for the spouses to stay and to furnish transportation from Denver or Colorado Springs and, if necessary, out to the facility. In addition, arranging for babysitting services if required. Last of all, preparations were needed for the meals to be served to the participants during the weekend. Some of the arrangements were seemingly impossible to accomplish, but God! I had a peace surrounding all these matters. A peace that is almost unexplainable except ….

"For this reason, since the day we heard about you, we did not stop praying for you, asking that you may be filled with knowledge of His will in all wisdom and spiritual understanding, that you may walk worthy of the Lord." (Colossians 1:9)

I must confess that from time to time during the course of the weekend, I noticed security staff peering through a side window. The couples attended the regular chapel Sunday service with the rest of the population. As part of this service, there was a renewal of wedding vows, which brought some of the men to tears and wives as well. From that day on there were numerous inquiries as to when the next marriage seminar would take place. What joy there was in my heart! At one point, a case manager asked if these marriage seminars could be held bi-monthly. That was not in reality at all remotely possible.

The chapel building project almost hit a snag relating to the carpet. Joan and I went to see my dear friend Dave McNab who, along with his wife, Elaine, owned a furniture store in Salida and asked him to provide a bid on the carpet. He said: "what is it that you want, and how many yards of carpet do we need?" I gave him the measurements and we looked at some carpet samples he had and picked out a few samples as possibilities.

"How soon do you need the carpet?"

I replied, "Yesterday."

Dave smiled in his unique way and said, "I will call the mill and get back to you in a few days." We then went to lunch.

I was on pins and needles that week until he called me the following Monday. I am glad that I was seated when he asked me if I would like the carpet "FREE!" "Are you kidding me?" Was this another WOW moment, God? Of course, it was. It just happened that the mill had an "end of the run" on a certain carpet style that was the exact amount of material we needed. I was rarely ever speechless in my life, but this was one. I was flabbergasted.

Then I heard Dave say: "Hello? Bill, are you there?"

After a quick recovery, I meekly responded, "yes." The carpet mill was in Georgia and the mill would ship it free to us, but it would not be until next month. "We can wait. At that price, we can wait." By the way, Dave McNab donated the glue for the installation. Oh my God, Joan and me were almost overcome at all the Lord continues to do. Miracles still happen, we just have to recognize them as a "God incident, not a co-incident."

"Blessed are those who have learned to acclaim you, who walk in the light of your presence, O Lord. They rejoice in Your name all day long; they exult in your righteousness." (Psalm 89: 15-16 NIV)

There was a brief discussion over the different types of seating arrangements for the chapel sanctuary area. I preferred pews over chairs. But there were going to be other uses of the chapel for facility events like graduation programs from the education department. Further, KAIROS Prison Ministry would need chairs for their program, as would most other ministries that would use the sanctuary as a multi-purpose room. So, chairs it was going to be.

You'd be surprised at the amount of chair types around. Using the DCMF resources that were available, I was able to locate a church chair supplier that would be able to deliver the number of chairs we needed (150) in short order. The price was within our budget, so we ordered them.

When the carpet arrived the following month, we were ready to install. The very next day the chairs arrived, although we had to store them for a few days so they were not in the way. The scheduled date of April 30 for the grand opening of the chapel would go as planned. *Yeah, God!*

"Because of the hope which is laid up for you in heaven, of which you heard before in the Word of the Truth of the gospel, which has come to you, as it has also in all the world, and is bringing forth fruit, as it is also among you since the day you heard and knew the grace of God in truth." (Colossians 1: 5-6 NKJ)

CHAPTER 24

By their Fruits …

"If you abide in Me, and My words abide in you, you will ask what you desire and it shall be done for you. By this My Father is glorified, that you bear much fruit; so, you will be my disciples."

- John 15:7-8 (NKJ)

I am awakened as the sun streams through the slats of the blinds in my bedroom. I say to myself: *Get up, self, this is the big day you and many others have been praying for.*

April 30, 1999, that is today and what a day this will be. Ever since the day that the ground was broken, there have been scoffers. If you recall, even the CDOC director did not think this would ever happen. It was back in 1994 that ground was dedicated and broken for this chapel. The CDOC directed that there would not be any debt incumbered on this building. All materials were to be purchased with cash. Duplicate receipts were to be kept on file. All the paperwork was completed as of April 28, 1999.

There was a lot to do this day before the actual dedication of the chapel at 1 p.m.. The RSVPs had to be checked and verified. The programs needed to be printed, and there was a choir practice at 9 a.m.. I made sure that I attended roll call that morning to answer any questions that security might have, and to my surprise Warden Green was there. Was there something going on that I was not aware of? As of this point, I was extremely nervous. Then I just went into a silent, short-but-effective prayer and the peace of God came upon me. (Roll Call went as usual.)

This was going to be a truly blessed day that God has brought forth from His mercy and grace.

Now, back to the mundane business at hand. At the last choir practice before this dedication day ceremony, I informed each choir member that if they were late for practice this day, they would be excluded from the program, no excuses, period. Of course, there is always one that comes in late and has a "story" to tell me. Not this time. I told them weeks before and at every practice session that was held: "the only excuse that IS acceptable to me is if you are "dead."

One offender was late, one of the lead singers (he had a great voice). But I did not bend the rule even for him. I have to admit that this was a difficult decision to make, but in order to maintain discipline within the choir, this had to be done. As God would have known all about this in advance, and He did, there was a plan "G" (or God's plan). Unknown to me, we had an offender who had recently arrived about three weeks earlier, and he had a beautiful tenor voice. Although he did not have a gate clearance to go out with the choir, he did not need one to sing with the choir because the chapel was on prison grounds. Just what the Master ordered. What a great spirit-filled ceremony we had. The chapel was filled with volunteers who were involved in the programming as well as volunteers who gave unselfishly to the chapel fund, and some of the local politicians and CDOC officials.

"Rejoice in the Lord always. Again, I will say rejoice!" (Philippians 4:4 NKJ)

The following day, there was another celebration. This was a service for the offenders. After that service we held an "open house" for all of the staff and inmates who wished to come and see what the Lord had done. A 5,000 square foot chapel. No debt encumbered, all manual labor by experienced inmate crews, with staff properly overseeing the work.

God does not stop, ever. Just another step closer to His coming again. This part was just the beginning. The wonder-working miracles were just getting started. During my time serving the Lord at CDOC central office, I had many opportunities to meet people from different parts of the country and Canada. I had joined a small group of professionals who supervised volunteers in their respective jurisdictions. This group was called the International Association of Justice Volunteerism. The purpose of this association was to network with like-minded others in order to share information. Through this group I welcomed all good referrals, contacts, and information. One of these men was Tom Beckner, who I had previously met. He and I worked together in creating a model for prison chaplains in Colorado (and hopefully eventually elsewhere), a Chaplains' Clinical Pastoral Education (CCPE), a program inaugurated within the Colorado Department of Corrections.

Additionally, he and I established a model for a life-long learning program (LLP) for offenders in state facilities, which was the only model for jailed offenders. The LLP was a brainchild of Good News and its author, Chaplain Cam Able. While this was a great model for county jailed prisoners, it was not a "good fit" for state-housed offenders. Tom and I agreed that there needed to be a different approach to this program model for state prison offenders. This agreement was as far as Mr. Beckner cared to get involved. Little did I know, at that time Tom was negotiating with Good News to join its executive staff as a region director.

One of my stumbling blocks was the author of the LLP. This was his "baby." While we wrestled with a modified version of LLP for state prisons, Chaplain Able told me, "Go ahead and adjust the program as you see fit, just keep me in the loop."

"Yes! I would keep you in the loop with detailed information as to content and result." By God's grace, and with the help of professionals from the western slope of Colorado, we did develop a comprehensive three-phase model comprising three 12-week sessions. Every inmate had to complete each phase they started. They could leave the program only after they have completed that phase. If they dropped out, they went on a labor crew for the remainder of the period for the completed phase they enrolled. Over time, while there were few dropouts, about six over a 12-year survey, over 2,000 inmates completed the program. Only six have re-offended. That makes a re-offender rate of .08%. What phenomenal glory to God?

One inmate in particular, I recall, and I would like to share what happened when in the middle of his third and final phase. Offender Matthew went back to court for a re-consideration of his initial court sentencing, meaning that he might have the remainder of his sentence dismissed. He came to me the night before he was to go to Denver and told me he would be gone for a week. He was concerned that he would lose his place in Life-Learning and have to start all over. I assured him that he would be able to make up the assignments he missed. He was so relieved.

When he went to court the judge said to him that he had fulfilled a sufficient amount of time based on the crime he committed and was free to go home. Upon hearing this, Matthew replied, "Your honor, I want to go back to DCC and complete the Life Learning Program before I go home!"

The judge was almost speechless. This was almost unthinkable, and surely unheard of, but in a moment or two the judge said: "WHAT! You want to go back to prison to complete a program? Why?"

Matthew then said something I thought was profound: "Sir, I have never completed any form of education before in my life and I need to complete this program for myself." The judge paused for a moment and then agreed, and Matthew came back to DCC. The rest of the story is that the judge called the facility and spoke to the warden, who referred him to me.

I explained: "Judge this is a 36-week life skills program based on biblical principles." After giving him a few more details, he wanted me to send him the full curriculum, which I did.

"Return to Me and I will return to you, says the Lord of hosts." (Malachi 3:7b) (NKJ)

About a month or so after, that same judge called me and indicated that he wanted me to make a full presentation to all of the CDOC case managers. He felt that this program was so important that all the state prisons should implement the program at their respective facilities. WOW! Another God moment.

I did make such a presentation, but sad to say, none accepted the challenge to institute the program. Some said that there was not enough adequate space at their prison, others just buried the information to the bottom of the pile. How sad.

There was another inmate I will call Barney. Now, Barney never had much of any kind of education. He was in and out of prison most of his life for one reason or another. He finally wound up at Delta. I was asked by his case manager if I had a place for him at the chapel.

"I could always use another custodian. If you can arrange that for me, I would be delighted to have Barney on my staff." She indicated that she would make it happen. And sure enough, Barney was assigned as a custodian in the chapel.

When I sat down with him and explained his duties, he was fully on board. I asked him if wanted to learn more about God? He said: "No, not now, maybe after I get more 'learn'n' I would like to get to know Him better."

"God can wait if you want, Barney, but He is wanting you now," I replied.

He starred at me for what seemed to be a long time, then he rather nonchalantly said, "Okay, I can start tomorrow." He smiled at me and left my office. That was that. I wondered what he was up to, this sly fox. Over the next three and a half years I found out the heart of this man was truly to seek God. Barney reminded me of the scripture "I will life up my eyes to the hills — from whence comes my help? My help comes from the Lord, who made heaven and earth." (Psalm 121:1-2) (NKJ)

Barney, you must read, and this was the book that he read. When he did not understand, he would knock on my door for an explanation (I might add, often). A pain in the neck for some, but I relished that time with Barney. He went on to participate in the LLP and graduated within the 36-week timeframe with an 88% grade. He was part of the choir and an outstanding witness for Christ.

Barney also went back to court for what he thought was a reconsideration of his sentence and he thought that he would be released. He packed up all of his possessions and left for court. Much to his astonishment, he was back to court considering an old charge against him that he thought had been thrown out. But the District Attorney refiled those charges and a judge found him guilty and gave him the "three-strikes" rule and sentenced Barney to life without parole. He was not going to return to Delta.

By some mix up in his paperwork, he was brought back to DCC instead of a more secure facility. No fences around here. The staff did not know what Barney's court outcome detailed. Barney told a few of his inmate friends about the judges' decision and asked them what he was to do?

Barney came into my office that night and told me what happened in court and what some of his "brothers in green" told him to do: Walk out of DCC after the 8 o'clock count. "What do you have to lose?" his "brothers" told him.

"What should I do, Chap?" he asked me.

"What would Jesus have you do?" was my reply to Barney. He paused for a moment and then he asked me to pray with him. We prayed for a few minutes and Barney said: "I have my answer and I now know what I must do." Barney left my office and went to his room, packed up his belongings and turned himself into Major Lisak. After roll call the following morning, the Major motioned to me to follow him to his office. He proceeded to ask me what happened that Barney would turn himself in? I replied: "But God" and left. Barney was placed in Administrative Segregation (lock-down) until he was sent back to a higher custody prison where he remains today.

"For this is the will of God, that by doing good you may put to silence the ignorance of foolish men — as free, yet not using liberty as a cloak for vice, but as bondservants of God. Honor all people. Love the brotherhood. Fear God. Honor the King." (1 Peter 2:15-17 NKJ)

One of the most difficult of time for inmates is around the holidays, especially Christmas. This is not only for the inmate, who often have said, "I did the crime, so I must do the time." Unfortunately, there are other people doing time as well. The family of an offender must deal with the crime, too. Rarely is there opportunity for celebration as a family when dad is incarcerated. Hard times befall most families during dad's imprisonment. The breadwinner is not there. Most families go on welfare. Children are often ridiculed by other children because dad is in prison.

Out at DCC, God inspired the outpouring of love to one and all. I briefly touched on this in an earlier chapter, but now I will recount in further detail. How God provides for people who love Him always has astonished me. Another case in point was the connection with Resurrection Fellowship (Rez) in Loveland. Whenever I contacted them about help with a particular matter, they always provided the requested help.

The first Christmas after the new chapel opened, God inspired Joan to provide Christmas stockings for all the children who come to visit their dad, from infant to teenagers, at Delta. I smiled and thought to myself: "the warden is not going to approve this one." But I said to Joan: "I will run it by Warden Green, and we will see. Great idea, sweetheart."

I must admit that it was a great idea, but how do we do this Christmas stocking for 20 to 50 children of all ages? First things first. The warden's approval. I set up an appointment with the warden. With some concern as to contraband, the warden gave "provisional" approval, pending assurance that guidelines would be in place for what could be included in the stockings. The list would be prepared by me and signed by the warden and the security manager.

The first thing I had to do was identify items that could and could not be included in the stockings. I used a list of recognized contraband items for my reference. Then I called the inmates on staff in the chapel and asked them what they thought should and should not be in the stockings. That is where I got some eye-opening information about what constitutes contraband. I submitted my formal request the next day and received the paperwork back before the day was over.

"APPROVED!" Never did I think this would be approved. What an outpouring of trust and faith in the system that things would work out. Only God. Thank you, Joan, for following the Lord's lead.

"Though the mountains be shaken and the hills be removed, yet my unfailing love for you will not be shaken nor my covenant of peace be removed," says the Lord, who has compassion on you." (Isaiah 54:10, NIV)

The call was made to my contact at Rez and she said she would contact the Women's Guild and run it by them and call me in a day or two. I was confused. In my first conversation with her, I thought she was going to do that at that time. Joan told me I worry too much. She was right. What do I do now? As Joan tells me: "Pray." I opened my Bible and started to skim through the pages. I stopped at the book of Romans and sure enough found my answer:

"And we know that in all things God works for the good of those who love Him, who have been called according to His purpose." (Romans 8:28) (NIV)

A wonderful peace came over me! The joy and love of God is awesome. To this day I wonder why I do not seek Him more often. What peace overcame me; the silence of that peace surrounds me. I was absorbed by His presence. Peace, peace, loving peace.

Mary, my Rez connection, did not call me 'til the following week. The Women's Guild agreed to take on the task of filling the stockings and included the shipping of the items to me. Another WOW! I passed that information along to security and the warden. Now the hard part began. We needed at least three weeks before Christmas to get all the information from the inmates as to how many children would be visiting them that weekend. This proved to be a disaster. Few inmates were able to provide the necessary information in a timely manner. The team had to make educated guesses as to the number of children (boys and girls and their ages) and forward those figures to Mary at Rez. She used that information to prepare stockings. The boxes, eight of them, arrived with plenty of time to sort through them and remove any nuisance contraband such as toy guns, caps for the guns, chewing gum matches, etc. Otherwise, all things checked out just fine.

The inmates were informed that if any of the children did not show up for any reason, those items, toys, and clothing alike would be donated to local charities. None would be given to visiting families to take home for children. Even though the inmates filled out gift requests, they understood that without the volunteers, their kids would have received nothing.

The Thursday before Christmas weekend, the inmates had a chance to wrap the gifts for their children, if they desired. There were volunteers available to help them, if needed. Most of them needed help as they had never wrapped a gift for their child. The tears flowed from their eyes as they saw firsthand that the gifts they requested were bought. Surprise was overcome with those tears of joy. The surprise that a person who did not know them or their family, would go out of their way to purchase those items.

Saturday arrived and the program went off without a hitch. The joy of the Lord filled this place.

Sunday visiting room had only a small group of people scheduled to arrive. A few children that were not there on Saturday did show up. We were thankful for the much smaller group, as there were some people who were not scheduled to come but came nevertheless, and we did not have gifts for them. But here is how God once again lets His presence be known.

In this group was a little girl, maybe eight or nine years old. She was not on the schedule and therefore we did not have any gifts for her. When I took the offender aside and spoke to him about this situation, he explained to me that he had no idea his family was coming to visit him that day. "I will see what we can find for your daughter." As I went over to the chapel and spoke with Joan to see what there was left, she said we would find something. In about 10 minutes, she had a bag full of small gifts for the girl. I went across the street and called the inmate over to me and informed him that we found some items for his daughter, he breathed a sigh of relief. With things being so difficult for his family, there were no toys for his little girl this Christmas.

I smiled and said I am sure she will be happy. She tore into those gifts as soon as her dad gave them to her. As I watched her finish opening her presents, she started to cry. I approached her and asked her, "What is the matter?"

She looked up at me and whimpered: "Jesus forgot me." I was shocked to hear her say that.

"Stay right where you are, I'll be right back." I went over to my office and grabbed some Christmas candy and brought that over to her and said, "Jesus did not forget you sweetheart, here is some candy."

She thanked me, but once again sadly remarked: "Jesus forgot me."

Feeling a little perplexed, I thought, what am I forgetting? Then it dawned on me: a Christmas stocking. I went to see if there were any left. I quickly scrambled over to the chapel and found the last box of stockings in my office. There were five or six in the box. I looked to see if there was a stocking marked girl, and there was just one. I pulled it out and went back to the visiting room and gave her the stocking. She went through it quickly; took out the coloring book, crayons, candy, and then with a great big smile on her face, jumping up and down, waving a pair of homemade knit gloves, shouted: "Jesus did not forget me! All I prayed for this Christmas was a pair of gloves to keep my hands warm." Tears running down her face and that of her family, the inmate included. I confess my eyeballs were sweating just a little too!

I went back over to her and said, "Jesus loves you, Sweetie." She kept repeating, "All I prayed for this year was a pair of gloves to keep my hands warm this winter." She then began shouting, "Jesus loves me!"

When I shared this story with the people at Rez, Mary checked with the Women's Guild. Only one pair of homemade gloves were made and put in a stocking, just one! God saw to it that those gloves were given to the right child. Another WOW moment, thanks be to God.

"This is the assurance we have in approaching God: that if we ask anything according to His will, He hears us. And if we know that He hears us, then whatever we ask, we know that we have what we asked of Him." (1 John 5:14-15, NIV)

CHAPTER 25

Shine Jesus, Shine

"I will love You, O Lord, my strength. The Lord is my rock, my fortress and my deliverer; My God, my strength, in whom I will trust; My shield and the horn of my salvation, my strong hold."

- Psalm 18:1,2 NKJ

On a Sunday morning in late July of 1999, while driving out to the facility I spotted in front of me at about 50 yards, a wild turkey in the middle of the road. As I came closer, I saw just how big that turkey was, I would estimate about 30 pounds. I continued to slow down, but that turkey was not moving over. I did come to a stop, got out of my car, and was going to chase that bird off the road, when he turned and looked at me as if to say, "you want a piece of me?" Then he turned and walked away.

I laughed to myself at that incident as I drove into DCC. It was about 8:30 a.m. when I approached the control center to sign in and get my keys. I asked the officer in control if the shift commander announced at roll call that the choir was going out that morning to a church in Montrose. All he said was "you had better talk to the shift commander. He is in his office."

At that point, I looked around and did not see any inmate activity in the yard. Something was up. Possibly a fight the night before? Or there was an escape or something? It appeared that the facility was in a lock down mode. *Okay God, let's see what is going on.*

I stopped for a moment inside the secure area behind the control center where the shift commander's office is and prayed. He was sitting at his desk, on the phone, and held his hand up in a "stop" motion. So, I waited. In a moment or two, as he was hanging up the phone, he motioned for me to come into the office.

He indicated that there was a fight the previous night and the facility was on lockdown. In addition, he said that he just got off the phone with the warden and they discussed the fact that the lockdown might go until noon.

I was thinking, Okay God, this was what I prayed to You before walking in here, but was that prayer too late? Did I make a mistake in stopping at McDonald's before coming out to work? Should I have run that big old turkey down on the road? Did I goof this morning? I should have been with the shift commander while he was talking to the warden. You knew Lord what was going down, I must learn to continue to trust and obey. There is a reason for these things to happen.

Then I remembered: "But as for me, I trust in You, O Lord; I say, "You are my God." (Psalm 31:14)

The shift commander shouted to me: "Are you awake or walking in your sleep?"

I shook my head. "I am awake, sir."

He said, "I was just on the phone with the warden, and he said to ask if you would be able to change the choir program to another day?"

I responded, "No can do."

He picked up the phone and called the warden. He also asked me to step out of the office for a moment while they talked. In what seemed like a blink of an eye, he called me back in and told me the warden said that although we were on lockdown (which was lifted at 10 a.m.), the warden gave permission to take the choir out as scheduled. WOW, there You go again, God.

I say all this because on that particular Sunday, at that particular church, there was a very special lady there who was a regular attendee of the church. After the choir program was over, she came to me and introduced herself.

"Hi, my name is Victoria. Do you need some help with the choir? If so, I would like to volunteer."

I did not realize at the time what a Big WOW of God this was to be. I almost exploded in joy. I wanted to give this woman one of the biggest hugs ever, but I said to myself: *Cool your jets. You do not know this person. Check things out before you start jumping for joy. Not yet, the prison has to check her out, do the background checks and all that before she would be able to come in and help with the choir.*

"Yes, ma'am, I sure can use some help."

To volunteer, you must apply to the CDOC with a volunteer application. I had forms in my briefcase, so I gave her one. She filled them out and had them back within a week. Two weeks later she was approved. Hallelujah! This wonderful woman not only would direct the choir, but she also became a member of my support council, a member of the Good News Board of Directors. In short, she was quite a blessing to us at the prison and beyond.

During her time volunteering at DCC, she had the opportunity to share with me her story of how several years earlier she vowed that she would never go into a prison again. You see, one of her siblings was wrongfully incarcerated for several years. When her sibling was released, she told God that she would never go into a prison ever again. I just chuckled and thought of the many times I have said "never" and God must have gotten a good laugh over that as well. Never say never to God, He will prove you wrong every time.

I had not encountered such a woman as her. She would hold each and every member of the choir accountable for their actions. If they were horsing around, she would call them out, even to the point to either sit out of part of the practice session or dismiss them and advise them to think about their actions and consider their motive for belonging to the choir. If they wished to return, they needed to change their ways.

She wanted those 20 or so inmates to know the importance of discipline and that it was a privilege, not a right, to belong to this group. With the more than 10 years of her volunteering to direct the choir, only one chastised offender never returned to the choir. The other choir members recognized what it meant to be part of a team. Not just the team-choir, but the team of Jesus Christ. To understand the victory in Christ was a life-long goal. Victoria was an instrument used of God to show the men of the choir what a true honor it is to be on God's team.

To God be the glory, great things He continues to do.

Chaplain Bill Potter & Victoria Hearst

Epilogue

There were many issues, problems, and obstacles over the 31-plus years of our service in prison ministry. If not for the "But God Factor" in our lives, we would have given up a long time ago. Whether I was a volunteer, contract employee, a CDOC employee, or even a "non-gratuitous employee, Jesus was always with us through it all and is with us today.

Texas was not my idea of the greatest place to retire. But things happen for a reason, and those reasons are part of God's plan for our lives and therefore, I'm in.. Joan and I were involved in a one-car crash on June 13, 2013, 17 days before I was to retire. At 77, I thought it was time to let go of the ministry and hand it over to the "younger generation."

We were traveling home from Grand Junction where I had just picked up a new set of trains for my model railroad I was building and planned to complete when retired. Joan was driving and coming around a curve, which was ironically known as Dead Man's Curve. Wind shears estimated at 60-plus miles took the car out of the lane we were in and, as it did, Joan over-compensated and crashed into a guard rail. The car flipped over and skidded atop that guard rail about 30 feet, then rolled over 2 ½ times and landed upright just 20 feet from going down a 50-foot ravine.

I was asleep in the passenger's side and did not wake up until the car was upright. Smoke was coming from underneath the dashboard, and the first thing I did was pray to God: "Lord, if that smoke is part of a fire going on in the engine compartment, please Lord, put it out."

Much to my surprise, the smoked stopped. I should have not been surprised, for the Word says, "For I am convinced that neither death nor life, neither angels nor demons, neither the present nor the future, nor any powers, neither height nor depth, nor anything else in all creation will be able to separate us from the love of God that is in Christ Jesus our Lord." (Romans 8:38-39)

What happened after that is just as wonderfully amazing. A car moving in the opposite direction on the other side of the highway saw the whole thing go down. They immediately turned around to help. Of the two passengers, one was a doctor and the other a nurse! They had been in Montrose area, the Black Canyon to be specific. They were going to stop at a restaurant there in Montrose, and at the last minute decided to drive back to Grand Junction and eat there instead. *WOW, God. Thank you.*

Coming behind them was a member of the Delta volunteer fire department. They all stopped to give assistance. We had On-Star installed in our car, and they immediately knew my location, that there was an accident, and had already called for an ambulance and asked if there was anyone else in the car with me. I told them that my wife was there, and they quickly said to me that they would call for another ambulance.

WOW, again. Only God could or would have set up something like this. I managed to open my car door and immediately was out on the dirt and was shouting that I had pains in my chest. Joan was in pain herself, being pinned behind the steering wheel. The doctor and nurse tried to calm us down and assure us that help was on the way. Joan's work colleague called our children and they came out to be by our side. Our daughters Lynn and Jennifer told us that when we retire, to move to Texas so that we would be 15 minutes away from them instead of 15 hours. We took that to heart, and we eventually moved there the following year.

DCC and Good News knew that I was planning to retire at the end of June. There were plans in place for a retirement party in the chapel on June 30. The retirement was postponed until July 30 because of the accident. It came across my mind that the inmate choir might also do something in the way of a surprise to send us off. Over the past 30 or so years, conservatively speaking, the chapel was blessed with 300-plus choir members. In all my years I could never had anticipated what this current choir group were planning.

My inmate staff, with the permission of the warden, prepared a DVD. It contained pictures of events over the years of our ministry at DCC. If ever something made tears flow, this did. Some of the events I did not recall until they flashed up on the screen. Others were so humorous that I almost wanted to forget them. But, it was all good. The background song of the DVD was unusual. It was as if the background music was chastising us for retiring? I had to stop and think about that even after the party was over and really listen closely to the words. One of the choir members composed an original song for the occasion. It was all good.

One of the administrative assistants made me a cute cake with a "Tommy the Train" on top of it, knowing that I was planning to build a model railroad. All in all, the party was a bittersweet departure.

This story does not end here. Nor did it end at the cross, for Easter points beyond the cross. It points us toward hope and eternal life. We must continue to spread the Good News of Jesus Christ until that day ….

"And behold, I am coming quickly, And My reward is with Me, to give to everyone according to his work. I am the Alpha and the Omega, The Beginning and the Last." (Revelation 22:12-13) (NKJ)

List of abbreviations

AAG   - Assistant Attorney General

ACA   - American Correctional Association

AG   - Attorney General

APB   - American Patriots Bible

AVCF   - Arkansas Valley Correctional Facility

CDOC   - Colorado Department of Corrections

CPE   - Clinical Pastoral Education

CSP   - Colorado State Prison

CTCF   - Colorado Territorial Correctional Facility

DCC   - Delta Correctional Center

DCMF   - Delta County Ministerial Fellowship

DMA   - Delta Ministerial Alliance

FCF   - Freemont Correction Facility

GNJPM   - Good News Jail and Prison Ministry

HCB   - Hollman Christian Bible

NKJV   - New King James Version

OVS   - Office of Volunteer Services

PF   - Prison Fellowship

REZ   - Resurrection Fellowship

RFRA   - Religion Freedom Restoration Act

SMCF   - Shadow Mountain Correctional Facility

CPSIA information can be obtained
at www.ICGtesting.com
Printed in the USA
LVHW101504100123
736853LV00006B/185